ANGLO-AMERICAN WOMEN WRITERS AND REPRESENTATIONS OF INDIANNESS, 1629–1824

For Sam and Will

Anglo-American Women Writers and Representations of Indianness, 1629–1824

CATHY REX

University of Wisconsin-Eau Claire, USA

Routledge
Taylor & Francis Group

LONDON AND NEW YORK

First published 2015 by Ashgate Publishing

2 Park Square, Milton Park, Abingdon, Oxfordshire OX14 4RN
52 Vanderbilt Avenue, New York, NY 10017

Routledge is an imprint of the Taylor & Francis Group, an informa business

First issued in paperback 2019

British Library Cataloguing in Publication Data
A catalogue record for this book is available from the British Library

The Library of Congress has cataloged the printed edition as follows:
Rex, Cathy.
  Anglo-American women writers and representations of Indianness, 1629–1824 / by Cathy
    Rex.
    pages cm
  Includes bibliographical references and index.
  ISBN 978-1-4724-3638-2 (hardcover)
  1. American literature—Women authors—History and criticism. 2. Indians of North
America—Ethnic identity. 3. Indians in literature. 4. Indians in popular culture. I. Title.
  PS151.R49 2015
  810.9'9287—dc23

                                                                          2015015282

ISBN: 978-1-4724-3638-2 (hbk)
ISBN: 978-0-367-88022-4 (pbk)

Contents

List of Figures

Acknowledgments

Portions of chapters 1 and 2 of this book appeared previously as "Indians and Images: The Massachusetts Bay Colony Seal, James Printer, and the Anxiety of Colonial Identity," *American Quarterly* 63.1 (2011): 61–93; and as "Revising the Nation: The Domesticated Nationalism of Ann Eliza Bleecker's *The History of Maria Kittle*," *Women's Studies: An Interdisciplinary Journal* 42.8 (2013): 1–23.

I owe my sincerest thanks to the many people and institutions that have made this book possible. Financial support was provided by the Virginia Historical Society, the University of Wisconsin-Eau Claire, and Auburn University in the form of fellowships, travel grants, and research stipends. I especially want to thank the Office for Research and Sponsored Programs at the University of Wisconsin-Eau Claire for granting me two University Creative and Research Activity Grants, and Dean Bernard Duyfhuizen and the English Department of UWEC for generously giving me two Duyfhuizen Research Professorships. I am also extremely grateful to the amazing librarians, archivists, and staff members at the Massachusetts Historical Society, the Massachusetts Archives, APVA Preservation Virginia, and the Virginia Historical Society for their assistance in finding the many images I rely upon in this work. I'd also like to personally thank artist and historian Mary Ellen Howe for speaking with me about her painting *Pocahontas* and sharing her research with me about the materiality surrounding this historic figure and image.

I would also like to thank many colleagues, friends, and associates for the tireless feedback and support they have provided as they read and re-read chapters of this work with enthusiasm and care. Hilary Wyss, Penelope Ingram, Cedrick May, and Craig Bertolet were some of the earliest encouragers and commenters, as was Paula Backscheider. Without their valuable input, things never would have progressed to this final point. Hilary Wyss, especially, has remained a steadfast supporter and friend, even when I have plagued her beyond all reason with questions, pleas for advice, and general moaning about the research and writing process. My anonymous reader at Ashgate Publishing was also immensely helpful as I shaped this project into its final form. José Alvergue, Stephanie Farrar, Stacy Thompson, Jan Stirm, Aram DeKoven, William H. Phillips, Eva Santos-Phillips, and other colleagues at UWEC have proven to be insightful readers and advisors as I revised this manuscript. Others, like Carey Applegate, Kate Hinnant, Michael Faris, and Alan Benson have provided the moral support, friendship, and humor I needed to carry this process through. And finally, I want to thank my sons, Sam and Will, who have handled their crazy, book-writing mother with grace, acceptance, and pride. I dedicate this book to them.

Introduction
Indians on Paper

On display in the Portraits Room at the Massachusetts Historical Society in Boston, there is a striking portrait of Pocahontas from the 1730s (see Figure I.1). This painting of the famous "Indian princess" was created by Mary Woodbury, a schoolgirl from Massachusetts and an untrained artist, who would have been in her early teens at the time the picture was made.[1] Aside from the title of the portrait, which designates the woman as *Pocahontas*, there are no markers of Pocahontas's Native American identity, stereotypical or otherwise, in the image. Featuring a stylized representation of Pocahontas in the folk tradition, the oil-on-paper image depicts Pocahontas seated in front of a solid, dark background. She is wearing a dark dress with a low-cut, rounded neckline that is trimmed with pretty floral lace, as are the ends of her three-quarter length sleeves. Her dark hair is done in an updo with a cluster of small flowers at the crown and her long, elegant neck is graced with a choker-style necklace that features a double row of beads and fastens in the back with a ribbon. Pocahontas's hands are resting lightly in her lap and she is holding a single flower in her left hand. The small, slight smile on her face is reminiscent of Western European ladies and the genteel expressions they adopted in their own portraits—and so is the obviously whitened, Anglicized appearance of the subject. The portrait overwhelmingly depicts an idealized form of eighteenth-century Anglo femininity. From the clothing to the hairstyle to shy smile and creamy pale skin, Mary Woodbury's *Pocahontas* is, indeed, white.

What would possess a young, Anglo woman from Massachusetts who is only in her teens to painstakingly paint a portrait of Pocahontas that in no way reflects any of the historic or ethnic realities of that figure? It cannot simply be due to ignorance, as the Pocahontas narrative would have been fairly well known at the time, with historic narratives about and engravings of her having been in print since the seventeenth century.[2] In fact, scholar Robert Tilton has suggested that

---

[1]   The Massachusetts Historical Society notes that Mary Woodbury was from Beverly, MA, and would have painted this "idealized depiction at a Boston finishing school in the 1730s" (Oliver, Huff, and Hanson 77). I use the terms "Indians" or "Indianness" to represent the Anglo, colonialist fantasy of a monolithic, stereotypical Native population. I use more culturally accurate tribal designations when available (Nipmuck, Mattaponi, Rappahannock, etc.) or the terms "Native Americans" and "Native Christians" to refer to the actual, historic people of Native ancestry. This distinction, while slight, is significant to underscore my desire not to reproduce the colonialist abstractions I am critiquing. However, when citing the work of other scholars, I have left their terms for referring to indigenous peoples unchanged.

[2]   Volume four of Theodor de Bry's *Grandes Voyages* series, *America* (1634), and John Smith's *The Generall Historie* (1624), for example, both featured narrative retellings and engravings of various events from Pocahontas's life, including the Simon Van de

Woodbury's portrait might have even been based on the 1616 Simon Van de Passe engraving of Pocahontas (the only life image of her known to exist) because of the European attire and similar composition, although he admits Woodbury's image "is in no way an attempt to copy the earlier portrait" (*Evolution* 111).

Woodbury would have been aware of the real, historic figure of Pocahontas—who she was, what she did, and when she lived—and undoubtedly wished to lionize or immortalize her image in a portrait, a portrait that is "certainly the first original depiction of Pocahontas produced in the New World, and almost surely the first done by a woman" (Tilton 111).[3] But why did Mary Woodbury create a Pocahontas that was fashioned more in her own image as an Anglo woman of the eighteenth century instead of a more accurate depiction of the actual Native American woman she sought to commemorate? Why would she meld Indianness and white femininity into a single identity in this image?

This entanglement or fusion of white womanhood with Indianness and the various ways in which Anglo-American women writers—and artists like Woodbury—sought to disentangle and even exploit it is the focus of *Anglo-American Women Writers and Representations of Indianness, 1629–1824*. Women writers of the seventeenth, eighteenth, and early nineteenth centuries were keenly

---

Passe engraving from 1616, which appeared in Smith's text alongside a similarly styled engraving of himself. Robert Beverly's *History and Present State of Virginia,* which was first published in 1705, also retells the story of Pocahontas and is, as Robert Tilton notes, "the first important colonial attempt to reconstruct the Pocahontas narrative" including her marriage to John Rolfe (3). Additionally, in their *Pocahontas: Her Life and Legend,* William Rasmussen and Robert Tilton note that Beverly's *History* was republished in a new edition in 1734 and had been advertised in the *Boston Gazette* "by means of an anonymous letter to the people which described Pocahontas as embodying 'virtue,' and 'greatness of Mind' and 'all that can be lovely or great in a Female Character'" (33). While it is not clear if Woodbury would have seen any of these texts or the letter in the *Gazette,* it seems unlikely that she would have been unaware of Pocahontas's historic identity. For more information on the progression and popularity of Pocahontas narratives, images, and folklore over time, see William M.S. Rasmussen and Robert S. Tilton's *Pocahontas, Her Life and Legend,* Robert Tilton's *Pocahontas: The Evolution of an American Narrative,* and Ann Uhry Abrams's *The Pilgrims and Pocahontas.* See also chapters 3 and 4 of this book, where I offer more in-depth readings of Pocahontas imagery, specifically of Simon Van de Passe's 1616 engraving and the *Sedgeford Hall Portrait.*

[3]   While Woodbury may have been the first female artist to create an original representation of Pocahontas in the New World, she certainly was not the first Anglo-European to visually connect Anglo womanhood with Indianness. Theodor Galle's engraving *America* (1580), based upon Jan van der Straet's drawing, which famously depicts America as a slumbering Indian woman awakening from her nap on a hammock at the beckoning of Amerigo Vespucci, is one earlier example. Theodor de Bry's engravings in his 1590 folio edition of Thomas Harriot's *A Briefe and True Report of the New Found Land of Virginia* also connect Indianness to Anglo womanhood through multiple images of Indian life and female roles but also with the centrally placed image, "Adam and Eve in America" which clearly works to connect white womanhood (via Eve's sin) to the New World colonial project and its inhabitants.

Figure I.1   *Pocahontas.* Oil on paper by Mary Woodbury, circa 1730.
Collection of the Massachusetts Historical Society.

aware of the connectedness between their own identities as white female Euro-
Americans and an indigenous, New World Native identity. They were also keenly
aware of the potency and utility this connection of Indianness and womanhood
could provide for them as authors. It could serve as a ground from which they
could contribute to the national struggle to organize a collective idea of not
only what the American nation should be, but also who they themselves were as
American women writers. At the same time, however, these writers understood

the injury this association with the "inferior" Indian other caused their own identities as Anglo women and potentially significant members of the forming American nation; consequently, these writers attempt to focus on the primacy of gender over race in their texts even as they bring Indianness to the forefront of them. The result is that these women writers were able to gain control over their own identities by exploring Indian topics in their writing. However, it was through the appropriation and the production of complex (mis)representations of that same Indianness they share a *de facto* connection with. Although sometimes ugly, sometimes problematic, and oftentimes patently racist, the Indian writings of these women writers are also transgressive and disruptive of patriarchal and nationalistic discourses governing American identity, an identity that has always had Indianness at its core.

Indians on Paper: Appropriating Indianness

While artistic license and authorial freedom are certainly possibilities that may explain young Mary Woodbury's departure from depicting the facticity of the "real" Pocahontas, there are more complex factors at play. By the time Woodbury began her painting, the Pocahontas narrative would have been stretched to such stereotypical and mythic proportions in multiple venues that the actual, historic figure would have been barely recognizable within those very texts. Perhaps Woodbury was simply following suit as a creative author of her own "fangirl" version of Pocahontas. Even if this were the case, I would assert that this portrait reveals a complex effort to create and assert an Anglo female identity through the representation of a Native one. Woodbury's image of Pocahontas enmeshes Anglo-American womanhood and Indianness in such a way that one identity becomes dependent upon the other for its meaning and value. Without the eye-grabbing, Indian title (and purported subject matter) of *Pocahontas*, the painting becomes just another image of generic Anglo female identity—a genteel but unremarkable image of womanhood which is notable only for its place in relation to the patriarchal hegemonies of its time. Without the appropriation of Indianness, Woodbury's painting probably would not have been so carefully preserved through the ages or deemed worthy of privileged display at the Massachusetts Historical Society, and it definitely would not be receiving critical attention from scholars like Robert Tilton, William Rasmussen, and myself.

However, without Woodbury's attention to white womanhood, if Woodbury had depicted her Anglicized conceptions about what Pocahontas "should" look like as an Indian, this portrait would potentially become just another naturalized image of colonialist-created Indianness—stereotypically "savage" or romantically noble. By appropriating Indianness and the specific identity of Pocahontas, and using them as props to highlight her own capabilities (and those of Anglo womanhood) Woodbury was able to promote her own identity as an artist into some level of prestige, originality, and immortality. Woodbury co-opted and revised the image of Pocahontas (and more broadly, Indianness) into an image of white female artistry and capability in order to posit her own identity as an Anglo-American woman; she produced a literal "Indian on paper"—a gendered version of a supposed Indian reality that simultaneously exploits and critiques the complex and problematic colonialist association of white womanhood and Indianness.

Since the earliest moments of New World contact, texts such as exploratory and colonial tracts, captivity narratives and historical novels, images on map cartouches, in political cartoons and paintings, and even figures on colonial seals and paper currency had all worked to inscribe Indians and women, or even Indian women, as connected to one another through their inherent subordination to white patriarchy. This idea of the Indian woman representing the New World can be seen in the depictions of the four "sister" continents, which symbolized Europe, Africa, and Asia, alongside America, as beautiful exotic women. Originating in sixteenth-century Europe, these male-authored and iconographic imaginings of the "four corners of the world" as women were characterized by stereotypical and racialized costumes, with America (or more broadly, the Americas) consistently being depicted in a feathered headdress or animal skins, holding a bow and arrow, and exposing her breasts. These depictions of America as an Amazonian "Indian Princess" persisted into the Revolutionary War and late eighteenth century when, as historian E. McClung Fleming has noted, this figure "evolved from a dependent daughter to a free sister of Britannia," becoming increasingly more Anglicized and civilized as her "savage" accoutrements were gradually replaced by "the liberty cap, the rattlesnake, and the American flag" (38).[4]

By feminizing Indianness and/or Indianizing white womanhood in these visual and narrative regimes, Anglo colonial patriarchy was assuring itself a position of dominance in the New World. As a result, Indianness and white womanhood came to be portrayed as interconnected, indistinct stereotypes that could by turns illustrate the patriotism, civic and moral virtue, and the fecundity of America and American identity, as well as the threat of "sexual temptation, immorality, and willful or unruly conduct" depending on the degree of Indianness or whiteness bestowed upon the female image (Day). The two identities became intricately and complexly linked with each other in the various discourses of nationhood and identity in New World texts that were undeniably male-controlled.

European explorers and colonists struggled to depict and define Indianness from the moments of initial contact with the indigenous peoples of the New World. However, because early Anglo-European conceptions of Indianness were only partially formed at these nascent attempts of colonization, much knowledge about

---

[4] See Clare Le Corbeiller's "Miss America and Her Sisters: Personifications of the Four Parts of the World" and Hugh Honor's *The New Golden Land* for further reading on the Four Sisters. For analysis of America as an Indian woman specifically, see E. McClung Fleming's "From Indian Princess to Greek Goddess: The American Image, 1783–1815" and John Higham's "The Indian Princess and Roman Goddess: The First Female Symbols of America." See also Louis Montrose ("The Work of Gender in the Discourse of Discovery"), Annette Kolodny (*The Lay of the Land*), and Anne McClintock (*Imperial Leather* and "'No Longer in a Future Heaven': Gender, Race and Nationalism"), among others, for a discussion of gender and New World discovery.

the "Native other" and his/her relationship to the Anglo-American self had to be produced. The early European residents of the New World struggled to control and understand the Indianness they encountered. Additionally, colonists were apprehensive about their great distance from England and the subsequent cultural alienation that geographic isolation entailed. They were anxious to maintain their English ways while appreciating the many freedoms that accompanied life in the colonies. However, the threat of becoming something else, something barbarous, was very real for the colonists, because in equal measure to their distance from England was their closeness to the Indians. Concrete, stable depictions of Anglo-imagined Indianness, therefore, were absolutely necessary as a means to establish a fixed Native identity that in turn was an attempt to fix the colonial identity. Such productions—whether visual, narrative, or both—sought to repair the colonists' loss of mastery and privilege invoked by the cultural isolation in the New World, but also to solidify their rightful place in and their autochthonous relationship with the New World. These images and texts, like Mary Woodbury's painting, produced the Natives as a visual, social reality, which was at once utterly "othered" and simultaneously knowable and visible, in order to disavow the racial, cultural, and intellectual differences the colonists saw of themselves in the colonized. By picturing and writing "Indianness" into record, these early Americans could more fully and easily understand their own uniquely new identity as discoverers and inhabitants of the New World. As a consequence, the burgeoning sense of the American "self" in the seventeenth, eighteenth, and early nineteenth centuries was intricately connected to and dependent upon the indigenous identity and colonial-created image of the Indian. There is much excellent scholarship that demonstrates these complex and fraught ties of Indianness and Americanness through various critical lenses.[5]

---

[5]   Authoritative texts such as Richard Slotkin's *Regeneration Through Violence*, Robert Berkhofer's *The White Man's Indian*, and Philip Deloria's *Playing Indian* have exposed the foundational link of Indianness to the conception of Americanness. Other works, such as Jared Gardiner's *Master Plots*, Renee Bergland's *The National Uncanny*, Laura Stevens's *The Poor Indians*, and Teresa Toulouse's *The Captive's Position* have examined how constructions of Indianness inform particular frameworks of American identity, including (respectively) whiteness, national pride and guilt, missionary roles, and the gendered understanding of captivity. Texts that address the role of Indianness in nineteenth-century American literature and culture include (but are not limited to): Lucy Maddox's *Removals*, Susan Scheckel's *The Insistence of the Indian*, Joshua David Bellin's *The Demon of the Continent*, and Laura Mielke's *Moving Encounters*. There have similarly been many excellent studies that examine Native American resistance to these colonialist forces in antebellum America, especially through writing, like Hilary Wyss's *Writing Indians*, Kristina Bross's *Dry Bones and Indian Sermons*, Maureen Konkle's *Writing Indian Nations*, Joanna Brooks's *American Lazarus*, Bernd C. Peyer's *The Tutor'd Mind*, Cheryl Walker's *Indian Nation*, Jace Weaver's *That the People Might Live*, Lisa Brooks's *The Common Pot*, and David Murray's *Forked Tongues*, to name just a few. In short, the scholarship on Indianness and its ties to American identity and literature is quite extensive, inspiring, and humbling.

However, the connection of Anglo women, particularly women writers in early America, to these representations of Indianness and American identity has gone relatively unexplored. Scholars such as Christopher Castiglia in his *Bound and Determined: Captivity, Culture-Crossing, and White Womanhood from Mary Rowlandson to Patty Hearst* (1996) and Rebecca Blevins Faery in her *Cartographies of Desire: Captivity, Race, and Sex in the Shaping of an American Nation* (1999) have both examined the relationships to and dependencies of white women on "the Indian Other" within the captivity genre. These very suggestive studies, which both utilize a wide historical range of captivity narratives, from seventeenth-century captivities, like that of Mary Rowlandson, to modern, pop-culture iterations of the captivity theme, work to expose the hegemonic discourses that underpin the processes of nation building, identity formation, and Anglo-female resistance to white patriarchy. Castiglia, for example, argues specifically that the experiences of white women during their captivities, their "trials in the wilderness," were liminal, marginalized experiences in terms of both race and gender, which allowed the captives to then make radical challenges to the key systems of male domination—imperialism and patriarchy—upon their return. Faery, on the other hand, exposes how the ideological and physical landscape of American identity was "mapped" onto women's bodies in order to define the nascent American nation as white, male, and Christian.[6] Pairing the stories of two iconic early American women, Mary Rowlandson and Pocahontas, Faery strives "to see the two figures as connected in the cultural work they have been made to do and to consider the ways the two figures have cooperated and intersected in the work of producing an evolving racially inflected and gendered nationalism" (13).[7]

My intervention into this conversation is to examine the nature of early American identity and the ways in which Anglo women writers participated in constructing it and the ways in which images and ideas of Indianness undergirded it, thus extending the work begun by Castiglia, Faery, and others. I want to bring texts by early American women writers and iconic portrayals of Indianness into focus together as texts that co-construct one another and actively participate in the revision of the racial, national, gendered, and historical discourses that underpin American identity, specifically American identity in its earliest iterations—from colonization to the formation of the early republic. The aim of *Anglo-American Women Writers and Representations of Indianness* is to show that these early American women writers co-opted and revised the prevalent images and ideas of

---

[6]   Karen Sanchez-Eppler's *Touching Liberty: Abolition, Feminism and Politics of the Body* does similar work to Faery's except her focus is on the nineteenth-century abolitionist movement and Black rather than Indian bodies.

[7]   Some other studies that examine the connections between Anglo female identity and racialized hierarchies in early America/the early republic include Pauline Schloesser's *The Fair Sex: White Women and Racial Patriarchy in the Early American Republic* (2001), Karen Anderson's *Chain Her By One Foot: The Subjugation of Native Women in Seventeenth-Century New France* (1994), and June Namias's *White Captives: Gender and Ethnicity on the American Frontier* (1993).

Indianness of their times, as well as the potential resistance these tropes contained, in order to posit their own identities as American women writers, to show how they produced flattened, one-dimensional versions of Native realities that would ultimately serve as the source for their own identities in print. This study examines how identity politics extend beyond imagistic portrayals of Indianness into the literature of women writers and the many ways in which these writers revise and expand male-controlled images, narratives, and subject-positions, creating their own complex (mis)representations of Indianness in response.

Iconography and Narrative

This study seeks to bring simultaneous, critical attention to both material, visual culture and print narrative. Instead of treating images and icons as ancillary to literary texts, I examine them as being in conversation with one another and as engaging with and obliquely critiquing larger discussions about race, gender, nationalism, and American identity. Because both iconography and narrative in the seventeenth, eighteenth, and early nineteenth centuries functioned within a colonialist, racist, patriarchal system, these modes of production played out the tensions between the promise of social opportunity of the burgeoning new nation and the overarching hegemonic constraints that controlled its formation. Iconographic images of Indianness and the responsive narratives of Anglo women writers delineate these tensions and, when read together, provide a richer context for understanding them both. It becomes clear that these Anglo female-authored texts are providing the dialogue, the back story, that these images of Indianness only suggest; furthermore, they are making explicit additions and strategic revisions to that story to include not only Anglo womanhood, but also Anglo female authorship.

Because of this focus on the interdependence of visual culture and narrative, I have organized *Anglo-American Women Writers and Representations of Indianness* into two halves. The first half focuses on the iconic image of the Massachusetts Bay Colony Seal and narratives of Anglo women that engage it, and the second, on images of Pocahontas and related women's narratives. The repeated headings of "Iconography" and "Narrative" within the chapters signal the ongoing structure of the book; they are also intended to reinforce my attention both to imagery and its historical context, as well as to how the female authors of the literary texts responded.

More specifically, the first half of this study, chapters 1 and 2, centers on the Bay Colony seal and its core elements of a nearly nude Native figure holding a bow and arrow and the words, "Come over and help us." Although these essential features have remained all but unchanged in the history of the seal's iconography, there have been striking alterations to the aggregate image throughout the years. By examining the historical contexts of and alterations to the seal, I trace in the first part of Chapter 1, "Iconography," how at different points in the colony's history, the residents inscribed the Indian of the seal as the cultural, racial, sexual, gendered, intellectual, economic, and religious other in order to stabilize their own identity. Using these identity politics of the earliest incarnations of the seal as a touchstone, I examine the complex relationship between the Christian Indian and printer, James Printer, and the Indian captive and author, Mary Rowlandson in the "Narrative" portion of this chapter. Although Printer served as translator and scribe during the negotiations for Rowlandson's return from captivity and as typesetter for the second edition of her 1682 narrative, *The Sovereignty and Goodness of God*, Rowlandson uses her newly granted agency to write Printer out of existence in her influential work by flattening out and erasing his and other Christian Indians' roles in her salvation/authorial self-creation, reducing Printer rhetorically to the iconic Indian on the Massachusetts Bay seal. I conclude that Rowlandson's creation of an authorial identity could not have been realized without a James Printer figure; however, she negates his role in order to justify her exceptionality as a female author.

In the "Iconongraphy" portion of Chapter 2, I move into analyzing a later image of the Massachusetts Bay Colony seal, the 1775 Paul Revere cut of the seal. While the Revere seal, which features an Anglo-American man clad in breeches and topcoat clutching a copy of Magna Carta and a sword instead of an Indian figure, reinforces the patriarchal discourses dominating the national dialogue, Ann Eliza Bleecker's 1793 captivity narrative, *The History of Maria Kittle*, challenges and ruptures them. I argue in the "Narrative" portion of this chapter how through the conscientious deployment of the trappings of the feminine sphere, Bleecker essentially writes the feminine and domestic into national existence in a system dominated and controlled by white patriarchal images like Revere's seal. Further, by masculinizing Indianness, and then bringing white womanhood into contact with it in an assertive, productive way, Bleecker is able to inscribe the feminine and the domestic with a new agency and even begin the visualization of a differently gendered national identity and of herself as an author.

The second half of my project, chapters 3 and 4, analyzes eighteenth- and nineteenth-century female-authored texts that play off images of Pocahontas and her foundational yet complex relationship to colonial identity. In the "Iconography" portion of Chapter 3, I examine the 1616 Simon Van de Passe engraving of Pocahontas. My analysis here asserts that this engraving, which depicts an "Indian princess" as an "English lady" disruptively suggests simultaneously that an "English lady" can be Indian. I assert that the melding of identities in this image fuses supposedly diametrically opposed cultures, races, and sensibilities through the filter of womanhood which endows Pocahontas's image and identity with a power Anglo women writers themselves sought and appropriated.

The "Narrative" portion of this chapter deals with the anonymous 1767 narrative, *The Female American*, which contains a feminine "mixed-blooded" character with an insurgent identity indebted to Pocahontas.[8] This text is purportedly

---

[8]   The vocabulary for describing people and fictional characters of mixed ancestry is, at best, problematic. Terms like *metis*, *mestizo*, crossblood, hybrid, and bi- and multi-racial

the autobiography of Unca Eliza Winkfield, a biracial New World woman who is the granddaughter of both Edward Maria Winkfield (more commonly spelled "Wingfield"), a founding father of the Virginia colony, and a powerful, Powhatan-like Indian chief of the region. I argue that the tension of Unca Eliza's "mixed-blood" position and her womanhood allows her to navigate among these many discourses of colonial containment and subvert them. To the colonial imagination, the construct of a "mixed-blood" Indian represented the possibility of the loss of the binaries that inscribed the colonists as "civilized" and "superior" and the Indians as "inferior" others. As a consequence, biracial Indians (particularly males, as I discuss in Chapter 4) were problematic for the master narratives of colonization because of their disruptive nature; they could be and were successfully deployed by female authors to rhetorically destabilize colonial hegemony. Unca Eliza's biracial identity and her gender, therefore, create textual slippages and ruptures that breach Anglo-American authority, as well as the anonymous author's, in ways that "pure-blooded" female characters simply cannot.

In the "Iconography" portion of Chapter 4, I examine the *Sedgeford Hall Portrait*, an image that purportedly depicts Pocahontas and her son Thomas. I argue that, although the painting's origins are apocryphal, it is the ambivalent presence of the biracial, "mixed-blooded" and male Thomas in the painting rather than its unclear provenance that makes the portrait "unacceptable" and incredibly threatening to Anglo-American audiences of the early republic. Alongside this portrait in the "Narrative" portion of Chapter 4, I examine Lydia Maria Child's 1824 novel, *Hobomok*. I argue that Child utilized the potency of her "mixed-blood" character, Charles Hobomok Conant, in her text to open a space within the white, masculine New World identity where white womanhood and female authorship could emerge. Child asserts that womanhood, when undergirded by the authenticating yet disruptive power of Indianness, could be inscribed as a significant and constituent part of American identity. Ultimately, however, Child

---

are other working phrases often employed to reflect racial mixture, but many of these underscore the "otherness" and perceived exoticism of "mixed-blood" people—at least to Anglo-American ears. They may also reflect the false notion that biologically pure races exist (as in bi- and multi-racial) or, as in the case of the term "hybrid," accentuate the colonial notion of racial contamination through "interbreeding"—a modern day version of the nineteenth-century pejorative for mixed-race Indians, "half-breed." In this book, I use the term "mixed-blood" alongside more mainstream designations like "biracial" because it seems less deterministic than other terms. As Thomas Ingersoll has argued, "mixed-blood" is perhaps "a helpful metaphor to express mixed ancestry precisely because blood itself is racially meaningless (for example, the basic ABO blood system is universal but its original function, for the most part, is unknown)" (xxi). Although the use of "mixed-blood" risks perpetuating the notion that racial differences can be traced to an essential, racial identity that exists in the blood at a cellular level, I would argue that it also, and perhaps more importantly, underscores the constructedness of Anglo-Indian identity within colonial discourse. Here, I use "mixed-blood" alongside more mainstream designations like "biracial" in order to emphasize the artificiality of a belief in pure races and racial identities.

backs away from her associations with "mixed-blood" Indian masculinity because of its potential to reinscribe the patriarchal structures she has so aggressively worked to disrupt.

The conclusion brings the entanglement of Anglo-American womanhood and Indianness into a twenty-first-century context with the examination of material manifestations of the legacies of the Massachusetts Bay Colony seal and Pocahontas. The fact that JC Penney and the Association for the Preservation of Virginia Antiquities museum store have breathed new life (and profit) into these emblems of American identity by turning them into commercial products specifically targeted to American women—window coverings and earrings, respectively—is significant to note. Clearly, Americans are still remaking and revisiting these originary representations of Indianness and hooking them into a feminine identity, underscoring the fact that we, as a nation, have not fully come to terms with our fraught and colonialist relationship to Native identity. The anxieties about and appropriations of Indianness from the earliest colonial encounters in the New World are still there. In the end, this work raises questions about and deepens our understanding of the complex ties between the visual and narrative regimes of colonialism, Anglo-female authorial identity, and representations of Indianness in early America.

Postcoloniality and Early American Studies

Because of the concepts that I examine in this study—nation, identity, gender, race—and the colonial/early republican time period that my study brackets, I necessarily invoke postcoloniality. The application of postcolonialism to early American studies has been of expanding interest in recent decades, with various scholars employing postcolonial methodologies as "a means of learning more about the intercultural and interracial matrices of the process of colonization and decolonization" in the Americas (Schueller and Watts 10–11). Collections of essays such as Edward Watts's *Writing and Postcolonialism in the Early Republic* (1998), Malini Schueller's *U.S. Orientalisms: Race, Nation, and Gender in Literature, 1790–1890* (1998), Robert Blair St. George's *Possible Pasts: Becoming Colonial in Early America* (2000), and Malini Schueller and Edward Watts's *Messy Beginnings: Postcoloniality and Early American Studies* (2003) represent just some of the scholarship that has brought together early American specialists with the singular goal of exploring and trying to understand the various forms of resistance enacted by colonized peoples in the New World and the entanglement of the colonizers within those resistances. Additionally, full-length monographs, like Andy Doolen's *Fugitive Empire: Locating Early American Imperialism* (2005), Ned C. Landsman's *Crossroads of Empire: The Middle Colonies in British North America* (2010), and Mark Rifkin's *Manifesting America: The Imperial Construction of U.S. National Space* (2012), among others, have also sought to interrogate the complex relationships of Anglo colonizers to the colonized, including the intricate ways in which the identities of the white settlers were shaped through the contact with, appropriations of, and occasionally even alliances with these discourses of resistance.[9]

Although Native Americans do not constitute the traditional definition of a colonized people, wherein an indigenous majority is invaded, ruled over, and exploited by a minority of foreigners in pursuits that are defined by a distant metropole, and, as many scholars have noted, there is no "post" to the "colonial," so to speak, for Native American nations in the United States, postcolonial theory is still decidedly useful for my methodology. The particularities of the fraught relationship between the United States government and Native American nations as well as the still-colonized status of tribal peoples have led to heated debates about the appropriateness of postcolonialism when treating early American/early Native American texts. Scholars such as Bill Ashcroft, Gareth Griffiths, Helen Tiffin (*The Empire Writes Back*, 1989), and Lawrence Buell ("America's Literary Emergence as a Post-Colonial Phenomenon," 1999) see American literature as postcolonial despite America's status as a settler nation, while other scholars, such as Amy Kaplan and Anne McClintock, have expressed concern about the appropriation of the postcolonial for settler cultures, with McClintock even specifically claiming that calling the United States postcolonial is a "monumental affront to Native American peoples" ("Angel of Progress" 87).[10] Peter Hulme, however, has suggested that postcolonial is a productive term for American studies in that it "refers to a *process* of disentanglement from the whole colonial syndrome, which takes many forms … 'postcolonial' is (or should be) a descriptive, not an evaluative, term" (emphasis in the original, 120). In a similar vein, scholars of Native Studies,

---

[9]   These edited collections of essays all cover a wide variety of texts from multiple colonized subject positions and early American time periods/genres. The monographs, of course, provide more specific, extended focus to a single region/subject position/topic and postcoloniality. Doolen's *Fugitive Empire* examines how whiteness came to be conflated with American national identity in the early republic in order to stabilize racial hierarchies and stave off challenges to national policies concerning slavery and expansion. Landsman's *Crossroads of Empire* traces how the middle colonies—New York, New Jersey, and Pennsylvania—became the center of imperial contests among European powers and various Native American nations. Rifkin's *Manifesting America* examines the legal rhetorics that allowed American expansion at the seeming "consent" of Native Americans and Mexicans who became incorporated into American authority.

[10]   Utilizing the earlier work of D.E.S. Maxwell, postcolonial theorists Bill Ashcroft, Gareth Griffiths, and Helen Tiffin define a settler nation or settler colony as a space in which land is occupied by "European colonists who dispossessed and overwhelmed the Indigenous populations. They established a transplanted civilization which eventually secured political independence while retaining a non-Indigenous language" (*The Empire Writes Back* 24). In "Angel of Progress," Anne McClintock expresses hesitance over use of the term "postcolonial" as though it describes a single condition because that "re-orients the globe once more around a single, binary opposition: colonial/post-colonial" ("Angel of Progress" 85). She resists the term for regions such as Australia, South Africa, and America in particular because, as she notes, the term is "prematurely celebratory" at best ("Angel of Progress" 87).

such as Jace Weaver and Gerald Vizenor (Anishinaabe) have proposed alternative terms that more accurately describe the colonized condition and identities of Native Americans—i.e., Weaver's "pericolonialism" (10) and Vizenor's idea of the "postindian" (7)—rather than disavowing the postcolonial altogether.

While these debates concerning the status of the postcolonial in early American studies—especially when discussing Native American texts and identities—are extremely valuable and necessary, I would suggest, like Hulme and others, that there is benefit in utilizing postcolonial theory to recognize and tease out the complexities of postcolonial resistance and identity in early America. Postcolonial theory, in its critique of the politics of knowledge and the functional relations of social, political, gendered, and economic power(s) that sustain the colonialist machinery, provides an interpretive framework through which we can understand a colonialist regime's representations of both the colonized and the colonizer. Because the burgeoning sense of the American self and attempts to establish a uniquely American literary tradition in the seventeenth, eighteenth, and nineteenth centuries were so intricately connected to representations of Indianness—both real and imagined, visual and written—postcolonial theory deconstructs and exposes the inherent ambivalences of these depictions. My object in *Anglo-American Women Writers and Representations of Indianness* is, therefore, not simply to expose injuries to white women in early America or to reclaim Anglo women writers as somehow being above and beyond the colonizer/colonized binary. Rather, my aim is to explore their entanglements with and the complexities and contradictions of the colonial-racial hierarchies in which these women intervened in order to demonstrate the ways in which these Anglo women writers and their Indian subjects destabilize the surety of the racist, sexist colonial hegemony. Although I do rely on the work of Native scholars, such as Vizenor, the frameworks and terminologies of the postcolonial theorists Edward Said, Homi Bhabha, and Rey Chow, while not strictly focused on the historic or geographical realities of early America, are especially productive for this goal.

In his landmark text, *Orientalism*, Edward Said establishes how the West constructs the "Orient" through various literary, cultural, and historical discourses, enabling the colonial conquest and subjugation of the East. Said argues that the resultant Western "Orientalist" fantasy reveals more about the West—its fears and ideals—than it does the East and serves to help define the colonial center of the West as "self" by virtue of the Orient's assigned position as "other."[11] Homi Bhabha, in *The Location of Culture*, extends Said's analysis by deconstructing these dichotomies of empire (West and East, colonizer and colonized, self and other, etc.) to propose that the relationship between the colonizer and the colonized is a complex mix of attraction and repulsion, recognition and disavowal. Nationalities and ethnicities, according to Bhabha, are characterized by "hybridity," a more

---

[11] Early American constructions of the Native other, such as those displayed in Mary Woodbury's portrait and in written texts, operate in a similar fashion of creating the other in order to define the colonial American self.

fluid, indeterminate sense of identity that emerges in and through the engagement between colonizer and colonized rather than essence.[12] The colonizer seeks to create compliant subjects who willingly accept and reproduce—"mimic"—the cultural identity of the colonizing force, but who do so without exact replication; perfect copies of the colonizing culture in the darker, more "savage" bodies of the colonized would simply be too threatening to imperial hierarchy. Consequently, Bhabha argues, there has to remain a difference between the colonizer and the colonized's mimicked performance of him; the colonizer's desire, therefore, is "for a reformed, recognizable Other, *as a subject of difference that is almost the same, but not quite*" (Bhabha, "Of Mimicry" 122, italics in original).

Because mimicry must always produce and perform its own difference as a blurred copy of the colonial original, the discourse of mimicry is necessarily generated out of ambivalence. Bhabha further notes, "in order to be effective, mimicry must continually produce its slippage, its excess, its difference ... [M]imicry is therefore stricken by an indeterminacy: mimicry emerges as the representation of a difference that is itself a process of disavowal" ("Of Mimicry" 122). Mimicry also is never very far from mockery, parodying what it imitates, and consequently, it is profoundly disturbing for colonial discourse because it continually suggests an identity that is not like that of the colonizer. Mimicry locates a rupture in the certainty of colonial domination, revealing its limitations; it pinpoints the uncertainty of colonization's control of the behavior of the colonized subjects because of their ambivalent fluctuation between resemblance and menace, and as a result, is always potentially insurgent. Rey Chow, in *Entanglements, or Transmedial Thinking about Capture*, extends this notion further, by focusing on the potency of the ambivalent, internally divided subjectivity of the colonized who at once desire to imitate the colonizer and become "white," but simultaneously feel self-loathing and abasement because of this desire. Chow asserts that through this introduction of desire,

> the entire question of mimesis [is transformed] into a fluid, because vacillating, structure in which the thoroughly entangled feelings of wanting at once to imitate the colonizer and to eliminate him become the basis or a new kind of analysis, with the tormented psychic interiority of the colonized as its theatrical nerve center ... the colonized's desire here makes way for a flexible, because mobile, framework for imagining alterity from within subordination. ("Sacrifice" 95)

---

[12]   I recognize that the use of the term "hybridity" is fraught with criticism. The term, when used to describe people of color, has often been criticized due to its inherently sexual overtones that suggest the replication of colonial culture through unions of the colonized and the colonizer. Hybridity has also been used to simply indicate cross-cultural exchange, thereby negating the imbalance of power between the colonizer and colonized. I am using the term, however, in the same way that Homi Bhabha uses it here—to underscore the interdependence and mutual construction of colonized and colonizer subjectivities. When figured in this way, hybridity asserts a shared postcolonial condition and consequently, contains the potentiality of reversing the hegemonic structures of domination in colonial discourse.

It is through these inherent "cracks" of colonialist discourse, the ambivalence of mimicry, that the colonized "others"—the Indians—were able to not only aggressively resist colonial domination, but also expose the inherent flaws within the system. Gerald Vizenor, an Anishinaabe writer and theorist, similarly argues that Native Americans are able to masterfully take advantage of the ambiguity of these colonialist "simulations." He writes, "the postindian warriors of postmodern simulations ... undermine and surmount, with imagination and the performance of new stories, the manifest manners of scriptural simulations and 'authentic' representations of tribes in the literature of dominance" (17).

Anglo women in the New World, through their de facto entanglement with Indianness and their embodied existence as females, were tied into these same colonialist discourses and the subsequent potential resistance embedded within them.[13] Anglo women in early America, particularly those within the Puritan tradition, were under the guardianship and tutelage of patriarchy and urged to uniformly submit to male authority in both social and spiritual matters and to exercise obedience and resignation in that respect. Noted historian David Hackett Fischer observes that ministers "preached that the husband ruled with God-given authority, and even represented divine sovereignty in the family" and that many Puritan New Englanders often "quoted the Pauline expression that the husband was 'the head of the wife'" (84). This is not to say the role and value of women went unrecognized or that women did not exercise some rights and agency within this patriarchal system. As historian Laurel Thatcher Ulrich posits in her now classic study of New England women's lives in the seventeenth and eighteenth centuries, *Good Wives*, the relationship of women and men was a covenant of unequals. She writes:

---

[13] Empire building has always been reliant upon the lived, bodily experiences of women. Anglo female bodies were the ones who brought "home" to the outposts and settlements of the imperial realm. The "proper womanhood" these white bodies represented became a fulcrum by which colonizing men measured themselves as well as those they colonized. Indigenous female bodies functioned as the antithesis to white womanhood and were marginalized, sexualized, and silenced within the colonialist systems. See Philippa Levine (*Gender and Empire*), Laura Donaldson (*Decolonizing Feminisms*), and the essay collection *Writing on the Body*, edited by Katie Conboy, Nadia Medina, and Sarah Stanbury (to name just a few), for more information on women, their bodies, and European empire formation more generally speaking. Much work has been done exposing and critiquing the multiple systems of oppression that bind women of color within colonialist systems, the ways in which feminism of the Anglo, Western tradition has neglected or overwritten indigenous/Third World subjectivities, and the subsequent resistance of these women. See, for example, the work of such postcolonial and intersectional feminists such as Chandra Talpade Mohanty ("Under Western Eyes"), Trinh T. Minh-ha (*Woman, Native, Other*), and Chilla Bulbeck (*Re-Orienting Western Feminisms*). There has also been much excellent work that specifically examines the resistance and agency of indigenous women of the Americas to these colonialist structures; Hilary Wyss and Kristina Bross (*Early Native Literacies in New England*), Mónica Díaz (*Indigenous Writings from the Convent*), and Drew Newman (*On Records*) are just a few examples.

the position of a wife was complementary and at the same time secondary to that of her husband. This was a function of not just ideology, but of the most pervasive realities of existence. Contradictory possibilities were built into a system which meshed law with sentiment, property with procreation, and gender specialization with communal obligation. (8)

Women, therefore, actually occupied a large, but domestically oriented, range of positions and roles within their communities and homes. Yet these roles and the agency that undergirded female identity were constantly subject to "embodiment," a process by which western patriarchy identified the woman (and often the indigenous population) with nature, the body, corruption, and irrationality. Feminist theorist Sidonie Smith argues that the act of embodiment is caused when a privileged subject reacts with revulsion to those he labels as "others"—either sexually or racially—and then projects his denied bodily experiences onto them (10).

Images and narratives of early America, like the Mary Woodbury painting and the other texts and images in my study, relied on this embodied connection of white womanhood and Indianness to buttress a sense of male American exceptionalism and to reinscribe the raced and gendered discourses of patriarchy. It was male explorers and leaders and scholars who were the authors of this fluctuating sense of Indianness and its connections to womanhood; however, it was Anglo women writers who exploited, appropriated, further racialized, and utilized that connection in order to separate themselves from it and establish their own authorial identities. It is the goal of this study to explore the various ways in which a selection of white women writers constructed themselves in an array of shifting relationships to the Indianness around them—Indianness that was the core of what was at stake in the New World colonial project and the core of these women's texts.

Chapter 1
Indians, Images, and Identity:
The Massachusetts Bay Colony Seal,
James Printer, and Mary Rowlandson's
Praying Indians

Part 1
Iconography: The Massachusetts Bay Colony Seal

Although the seal of the Massachusetts Bay Colony is a familiar sight to scholars of early American history and literature, this iconic image of imperialism and colonialism has served as little more than an interesting footnote in the annals of early American scholarship. As scholars, we are all familiar with the stark imagery of the seal: a nearly nude, Native figure holding a bow in one hand and a down-turned arrow in the other with the appeal "Come over and help us" issuing from the mouth,[1] and we have seen it prominently displayed as a frontispiece or as a key illustration in various academic texts (see Figure 1.1).[2] In such texts, the detailed image of the seal is often accompanied by rather basic annotation which notes the seal's imperialistic overtones and perhaps its dates of use, but then the pace of the work surrounding the image resumes, as if to move on to what "really needs to be said" about more pertinent topics, suggesting the seal itself is an interesting visual relic but an open book. It is a text about which all is transparent and readily evident to the viewer. Its motives and intent are obvious; and while arresting, there is nothing else to say or that can be said about it, really.

---

[1] As of yet, I have been unable to definitively identify the creator/owner and exact dates of usage of this seal (Figure 1.1), although preliminary research indicates it is also a printer's cut commissioned by John Usher, a Boston bookseller and active businessman who had mercantile connections in London and, on occasion, served as agent for the colony. However, more research needs to be done on this image's origins and use. In a further twist of ambivalence, I am unclear on whether this image depicts a feminized, adolescent male or a female figure, a point which further illustrates my claims.

[2] See, for example, the image as pictured in Francis Jennings's *The Invasion of America: Indians, Colonialism, and the Cant of Conquest*; in Neal Salisbury's excellent introduction to *The Sovereignty and Goodness of God* by Mary Rowlandson; in Susan Castillo and Ivy Schweitzer's *The Literatures of Colonial America: An Anthology*; in Jill Lepore's *The Name of War: King Philip's War and the Origins of American Identity*; and in James Axtell's *The Invasion Within: The Contest of Cultures in Colonial North America*. See also Kristina Bross's "'Come Over and Help Us': Reading Mission Literature," which provides the written equivalent to such visual glosses of the seal.

Figure 1.1   Massachusetts Bay Colony Seal, 1629. Courtesy of the
                Massachusetts Archives.

Yet, for all of this apparent lack of complexity and depth, this seal has been an enduring and near-constant element of the authorized and official identity of the Massachusetts Colony/Commonwealth. From King Charles's charter of the Massachusetts Bay Plantation on March 4, 1629, until today, there has nearly always been an official seal in active usage that depicts some variation of a Native figure holding a bow in its left hand and a down-turned arrow in the right.[3] Granted, the seal of today features a Native figure now clothed in more accurate garb of shirt and moccasins who is no longer crying out for help, but the figure still stands alone on a field of blue, grasping a bow in one hand and arrow in the other (see Figure 1.2). It is practically the same image from nearly 400 years ago. Obviously then, this seal is more than simply a footnote of American history; it is a powerful testament to the identity, culture, and self-perception of the people who have lived and live now under its auspices. It is an official statement of the authority, unity, and individuality of the residents of the Commonwealth, and according to William Francis Galvin, the current Secretary of the Commonwealth of Massachusetts, it also "is rich in Massachusetts culture[.] [T]he images are traceable from century to century, and the value has survived the test of time. Indeed, its authenticity and usefulness can be seen in the many documents that bear its certification" (Galvin 2). While Secretary Galvin's statements are certainly open for lively critical debate and interpretation, his final point about the "usefulness" of the seal, even from its origins in 1629, is accurate. It was a very useful tool for the colonial enterprise. Colonial epistemology began with Europeans' production of cultural, historical, and political representations about the Indians of North America as "inferior," ahistorical, and elemental beings who were deserving of, and in the case of the Bay Colony seal, even pleading for, the domination of Europe. This production of knowledge began not only with written accounts of New World exploration and settlement, all of which were contingent on a literate population with access to texts in order to absorb the knowledge, but also on visual markers that legitimized these New World ventures and attempted to fix Native and colonial identity, such as the Bay Colony Seal. This symbol, which would have been in use not only on the official documents of the colony, but also on correspondence with other colonies and governments, public notices, and even the individual governors' personal messages within a month after the colony's charter, would have been a highly visible, and visual, representation that did the work of imperialism in an effective yet simple manner on both sides of the Atlantic. It would have served to stabilize the identities of English colonists and their understanding of the Indians, which were only partially formed in the colonizers' minds during these initial colonial encounters. The various renderings of the Indians and New World

---

[3]   Only between the years 1686 and 1689 when Governor Edmund Andros ruled the colony under a charter from King James II, and again between 1692 and 1775 when the Province of Massachusetts employed the royal coat of arms of England combined with a motto specific to the reigning monarch, did the seal of the Massachusetts Colony/ Province deviate from the formula of depicting a single "native" figure wielding weaponry. Interestingly, after the break with England, the Massachusetts General Court adopted a new seal, which depicted once again a single figure facing outward grasping weaponry in either hand. However, as Secretary of the Commonwealth William Francis Galvin notes, this time the figure was that of an "English-American man holding the Magna Carta in his left hand and an upraised sword in his right" (Galvin 4). I discuss this seal, most commonly known as the Revere Seal in honor of its engraver, Paul Revere, at length in Chapter 2.

Figure 1.2   The present Great Seal of the Commonwealth of Massachusetts.
Courtesy of the Office of the Secretary of the Commonwealth
of Massachusetts.

landscapes on the seals were attempts to calcify a representational reality and to define the colonizers and their mission.

However, because of the colonists' unclear and fluctuating sense of themselves, as well as their identity in the New World and their relationship to the Native Americans (real and imagined) around them, the "stable" image of the Massachusetts Bay Colony seal was constantly changing. The core image of the Indian and the landscape around him becomes muddied and diffuse as the cultural and gendered markers of the figure fluctuate from seal to seal. This interplay of civilization and gender at the core of the seal embodies the anxieties about identity and the colonists' ambivalent position in the New World. These images are fascinating and troubling on so many levels because of the mixed and even contradictory messages they seem to send about the identity of the Native inhabitants of the New World as well as the people who designed and used the seal, the colonists themselves. The fears and prejudices of the Bay Colony settlers are evident as they are projected onto the raced and gendered body of the Native figures of these seals; however, the colonists' unclear and fluctuating sense of themselves, as well as their identity and role in the New World also become painfully clear through the various representations of the primary image of Indianness. This image becomes a barometer of sorts, reflecting the diffuse and fluid nature of colonial identity, and the conflicted repulsion from/desire for the Nativeness that not only underpins that identity, but gives it existence.[4] The seal becomes a representation of the ambivalence, fragmentation, and instability that necessarily accompanied the formation of a colonial New World identity. It exposes the fraught and fluctuating conceptions of race, gender, and cultural superiority that undergirded Anglo-European understanding of identity. Perhaps more provocatively, however, such an image exposes the colonists' own uncertainty in their control over the colonized Natives, revealing a crack through which Native Americans, particularly transculturated Native Christians, could critique and ultimately disrupt the conviction—and fantasy—of colonial dominance.

A Native American who had adopted all of the cultural trappings, beliefs, and abilities that were the hallmarks of English superiority, yet was still so obviously not-English, would have been extremely threatening to colonial dominance. Such a figure would have been Bhabha's "almost but not quite," that colonized object who simultaneously attracted the colonizer's attention because of his successful assimilation and conversion, but also repelled them because of the inherent ambivalence in his position. Such a person, like the Native Christian and Bay Colony resident James Printer, whom I discuss later in this chapter, would have been a constant, living, breathing enactment of the identity issues plaguing these no-longer-English but not-yet-American pilgrims in the wilderness. He would have reflected the very complexities inscribed on the colony's seal, but because of Printer's actual historic existence and active resistance to the colonial project during King Philip's War, the cracks already inherent in colonial discourse are perilously destabilized and readily exploited. Native Americans with acculturated knowledge of the system, like Printer, could disrupt and deconstruct the raced and gendered system of colonization. Anglo women writers who were closely associated with both Native Christians and these fraught ideas of Indianness, like the famous Indian captivity survivor, Mary Rowlandson, could also capitalize on these exposed cracks in the colonialist system, using the stereotypes of the "paper Indians" from the seal to write themselves into existence while intentionally writing Indian and Native Christianity out.

---

[4] There is much scholarship on the textual representation of the Native/Indigene and the colonist/settler response to, articulation of, and appropriation of it. See, for example, Scott Lauria Morgensen's *Spaces Between Us: Queer Settler Colonialism and Indigenous Decolonization*, Terry Goldie's *Fear and Temptation: The Image of the Indigene in Canadian, Australian, and New Zealand Literatures*, and Penelope Ingram's "Racializing Babylon: Settler Whiteness and the 'New Racism'" and "Can the Settler Speak? Appropriating Subaltern Silence in Janet Frame's *The Carpathians*."

Understanding New World Anglo Identity

The colonists of the New World, already apprehensive about their great distance from England and the subsequent cultural alienation that that entailed, were anxious to maintain their English ways while appreciating the many freedoms that accompanied life in the colonies. The threat of becoming something else, something barbarous, was very real for the colonists, because in equal measure to their distance from England was their closeness to the Indians. As historian Jill Lepore has noted, this aroused serious doubts for the colonists about their own identity because

> [e]ither the Indians were native to America ... or else they were migrants from Europe or Asia.... If native, the Indians were one with the wilderness and had always been as savage as their surroundings.... But if the Indians were migrants from Europe or Asia, then they had changed since coming to America and had been contaminated by its savage environment. If this were the case, as many believed, then the English could expect to degenerate, too. (Lepore 5–6)

Therefore the seal, even in its various permutations, presented a fixed Native identity that in turn was an attempt to fix the colonial identity, to repair the colonists' loss of mastery and privilege invoked by the cultural isolation in the New World, but yet solidify his/her rightful place in and his/her autochthonous relationship with that New World. These images produced the Natives as a visual, social reality, which was at once utterly "othered" and simultaneously knowable and visible, in order to disavow the racial, cultural, and intellectual differences the colonists saw of themselves in the colonized. As historian Robert Berkhofer has observed in *The White Man's Indian*, these "counterimages" were used by Anglo colonists to "define White identity or prove White superiority over the worst fears of their own depravity" (27). The Massachusetts Bay Colony seal was one such image.

From its charter on March 4, 1629, the Massachusetts Bay Plantation was authorized by the New England Company to establish one common seal, and by April 30 of that same year, the warrant of Richard Trott for making two seals in silver was approved. The seals were most likely completed by April 17, 1629, because in the first General Letter to Governor John Endecott, who was still in England, it was noted by his council that two duplicate silver seals had been made.[5] These two identical seals were made for wax impressions (see Figure 1.3) and displayed "a human figure holding a straight back Indian bow in its left hand and an arrow in the right hand"; this image was the governor's official signature for the colony and its inhabitants for some 33 years (Jones 15). The seal also functioned on a broader level, beyond the colony and governor, to validate the communal,

---

5   John Endecott had previously helped lead the Dorchester Bay Company's settlement on Cape Anne in the 1620s and served as the Bay Colony's governor for only a year until he was replaced by John Winthrop in 1630. Having earned the colonists' respect for his leadership during that first winter, however, he remained active in the colony's politics and was elected governor again in 1644, a position in which he served almost continuously until his death in 1665.

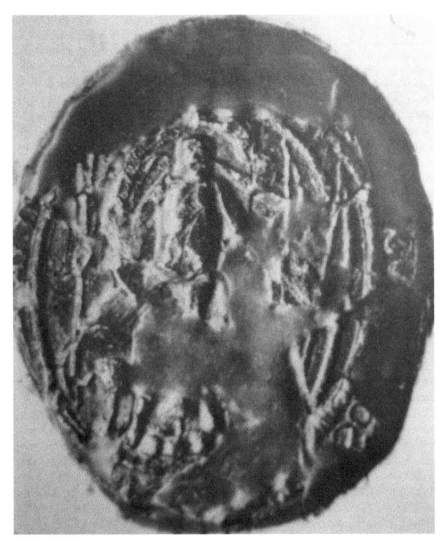

Figure 1.3   Photograph of wax impression of Massachusetts Bay Colony
Seal, no date. From the Stewart Mitchell Papers. Collection of the
Massachusetts Historical Society.

political identity of Massachusetts Bay and make it "official" in the eyes of
the world. Today, as in the seventeenth century, a seal is defined as "a device
impressed upon wax or other plastic material … as evidence of authenticity or
attestation" and as "a token or symbol of a covenant; something that authenticates
or confirms; a final addition which completes and secures" (OED). As such an
authenticating tool, a seal must be able to translate intangible principles and ideals
into consistent, graphic symbols that are readily interpreted and understood by all

who view it. For centuries, seals were used to indicate an individual's acceptance of a document, as in the case of a signet ring or familial crest impressed into wax, or to verify the sovereign authority's acceptance of official documents of state, such as proclamations or deeds, as with a royal coat of arms, an official presidential crest or other heraldic seal that would be embossed onto paper or sealed into wax. The image or emblem on the seal served as a fixed representation of the authority figure behind it; it was a visual symbol of the unalterable facticity, as well as the lineage, cultural heritage, title or rank, of the person or group of people authorized to use it. The Bay Colony's seal and its variations were visible, sanctioned markers of assurance; they were confirmations of the legal and official authority of the newly formed colony and its government, markers that testified to the "truth" of the cultural and communal identities of the citizens under its jurisdiction.

The earliest seals of the Massachusetts Bay Colony were impressed into wax or embossed onto paper by method of some sort of mechanical screw press and they validated acts of the General Court and certified proclamations and commissions; they would have served on both sides of the Atlantic as a tangible and acknowledged representation of the governor of the colony and his authority (and the king's sanctification of that authority) *in absentia*. In 1672, however, the original silver seals were replaced with a newer version (see Figure 1.4), one that, according to the records of the Bay Colony, was "used with a skrw, much more convenient then [sic] the hand seal" and coincided with the administration of Governor John Leverett (1672–1679) (Jones 14).[6] Although the Leverett seal was primarily created and instituted for its technological advancements and not documented as an intended revision of the original seal, it does manifest an interesting difference from Trott's silver seals.

Although it is nearly impossible to speak definitively of the differences between the original 1629 seals and the Leverett seal because the original seals are so badly broken, it appears the bow of the Native on the original seals was depicted as a straight-back Indian-style bow, while in the Leverett seal, the bow is now presented in the curved English style. Such a revision to the Native figure on the seal, even at the risk of verisimilitude, indicates the complex colonial relationship to both England and the native life around them, as well as the accompanying ambivalent anxiety. Were the Natives becoming more English and adopting English tools and technology or were they inaccurately mimicking, corrupting, that English sensibility? Both of these seals, however, still reflect nearly identical images of a stiff-legged, unyielding male Native figure, clutching his bow and down-turned arrow and crying out for assistance from within a neat circle of the colony's Latin motto: *Sigillum Gvb et Societatis de Massachusetts Bay in Nova Anglia*—Seal of the Governor and Society of Massachusetts Bay in New England. These images of the rigid Natives with unreadable faces, prominently yet peacefully displaying their weaponry, and willingly attempting to interact with the colonial viewer through pleas for aid, seem to have been satisfactory self-representations for

---

6   Here, as in other places where I quote archival texts, I have left the idiosyncratic spelling and wording of these early American texts unchanged.

Figure 1.4   Photograph of Massachusetts Bay Colony Seal (Governor Leverett Seal), circa 1678. From the Stewart Mitchell Papers. Collection of the Massachusetts Historical Society.

the Bay Colony residents. In fact, one or both of these seals were used almost exclusively between the years 1629 and 1692 when William and Mary assumed the charter for the crown. Except for the three years between 1686 and 1689 when President Dudley and Governor Andros introduced new official seals to the colony,[7] this was the unquestioned representation of the static, unchanging Native

---

7   Sir Edmund Andros, governor of New England between 1686 and 1689, had a more elaborate seal than had previously been used in the colony. It had two sides, one picturing King James II's effigy in full panoply with an Englishman and Indian kneeling beneath him and a cherub floating above. The motto that encircles this side of the seal reads, "Iacobvs II D G Mag Brit Fran Et Hib Rex Fidei Defensor" ("James II By the Grace of God King of

other who simultaneously posed the possibility of violence and resistance as well as an opportunity for colonial instruction and civilization. More significant, however, is the fact that that unchanging Native was male; the authorized mark of the colony was from its inception inextricably tied to Indianness and maleness.

During the 1670s and 1680s, however, there were several semi-official printers' cuts sanctioned for use on the colony's official printed materials. These "semi-official" versions of the original, gubernatorial seal were designed for use in printing and were consequently engraved onto either wood or soft, brittle metal and commissioned by the owners of various printing houses for use on their presses' versions of official colony documents as well as on some of their own personal enterprises. Each printer would have designed his own unique version of the seal and that image would have been tied inextricably to his work and his individual press as well as the colony and its dominion. Not only were the impressions of these printer's cuts far more detailed and easier to read than the official governors' seals because they are carved into a solid surface rather than raised from that surface as if produced in a mold, their impressions were also left in ink on paper, a form that could be quickly and easily reproduced for dissemination to a larger audience. Only high-ranking officials and the governor's personal acquaintances would have ever viewed the impressions of the colony's official seals, while the printer's cuts would be seen by nearly the entire population of the colony. Consequently, the colonial presses "took on some of the features of a mint, setting an official seal of authenticity on a text" through their specialized versions of the gubernatorial seal (Amory, "Printing and Bookselling" 84). Used to validate published broadsides, declarations, and the "authentic" version of an event, the printer' cuts of the seal functioned *in absentia* of the legitimate colony seal, which functioned *in absentia* of the embodied authority of the governor himself. On the surface, this relational continuum of seals seems to represent a direct and stable line of authority from its source—the individualized seal of each governor—to the masses—the publicly produced images of the seal that appeared on various publications from various printers.

The first of these cuts was commissioned in 1672 by the Cambridge Printer Samuel Green (see Figure 1.5). Green's cut of the seal conscientiously reproduces the key images of its gubernatorial forbears, with one not-so-minor exception: the Native figure in the center of the seal is now a woman.[8] She is clothed in

---

Great Britain, France and Ireland Defender of the Faith"). The other side of the seal features the King's arms with his garter, crown, supporters, and the motto, "Sigillum Novae Angliae in America" ("Seal of New England in America"). Andros was overthrown by the Puritans in the "American version of the Glorious Revolution" in 1689. See Richard Slotkin's and James K. Folsom's *So Dreadfull a Judgment: Puritan Responses to King Philip's War, 1676–1677*, 10.

[8]   This cut of the seal was most likely commissioned by Green from an engraver in England, because as Matt B. Jones has noted, there is a small break in the right-hand edge of the seal "as though a piece had been broken out and rather clumsily replaced" (21). Because this defect is irregular in form with two sharp angles, Jones asserts that this cut must have been produced on a metal surface, because a break in a wooden cut "would have followed

Figure 1.5   Massachusetts Bay Colony Seal (Cambridge Cut). Detail from *At a Council, held at Charlestown, June the 20th, 1676*. Broadside. Collection of the Massachusetts Historical Society.

a pleated skirt of fabric or animal skin that barely skims the top of her ample thighs and is holding an English style, reverse-curve bow in her left hand and the downward pointed arrow in her right. Her hair is long and loose and her breasts are fully exposed to the viewer. She is standing with her legs apart, but with one foot positioned slightly in front of the other and a slight bend in her right knee. Such a stance, while definitely giving her body some movement and life as opposed to the rather rigid figures depicted in the earlier seals, also gives her a relaxed, natural pose, revealing the contrapposto of the human form. Her hands are similarly relaxed around both the bow and arrow that she holds. Her forefinger and thumb on both hands are pointed outward from her body; they extend away from the rest of her hand instead of folding back toward it as when making a fist to grasp something tightly. This woman is clearly not holding her weapons firmly or standing rigidly in a show of anxiety or tension. She may even be simply holding these items, unsure of how to handle them or what to do with them, until someone else can relieve her of them. The fact that this feminine figure is holding weapons (no matter how leisurely) reflects dissonance with the gendered codes of both the regional Native American tribes of southern New England and the English colonists. As anthropologist Kathleen Bragdon has noted,

> Women and men among the Massachusett … seem to have participated in separate spheres of activity … Women were responsible for farming; child care; gathering wild plants … making clothing … cooking; and serving meals. Men were responsible for hunting, fishing, manufacturing most tools, trading, diplomacy, and warfare. (Bragdon 576)

English society similarly dictated "separate spheres" for the genders, with women's roles being defined by "a space (a house and surrounding yards), a set of tasks (cooking, washing, sewing, milking, spinning, cleaning, gardening), and a limited area of authority (the internal economy of the family)" (Ulrich 9). This representation of an armed feminine figure, while still working through the anxieties expressed on the earlier seals about the threatening-yet-submissive nature of Indian identity, is now also working through the gendered implications of that same identity. If the Indians were the antithesis of the colonists—the "savage" to their "civilized" and "heathen" to their "Christian," then couldn't Indian women be the antithesis of English women—war-like, aggressive, and more sexualized? Could these women challenge colonial stability and identity, too? Native women had long been stereotyped in widely circulated Anglo-European exploratory reports and captivity narratives as being as ferocious and cruel as the men—even vaguely Amazon-like in their threat to Anglo males. For example, in his 1557 narrative *Veritable History and Description of a Country …*, the German adventurer Hans Staden reports that it was the women of the tribal peoples he encountered who would torture a male prisoner by "run[ning] around

---

the grain of the wood and would have been substantially a chord of the curve" (21) as it was the custom of engravers at that time to make the engraving upon the flat side of a board, "longitudinally with the grain" (Jones 21).

him boasting that they will eat him" and then after his death, "scrap[ing] off his skin, making him quite white and stopping up his fundament with a piece of wood so that nothing of him may be lost" (109–10). Girolamo Benzoni, a Spaniard, similarly describes very warlike and violent women in his 1565 *La Historia del Mondo Nuovo* by simply stating, "When [the Natives] go to war, the women fight as well as the men. Their arms are poisoned arrows. They eat their enemies and have eaten many Spaniards" (148). Clearly, this woman's stance and her weaponry were densely loaded and conflicting images for the colonial viewers.

In contrast to her armed and threatening appearance, this female figure is submissively pleading for aid, even domination. Just as the male Indians on the two earliest seals had banners reading, "Come over and help us" issuing from their mouths, so, too, does this woman. This quote, which is from Acts 16:9 of the Bible, reads in its entirety: "Where a vision appeared to Paul in the night. There stoode a man of Macedonia, and prayed him, saying, Come into Macedonia, and helpe vs."[9] This dream occurs during Paul's second missionary journey and the first-ever Christian mission into Europe. Paul was himself, of course, converted through the medium of a vision, so the visionary power of this verse is especially important to note. Also interesting is the fact that Paul and his companions' first convert to Christianity in all of Europe after their arrival in Macedonia is a woman, Lydia, the seller of purple, which perhaps accounts for the sudden use of a female Native figure on Green's iteration of the seal. Yet even with this implicit missionary background, the quote itself is confusing, even conflicting, in this New World context. Who is calling to whom for assistance? Are the colonists of Massachusetts Bay (who are represented by this seal) calling for other colonists from Europe to come and aid the missionary efforts in the New World? Or are the unschooled "savages" calling for something they are generally as of yet unaware of? Ostensibly, it is the Native figure beseeching good European Christians, as the Macedonian man did the apostle Paul in his vision, to travel to the New World and convert the "savages" to Christianity, as the direct biblical quote would indicate. However, Paul's caller was a figment of a dream, a vision received in the night. While this visionary element does not make Paul's calling to venture into Europe any less inspired (spectral evidence like a dream was, in fact, quite meaningful in this time period), the fact remains that actual Macedonian citizens did not request Paul's missionary efforts into Europe; a specter (divinely inspired or

---

[9]   This quote is taken from the first full version of the Geneva Bible, published in 1560, which preceded the authorized King James version by 51 years. The Geneva Bible was one of the first mass-produced bibles made readily available to the public that contained various study guides, cross-references of verses, woodcut illustrations, and introductions to each book of the bible. John Calvin's involvement in the production of the bible, as well as its strongly Puritanical and Calvinist annotations, made it very popular among Puritans and the version most likely consulted by the founders of the Bay Colony. The same passage from Acts 16:9 in the King James Bible, which would have also been in usage during this time, reads: "And a vision appeared to Paul in the night: there stood a man of Macedonia, beseeching him, and saying, Come over into Macedonia, and help us." The differences in the passages between the two bibles are minimal, but certainly could invite more analysis.

otherwise) did. If the Native in the seal is analogously recognized as a fantastical vision like Paul's, the stability and facticity of the seal become even more confused and threatening. The official identity of the colony, the seal, is not based on the fact of "real" Indians that desire European Christianity and welcome missionaries and colonists with down-turned weapons, but a spectral, colonist-generated fantasy. The "truth" and authenticity depicted in the seal, while biblically and doctrinally accurate, is based upon a dream.

The placement of the banner that contains this plea issuing from the mouth of Green's female figure now extends from the left side of her mouth, around her head to end in a gentle curve beside her right cheek rather than trailing off to the side and down toward her weapon as in the Leverett seal. It encircles her head and very becoming face, which unabashedly looks directly out from the seal, a slight smile playing about the full and richly darkened lips. Jill Lepore has noted, "The face, the English believed, 'is a special glass wherein the glory and Image of God doth shine forth and appeare,' and to obscure it in any way was of offense against God" (*The Name of War* 93). Because this figure's face is not obscured, even though her hair is loose and unbound, her welcoming appearance is enhanced. The banner is clearly calling attention to the face and features of the woman rather than weaponry she holds, making the plea, originally delivered by a male figure, rife with sexual innuendo. This woman is a welcoming, non-threatening figure. She is alluring, sexual, even a bit coy, as she stands waiting to receive the colonists (with literal "open arms") and turn over her weapons, perhaps even her body, to them when they arrive to render the help she has requested.

The overt sexuality of this female Native and her seductive plea complicates the meaning of the seal. When a male Indian was the central figure, the intentions (conversion) and the problems (war, resistance) of the colony were satisfactorily evident. Now, however, with an overtly sexual and simultaneously threatening woman at the center, pleading for domination, the added dimensions of reproduction, rape, seduction, and miscegenation become evident. Kathleen M. Brown has noted in her book *Good Wives, Nasty Wenches and Anxious Patriarchs*, which examines race and gender relations in colonial Virginia, that very often in accounts of the New World there are embedded

> clearly cautionary [messages].... Indians are represented literally as feminine
> seducers capable of trapping English men in the web of their own sexual
> desires ... Exploiting English men's hopes for colonial pleasures, Indian women
> dangled before them the opportunity for sexual intimacy, turning a female
> tradition of sexual hospitality into a weapon of war. (67)

This woman is an amalgamation of New England reality and English fantasy; she is another permutation of the allegorical personifications of America as a welcoming, nude, Indian woman that were appearing on map cartouches, engravings, and paintings throughout Western Europe by the 1570s.[10] Her image, as Louis

---

[10]   Here, I am referring to such images as Theodor Galle's quite famous engraving of Jan van der Straet's drawing, *America* (1575), that depicts Vespucci discovering a nude, just

Montrose has argued of other similar images, is an instance of "the gendering of the New World as feminine, and the sexualizing of its exploration, conquest, and settlement" (Montrose 2). Her image simultaneously reflects the tensions between the colonial desire for the misogynistic fantasy of a feminized and sexually compliant Indian other and the very real threat of the "savage" and the feminine combined. Additionally, her presence on the seal underscores the absence of the male Native, and the erasure, or at least denial, of his gendered threat to imperial power and the missionary effort. Yet, her presence also complicates the embedded threat of the violent Indian male by enlarging it to include the dual threat of the Indian female—Amazonian-like violence and miscegenetic seduction.

In use alongside Green's Cambridge cut was another printer's cut featuring a youthful-looking male figure. John Foster's Boston Press cut seems to have been created in 1675 by Foster himself and is reminiscent of the colony's original silver seal and the Leverett seal because it depicts a long-haired male figure with the same bow and arrow (see Figure 1.6). Matt B. Jones notes that "this image is clearly a woodcut engraved on the flat side of a board, as Foster is known to have done, and as was the general custom of wood engravers at that time. It was undoubtedly cut by [Foster] ... for his own use in connection with the press which he had started in Boston" (22). Additionally, Foster must have cut several versions of the seal because slight variations appear in the seal's image on different editions of Foster's documents, such as the Colonial Laws (Littlefield 6). Although both Green's Cambridge cut and Foster's Boston cut were used with comparative frequency between 1675 and 1678,[11] and did appear on printing specimens until the Andros government of 1686, after 1678, Foster's Boston Press cut "appears on a very considerable number of documents ... [indicating] that nearly all official printing went to him after that date" (Jones 40).[12] These two printer's cuts, although essentially interchangeable in the eyes of the colony leaders for authenticating colonial documents, are vastly different and present competing, if not contradictory, versions of colonial identity.

By 1675, New England was about to enter into King Philip's War. King Philip's War, also known as Metacom's War, lasted from June of 1675 to August

---

awakening Native American woman in a hammock upon his arrival in the New World. See Hugh Honour, *The New Golden Land: European Images of America from the Discoveries to the Present Time*, and Louis Montrose, "The Work of Gender in the Discourse of Discovery," for more on images such as these.

[11] Green's Cambridge cut of the seal first appeared on "The General Laws and Liberties of the Massachusetts Colony" in 1672, while Foster's Boston cut was first put to use on "Severall Lawes and Ordinances of War past and made the 26th October 1675." See Jones's "Early Massachusetts-Bay Seals" for a listing of the many various documents on which these two versions of the seal appeared.

[12] William Reese notes that government printing contracts were of crucial importance to Massachusetts printers. He states that before about 1720, "Boston was unable to support printers who did not have some kind of subsidy from either governor or legislature to do the official printing, and for the entire period [first 100 years] it was the most lucrative single contract a printer could hope to have" (5).

Figure 1.6   Massachusetts Bay Colony Seal (Boston Cut). Detail from
*At the second sessions of the General Court held at Boston
in New-England.* Broadside. Collection of the Massachusetts
Historical Society.

of 1676 and was "the bloodiest and most destructive war in American history …
Metacom's War took the lives of about five thousand of the Indians and about two
thousand five hundred of the English, roughly 40 and 5 percent, respectively, of
the two peoples' populations" (Salisbury 1).[13] Prior to the conflict itself, tensions

---

[13]   See Neal Salisbury's excellent introduction to Mary Rowlandson's narrative; Jill
Lepore; Eric B. Schultz and Michael J. Tougias in *King Philip's War: The History and
Legacy of America's Forgotten Conflict*; Jenny Hale Pulsipher's *Subjects unto the Same*

had been building for some time between the colonists, who were "pressuring natives to give up yet more land as well as control over their own communities," and the various tribes who "equate[d] English encroachment on their land with the death of their cultures" (Salisbury 2). The peaceful coexistence that had been maintained on unwritten terms for years in the past was now breaking down, leaving people on each side feeling "that the other had betrayed them ... Such feelings undoubtedly heightened the animosity and cruelty that they visited on one another" (Salisbury 5). Additional issues such as a devaluation of Native American wampum due to a decline in demand for imported beaver pelts; a colonial English baby boom in the 1630s and 1640s that increased English land acquisition in the New World; and the subsequent increase in outlying settlements, trading posts, and the clearing of fields to support growing numbers of imported livestock, also contributed to the tense and trying relationship between the English and Native Americans.[14] Historian William Cronon summarized the culmination of events leading to King Philip's War as being at their core a struggle over "how two peoples conceived of property, wealth, and boundaries on the landscape" (53). With the tension increasing daily between these neighbors, there are, consequently, some significant changes to Foster's Boston cut of the seal from Green's previous version. For example, the central figure of the image is now an adolescent-looking male, clothed in an apron of leaves. His hair is long and shaggy, hanging over his shoulders to the front, lying alongside his cheeks and trailing down along his right arm. Jill Lepore writes:

> Long hair in [English] men, or wayward hair in women, was considered excessive, 'when it is so long, that it covers the eyes, the cheeks, the countenance, &c God hath ordeined those parts to be visible.' Long hair was considered a 'badge of cruelty and effeminacy' and was even vaguely associated with cannibalism. (93)

Clearly, this young man is meant to portray the "savage" nature of the Natives in its most significant, recognizable forms to the colonists. His wild hair and Edenic loincloth of leaves would undoubtedly speak to the colonial perceptions of the Indians as being one with the wilderness, allowing them to disavow any bond with these others. However, the clean-shaven status of the Native man on this cut would deliver a divergent yet equally potent message to the colonists. Kathleen M. Brown points out that

> The native male fashion of being clean-shaven ... clashed with English associations of beards with male political and sexual maturity, perhaps diminishing further Indian men's claims to manliness in the eyes of the English. It probably did not enhance English respect for Indian manhood that female barbers sheared men's facial hair. (58)

King: Indians, English, and the Contest for Authority in Colonial New England; and Daniel R. Mandell's *King Philip's War: Colonial Expansion, Native Resistance, and the End of Indian Sovereignty* for further details of the war.

[14] See Schultz and Tougias for more detail on these many factors contributing to the war.

This figure, through the presence and/or absence of body hair, is depicted simultaneously as wildly chaotic and threatening, yet physically immature and even effeminate. His gender would have signified even further disarray for the colonists because "[m]ale Indian bodies were seen as disorderly, savage, and lazy because they 'ranged the forests' for fish and game, while women performed the horticultural labors" (Finch 53).

Additionally, the bow the man is clutching in the Boston cut has also been altered; it is once again depicted as the straight-back style of the Native Americans which appeared in the original silver seal of the colony, and he is grasping it firmly in his left fist. In his right hand, the figure holds an arrow in a peculiar fashion, with his forefinger and thumb extended, almost as if he is preparing to load it into the bow and draw it back for a shot. The banner, which still extols the "Come over and help us" plea, also has been altered. Although still extending from the left side of the Native's face and encircling his head to the left, the tail end of the banner now swirls around the feathered end of the arrow, calling attention to its very large presence. In all, this figure is far more overtly aggressive and barbarous than his female counterpart in the Cambridge cut, but still just as strangely grounded in fantasy. By the time of King Philip's War, "most native warriors had flintlock muskets or carbines, as opposed to their more traditional bow and arrow weaponry ... [and] were often more adept with European technology than the English themselves" (Schultz and Tougias 16). This iteration of the seal is clearly attempting to mediate the growing threat of the ever more resistant Native Americans by "regressing" the male figure to a more primitive and uncivilized state. Yet the same image is simultaneously asserting the right of and the need for the English to defend themselves, or even possibly initiate an assault, by insistently underscoring that same threat that is neutralized.

The Native figure on this Boston cut of the seal depicts the deep confusion, fear, and loathing with which the colonists viewed their Indian neighbors as well as their own desperate attempts to master their own identities by denying any affinity with—and asserting a mastery over—these others. It also places into stark relief the desire and more confident imperial attitude with which the female figure of the Cambridge cut is depicted. Clearly, colonial interpretations of Indianness varied depending upon the gender of the Native other; perhaps not as obviously, however, were the fluctuating definitions of the colonial self that accompanied the changes in the Native other's gender. While femaleness imparted a colonial identity filled with yearning for a carnal and masterful relationship with the autochthonous land and other, it also revealed the accompanying anxiety to such a union: the fear of violence and reciprocity, that just as the English could adopt, adapt, and erase Indianness, so, too, could the Indian usurp or devour Englishness. Correspondingly, maleness of the Indian figure imparted fears of dominance and erasure by the "inferior" other; however, it also communicated the political, economic, and religious authority of the colony in tacit terms, even if inextricably connected to an Indian body. These ambiguities, these fluctuations between desire for and repulsion from Indianness, are telling markers of the diffuse nature of colonial identity. The anxious return to and repetition of this image, through broadsides, official paperwork and even the early paper money,[15] as an attempt to master and permanently fix it in otherness and stabilize one's own identity ultimately undermines itself because of the image's own fluidity and lack of a fixed central core of meaning. Bhabha identifies this tension as the

> *productive* ambivalence of the object of colonial discourse—that 'otherness' which is at once an object of desire and derision, an articulation of difference contained within the fantasy of origin and identity. What such a reading reveals are the boundaries of colonial discourse and it enables a transgression of these limits from the space of that otherness. ("The Other Question" 67, italics in original).

The Native image and form became a slippery, even dangerous, prospect for colonists to imagine and depict because it was so uncontrollable and could transgress the limits set upon it by colonial discourse. In attempting to revision and re-fix the colonial identity through depicting gendered variations of Indianness, these printer's cuts of the seal ultimately produce an even more conflicted sense of the colonial self and its complex relationship to indefinable Indianness.

Containing the Uncontainable Indian

Perhaps even more revealing than the central, Native figures of the Bay Colony seals are the ways in which the borders and backgrounds of these various seals attempt to contain and ground the uncontainable Indian of the image. From the original silver seals created in 1629 until 1692, there has always been a Latin motto containing a prominent Maltese cross and ornate garlands encircling the motto and image at the center of the seal; even the double-sided Andros seal, which departs greatly from the lone-Indian motif of the other seals, contains a Latin motto on both of its sides. Additionally, each of these Native-figure seals portrays some sort of natural, physical background, a New World landscape that provides further insight into the efforts to enclose and validate a very slippery sense of the colonists' identity and place in the wilderness of America.

The images of the original silver seal are really too badly broken to reveal much more than the central Native figure clutching a bow and arrow and the presence of the motto, but the Leverett seal, a direct descendant of the original seal, more clearly reveals the image of two pine trees, one on either side of the Native's legs, but within the umbrella of the extended weaponry in the figure's hands (Figure 1.4). Placed in perspective to the viewer, the trees appear small beside the figure, as if at a distance, and there does appear to be some sort of ground or horizon beneath the figure's feet. In all, this is a very basic representation of the flora and the fauna

---

[15]   Many variations of the colony's seal were featured on paper currency. Eric Newman notes that in December of 1690 Massachusetts authorized "$7,000 in indented Colony or Old Charter Bills, [which was] the first authorized public paper currency issued in the Western World" (158). The faces of the bills were "printed from an engraved copper plate containing four denominations" (E. Newman 158).

one could expect to encounter in the colonies of the New World: virgin native pine trees for lumber as well as tar and resin for ship building, land for settlement and agriculture, and uncorrupted, peaceful Natives, ripe for missionary efforts and conversion. The motto is very basically surrounded in concentric, raised lines that frame it and differentiate it from the interior image of the seal.

The 1672 Cambridge cut of Samuel Green also bears the ornate and traditional double circle of leafy garlands on either side of the Latin motto (Figure 1.5). The garlands of Green's cut are quite detailed, depicting three-leafed clusters, almost wheat-like in appearance, that encircle the figure in an orderly clock-wise fashion on the innermost circle, and proceed counter-clockwise on the left side of the outermost circle and clockwise on the right. Where the two garlands meet at the very top and bottom of the oval on the outermost circle, a small sheaf of some sort of grain, perhaps wheat, joins the two opposing garlands into a unified and stately frame for the entirety of the image. The Latin motto also reflects some artistic adaptation. Although it still reads "Seal of the Governor and Society of Massachusetts Bay in New England," a small Maltese cross has been added to the top center ring of the motto. This cross clearly indicates not only where the motto begins and ends, as it appears directly between the words "Anglia" at the end of the motto and "Sigillum" at the beginning; it also appears directly beneath the topmost sheaf of wheat on the outermost ring and above the head of the Native figure in the center of the image. The cross is significant for its reinforcement of the missionary designs of the colony, and its conspicuous position at the very center and top of the seal and directly over the head of the figure gives it a prominence in the image that cannot be overlooked. Although previous seal images do appear to have some sort of cross-like symbol at the top of the image, separating the beginning and ending of the motto (the original silver seal and the Leverett seal), none are as eye-catching as the boldly outlined Maltese cross in the Cambridge cut.[16]

These changes to the framing of the Cambridge image, while relatively minor, do suggest significant motives. The much more ornate and traditional garlands that proceed orderly around the outer edges of the seal appear in sharp contrast to the "savage" figure in the center and the three deciduous trees that surround her legs in the background. The three trees, which are notably changed from the

---

[16] The Maltese cross is identified as the symbol of the Knights of Malta, also known as the Knights Hospitaller, which was an order of Christian warriors founded in 1080 in Jerusalem to provide aid to poor and sick pilgrims to the Holy Land. The eight-pointed star is formed of four V-shaped arms joined at their tips with each of the eight points symbolizing one of the chivalric virtues. Today, it is closely associated with firefighters and serves as a symbol of honor, courage, and dedication. In the seventeenth century, the cross was used in a variety of iconographic ways to indicate religious and/or imperialistic enterprises that carried a "charitable" intent. For example, Catherine Armstrong notes that John Smith's 1608 map of Virginia, which was widely reprinted and became "a source for all maps of Virginia for sixty years," featured a Maltese cross at each river, pointing to "show the point at which English exploration had stopped. Any information about landscape features and settlement beyond those points had come to Smith from his Native American contacts" (44–5).

very American pines in previous images, now appear to be English oaks with full, puffy canopies.[17] Also, a third, rather phallic tree has been added directly between the legs of the woman whereas previous images only displayed two trees on either side of the figure's legs. The ground beneath the trees is also evident now in the Cambridge image, where in other seals it was not. The ground beneath the Native woman's feet is rich and dark, curvaceous and hilly. It appears to be unplanted and unleveled for agricultural purposes; the land is as virginally appealing and "wild" as the female figure standing on it. This landscape envisions, as feminist literary scholar Annette Kolodny has observed of other texts, the colonialist fantasy of "the white male imagination [which] continued to project ever westward, its endless dream of rediscovering Paradise" (Kolodny 29).

The contrast between the "untamed" vision of nature within the central area of the seal and the very "civilized" garlands and Latinate motto on the perimeters also reflect the polarized metaphors for "wilderness" and "garden" that were so central to the Puritan beliefs about their mission in the New World and their ties to civilization in the old. Martha L. Finch notes that the rhetorical interpretations of the landscape by the Puritans can be "transposed into other familiar dichotomies: nature and culture, wild and civilized, space and place. Collapsing these dichotomies involves focusing on lived experience, investigating how human beings go about organizing the world, turning unstructured, frightening space into familiar, meaningful place" (45). Kathleen M. Brown also observes that land use was one of the important ways in which the colonists distinguished themselves from the Indians. She writes, "Herding and hunting economies, with their transient settlements and low population densities, contrasted sharply with the English visions of shining cities, well-cultivated countrysides, and burgeoning populations" (55). This is exactly what is occurring in the Cambridge cut of the seal. By juxtaposing a wild image of the uncultivated wilderness with the tradition and order of a garland/garden and the erudite Latin motto, the visceral landscape of the New World has been effectively enveloped and contained by English tradition and sensibility. The transformation of the "untamed, chaotic, raw environment" into the "civilized, ordered, productive farms and villages" has been effectively envisioned and expressed in this image and further establishes the world of difference between the colonists and their barbaric neighbors (Finch 45). However, it still very pointedly features the larger-than-life image of the Indian, the one major obstacle in realizing these colonialist fantasies.

Although the Cambridge cut attempts to reconcile these two divergent identities/realities within its parameters, the marriage is not fully and confidently

---

[17] Traditionally, oaks are symbols of strength and endurance as well as being the national tree of England. Oaks were also used in the construction of ships and timber framed buildings in Europe until the nineteenth century. Oaks are also tied to two famous Anglo-European landmarks: the "Royal Oak" of Boscobel Wood in England where King Charles II hid to escape the Roundheads following the Battle of Worcester in 1651 and the "Charter Oak" in what is now Hartford, Connecticut, where colonists supposedly hid the charter of the Connecticut colony from Governor Andros when he arrived in October of 1687 to confiscate the document.

realized within the cut. There is still confusion and dis-ease in the message of the seal. Were the colonists the tamers, the guardians, of this promising "errand into the wilderness," or were they subject to it, victims of war and Native threat? They almost seem consumed and dwarfed by New World realities. And beyond the corporate, colony-wide identity manifested by the seal is Samuel Green's own, individual identity. Green chose these images to identify his press and its singular imprint among the other colonial presses of the period. Its female and sexual nature certainly sets Green's version of the seal apart from the legion of male warriors featured on other seals. Green's rendition of the seal presents a more feminized, more sexual, more wild vision of the New World that the classical, Latinate containment and English sensibility that the frame and background attempt to provide. However, the cogency of those English fortifications to the seal was questionable. The struggle to define and control just what was going on in the New World is readily evident in the Cambridge cut of the Bay Colony seal.

Whereas in the Cambridge cut, the landscape was fecund and slightly British, the Boston cut of John Foster portrays a much wilder, thoroughly American vista (Figure 1.6). Three trees are again depicted on either side of and in between the figure's legs, but this time they appear to be elms, an indigenous New England tree.[18] The land beneath the Native's feet is again hilly and rolling as in the Cambridge cut, perhaps indicating the lack of agricultural development, but this time it is scattered over with sprouts of grasses and small, bushy plants that do not appear to be of any uniform arrangement or type. They are clustered all about the Native's feet and are of such a jumbled layout that it is really hard to even identify where one plant begins and another ends. Some, to the lower left of the image, might even pass for small animals because they are so ill-formed. Such "messy" renditions of the American landscape may simply reflect the inability of John Foster to create a sophisticated and clean cut of the seal, or, as I would suggest instead, they reflect the disarray of the current colonial state in 1675. With King Philip's war looming on the horizon and Native populations becoming more and more belligerent toward colonial intervention, the once promising landscape of New England probably seemed much more wild and ungovernable to the colonists. The framing of the Boston cut, however, still depicts the orderly

---

[18]   The elm tree is the traditional symbol for wisdom and respect. Throughout the Middle Ages, elm wood was utilized for chair seats, wheels, coffins, and water pipes due to its interlocking grain and resistance to splitting and decay when permanently wet. It was also a widely planted ornamental tree in both America and Europe until Dutch elm disease devastated the elm populations in the twentieth century. In Boston at the time of the American Revolution, the Liberty Tree was a famous elm in the commons from which the Sons of Liberty hung two tax collectors in effigy in demonstration against the Stamp Act. The tree then became a rallying point for assemblies and the venting of emotions in pre-revolutionary America; it also became a meeting place for the Sons of Liberty where they could maintain the appearance of "chatting" casually beneath its boughs instead of holding an illegal unauthorized assembly. Once word of Boston's Liberty Tree spread, most other American cities designated a Liberty Tree of their own as well.

garlands and Latin quote of the Cambridge cut and earlier seals, suggesting the colonial attempts to maintain their civility and contain the "savagery" of the New World within a classical frame. However, the "savagery" and "wildness" of the central image seem to overwhelm and nullify this attempt at containment. It is the disorder and stereotypical "Indianness" that dominates this and other images of the seal, leaving the viewer with a sense of the consuming, threatening nature of the native landscape and the equally threatening duality of Indianness. The Indians could be everything and nothing the English wanted them to be, which undermined any chance of the colonists achieving a coherent understanding of themselves through the use of their imagined version of Indianness.

While these iconic seals of the colony self-consciously proclaim the inhabitants to be not "Indian" and not "savage," they also just as loudly proclaim them to be not "English." And it is only through a careful balancing act of maintaining classical, "civilized," English markers, which enabled the colonists to effectively distinguish themselves from the barbarism of the New World, and appropriating images of "Indianness," which enabled the colonists to distinguish themselves from all that was English, that a somewhat stable and unique identity can begin to be formed. Or could it? Scholars have often claimed that without its Indian heritage, "America was only a more vulgar England, but with it, America was its own nation, with a unique culture and its own ancestral past" (Lepore 200). However, with its Indian heritage, American identity becomes a problematic mélange of anxious repetitions of stereotypes and fetishized representations that

> giv[e] access to an 'identity' which is predicated as much on mastery and pleasure as it is on anxiety and defence [sic], for it is a form of multiple and contradictory belief in its recognition of difference and disavowal of it ... For the scene of fetishism is also the scene of the reactivation and repetition of primal fantasy—the subject's desire for a pure origin that is always threatened by its division, for the subject must be gendered to be engendered, to be spoken. (Bhabha, "The Other Question" 107)

In short, it is an identity that contains the seeds of its own undoing because beyond the fixed image of the "paper Indians" of the seal were the realities of the Indians in the New World, those "reformed, recognizable Other[s], [functioning] *as ... subject[s] of a difference that is almost the same, but not quite*"; there were the Native Christians like James Printer (Bhabha, "Of Mimicry" 122, italics in original).

Part 2
Narrative: James Printer and Mary Rowlandson

Native Christians, also called "Christian Indians" or "Praying Indians," lived in both Anglo and Indian worlds. They were the products of the Massachusetts Bay Colony's overtly missionizing intent so boldly emblazoned on its official seal. These Native American converts would have spoken and been literate in English to varying degrees, would have adopted some level of Anglo dress and lifestyle, often living and working side by side with the colonists, and they would, of course, have accepted Christianity and many of its mores. Most often organized into "praying towns" which were situated on the outskirts of English settlements throughout central and eastern Massachusetts, Praying Indians and their residences served as buffers between the sanctity of English "civilization" and the untamed wilderness that surrounded it. They also fulfilled a complex and often contradictory role within English imagination, at once potentially representing descendants of the lost tribes of Israel who must be actively brought to Christianity in order to usher in the millennium and Christ's second coming, but simultaneously being viewed, as William Hubbard writes in his *A Narrative of the Troubles*, as "children of the Devill, full of all subtlety and malice," especially during times of conflict (42).[19] Subsequently, a Praying Indian identity was one necessarily maintained, as Kathryn Gray notes, through "a complex network of performances" that had to be carefully mediated by religious authority in order to "accommodate concerns of New England's errand into the wilderness, as well as England's revolutionary spirit and its attempt to dominate the New World" (xiii).

These individuals, who culturally resembled the colonists more than they differed from them, would have fractured the various attempts made on the seals to stabilize a dominant colonial identity. On the one hand, they represented a threat. On the other, however, these Indians were colonial success stories; they represented the construction of a solid religious foundation through which English colonists could claim providential authority over the colonial landscape and England could rebuild her reputation as a significant presence in the Atlantic world. Highly literate and successful Praying Indians, like James Printer, a Nipmuck typesetter and printer who was a key player for both sides of the conflict during King Philip's War (1675–1676), would have stood in sharp contrast to the "uncivilized" and "unholy" Indian depicted on the Bay Colony's seals as scantily dressed and clutching rudimentary weapons, yet still so clearly not white. An individual like

---

[19]   Millennial Puritans believed "that they would live to see (or were already living within) the millennium, the thousand-year rule of saints prophesied to precede or, depending upon one's interpretation of difficult scripture, to follow Christ's second coming" (Bross, *Dry Bones* 12). This rather radical religious belief, which rose to popularity in the 1640s and 1650s, stemmed largely from the writings of Thomas Brightman and hinged on the conversion of the Jews, hence the emphasis on Native Americans as one of the lost tribes of Israel. Most Puritans did not subscribe to these beliefs, but instead viewed the Indians as descendants of Tartars or other gentiles, and subsequently felt the millennium could still be in the very distant future. Regardless, conversion of the Indians for both groups was a necessity as it would indicate the growth in Christ's dominions and reaffirm Anglo/Christian superiority. See Lepore, Wyss, Kristina Bross's *Dry Bones and Indian Sermons*, Kathryn Gray's *John Eliot and the Praying Indians of Massachusetts Bay*, and Richard Cogley's *John Eliot's Mission to the Indians Before King Philip's War* (among others) for more on Praying Indians and the bifurcated view the colonists held of them. William Hubbard was a Puritan clergyman in Ipswich, Massachusetts, who wrote an account of King Philip's War (*A Narrative of the Troubles*) published in Boston, 1677, that vilified Native Americans and Praying Indians in particular.

Printer would throw the meanings of the already complex and ever-fluctuating seal and identity stabilizing endeavor into disarray because he simultaneously was and was not the Indian depicted on it.

Born in the praying Indian town of Hassanamesit (near what is now Grafton, Massachusetts), James Printer was the son of Naoas, one of John Eliot's converts and a leading member of the Christian Native church in the settlement. Eliot, who founded numerous praying towns, devised an orthography for the Massachusett language based on the Roman alphabet, and produced a large set of works in Massachusett known as the "Indian Library" that included primers, catechisms, and religious tracts, as well as his Indian bible, was a successful and influential English missionary among the Native Americans in New England around the Boston area beginning in the 1650s.[20] Printer's indoctrination into English Christian culture was, consequently, immediate. How could it not be? Born into a Christian Native town that was inundated with English influences, yet was still defined as Indian, Printer was bicultural from birth. It is unclear, however, when Printer's process of "civilization" moved from the liminal grounds of the praying town of Hassanamesit to the official world and historical records of the colony proper. It is possible he was bound out as a young boy to an English family where he was taught to read and write, even enrolling later in a Cambridge grammar school between 1645 and 1646;[21] however, it may be more likely that his formal process of indoctrination began when he was apprenticed in 1659 as a printer's devil/typesetter to Samuel Green of the Cambridge Press where he became an accomplished typesetter and printer, a career he retained for most of his life. He was the "perfect" result of the rigorous process of colonial indoctrination, living and working among the English for nearly his entire life. He was, for the most part, the "model" seventeenth-century Indian; Printer was the Indian from the seal, the willing colonial subject, come to life.

However, through his complex actions toward and reactions to English society during King Philip's War, James Printer exposed the limitations of colonial dominance and the cracks in colonial identity—the very same entanglements the imagery of the Massachusetts Bay Colony seal struggled with since the

---

[20]   See Gray and Cogley among others for a more detailed treatment of Eliot's mission and works.

[21]   See Margaret Szasz's *Indian Education in the American Colonies, 1607–1783*, 115–20; George Winship's *The Cambridge Press 1638–1692*, 69; and George Littlefield's *The Early Massachusetts Press 1638–1711*, vol. 2, 77. Hugh Amory, however, posits that Printer's formal association with the English could not have begun before 1649, because until that point, "the Nipmucks did not 'submit' to English jurisdiction … and would hardly have entrusted their children to an open enemy" (41). Others, such as Hilary Wyss (*Writing Indians*) and Jill Lepore, similarly indicate Printer's first, formal, extended cultural exchanges with the English began with his conversion to Christianity and association with John Eliot. I would add that because of his upbringing in Hassanamesit and early exposure to the Christian religion, English culture, and legal codes endemic to the praying towns that the "informal" process indoctrination would have begun with his birth. Colonization was the "always already" in Printer's case.

colony's inception. Consequently, he was an ambivalent figure for the colonists, a figure who, because of his "imperfect" civilized status, could and did exploit the dis-ease the colonists felt about their place in the New World. James Printer was also an ambivalent figure for Mary Rowlandson, the wife of a Puritan minister living in Lancaster, Massachusetts, and the famous survivor of an 11-week captivity among the Nipmuck, Narragansett, and Wampanoag people during King Philip's War. Rowlandson's ransom from captivity and her subsequent narrative account of it, *The Sovereignty and Goodness of God*, published in 1682, were deeply dependent upon the ambivalent, bicultural identity of James Printer for their existence. Yet, this was a dependency Rowlandson aggressively denied and erased within her text in order for her own authorial identity to emerge.

James Printer: The Seal Come to Life

James Printer would have been working as a typesetter and printer's devil for Samuel Green's Cambridge press during the mid-seventeenth century, both before and after King Philip's War when both of the printer's cuts—Green's and Foster's—were in use. Printer was initially brought into Green's press to aid with the production of John Eliot's great Indian Bible. Because of the massive and atypical nature of this job—it was the first entire Bible printed in North America in any language—it was nearly published in England, especially since it was entirely subsidized, even down to additional printing equipment and funds to repair damaged equipment already in place, by the English-based Corporation for Propagation of the Gospel among the Indians in New England of the New England Company. Ultimately, though, the project was granted to Green's Cambridge Press, located in a building at Harvard Indian College, because, as Isaiah Thomas has noted in his *The History of Printing in America*, the Indian youth of that area "had been taught to read &c., at the school at Cambridge, established for the purpose, and Mr. Eliot and Mr. Pierson had translated Primers and Catechisms into the Indian language for the common use of the Indians … [therefore] it became necessary that these works should be printed in America, under the inspection of the translators" (59). Additionally, the experienced English master-printer, Marmaduke Johnson, was imported to the colonies, along with a new press and other printing materials, at the behest of John Eliot to lend his expertise in the Cambridge Press's production of the Bible. This transatlantic move of Johnson and the press is especially interesting because it is essentially the center moving toward the periphery. A "civilized" printer of England is being relocated to the New World wilderness in order to have access to Indian expertise and produce an inaugural Indian language text.

By the completion of Eliot's first Indian Bible in 1663, Printer had had a hand in producing two editions of an Indian primer and two books of psalms, as well as the bible itself. He was arguably Eliot's most accomplished interpreter and did more than any other translator to help Eliot in the production of his bible.[22] Printer most

---

[22] See Meserve's "English Works of Seventeenth-century Indians," 267; and Littlefield, 77.

likely functioned in the capacity of master typesetter and editor in the production of these texts. Job Nesutan (Nipmuck) and John Sassamon (Massachusett), both former students of Eliot's and schoolmasters, functioned as translators, although Printer probably helped to smooth out and regulate their translations. Printer is also recognized as being indispensable to Eliot in the publication of his second Indian Bible between 1680 and 1685; Eliot himself noted in a letter to Robert Boyle in London in 1683, that he had "but one man, viz. the Indian Printer, that is able to compose the sheets, and correct the press with understanding" (as qtd. in Littlefield 77). James Printer was clearly someone who had a mastery of a wide range of literacies—both Native and English—that ranged from alphabetic knowledge to higher-level skills that required comprehension, intellectual engagement, and the ability to make use of the technologies of literacy, like the printing press. To utilize the terms of Hilary Wyss in her *English Letters and Indian Literacies*, he would have been both a "Readerly" and a "Writerly" Indian—someone who was both a passive, docile figure absorbing the indoctrination of the English (or at least appearing to) and someone who was a "speaker and actor fluent in the cultures and conventions of colonial society but also ... fully committed to Native community as an ongoing political and cultural concern" (6). While missionary fantasy pursued the production of "Readerly Indians" in order to maintain the power dynamic of Anglo superiority within colonialism, the inevitable outcome was "Writerly Indians," like Printer, who "used discourse to manage their own sovereignty in ways that often challenged, confused or contradicted missionary desire" (Wyss, *English Letters* 7).

James Printer embodied both of these identities. Not only was he the ideal colonial subject himself, mimicking Englishness and Christianness with success, but he was also a useful tool in the continuing expansion of colonialist efforts in the New World. Eliot clearly could not have translated and produced his Bibles without him, although not surprisingly, credit for this period of unparalleled production of Indian texts by the Cambridge Press has generally been given only to John Eliot, not his Indian aides. Printer was the "good Indian" from the seal, desiring and achieving both conversion and acculturation in order to better serve English purposes. He was a success story in the colonialist New World narrative.

However, Printer was also a threat to these successes; he was also the "menacing Indian" from the seal. Because of his abilities to so successfully acculturate and excel in the performance of "Englishness" while still inhabiting his darker, Indian body, he challenged the colonialist binaries of assumed "superiority/inferiority" and "civilized/savage." Beneath that veneer of assimilation was still the fact of his Indianness; and no matter how unambiguously "English" Printer became and appeared, he was never able to pass as English. He was an ambivalent figure, at once signifying the mastery and control of the English over the other, but also signifying the limits of that control as he adopted and adapted their "inherent" culture to an Indian body. Printer and other Praying Indians like him illustrated how "the colonists still depended, in certain crucial ways, on Indians who embodied cultural and political ambiguities" (Salisbury, Introduction 49). As Homi Bhabha has stated, "Mimicry is ... a sign of the inappropriate ... a difference or recalcitrance which coheres the dominant strategic function of colonial power, intensifies surveillance, and poses an immanent threat to both 'normalized' knowledges and disciplinary powers" (Bhabha, "Of Mimicry" 122–3). In short, Printer embodied both resemblance and menace in a single colonized body, much as the Indian figures of the seal did; only now, James Printer was real. He was, as Rey Chow notes, "the sign that remains—in the form of a literal being-there, an externalization and an exhibition in the aftermath of the process of a sacrifice" (90). He was a visible remnant of the transaction of mimesis, but also an actual actor in the colony's struggle for identity and survival, someone who exposed the ruptures in the surety of colonial dominance. He was not the flattened and revisable Indian of the seal, a two-dimensional fantasy that could (conceivably) be fixed and contained.

Printer's Rebellion and Redemption

In 1675 prior to the publication of the second Eliot bible, however, James Printer revised his assigned role as the perfect Indian convert and colonial subject to assert another, more complex self-identity. With the onset of King Philip's War and the increased tensions and violence between English and Indian communities, Printer left behind his English identity to join with King Philip and his allies in the fight against the colonists. His once ambivalent position as the ideal imagined Indian, a "mimic man," now became an overtly aggressive one toward the colonists; Printer became the stark realization of just how loosely the ties of colonization bound those under its thrall.

While it is unclear exactly why Printer's "defection" to Philip's army occurred—whether it was out of familial loyalty and responsibility, or due to coercion by an attacking band of Nipmucks who raided Hassanamesit in 1675—the fact that Printer's identity as a colonial subject could become so drastically altered and effectively insurgent is important.[23] Printer went from being a colonial success story to a reviled turncoat, a threatening and ominous figure of what the Indian could become post-assimilation. He is described in the anonymous *A True Account* as "a Revolter ... and a fellow that had done mischief, and staid out as long as he could" (5) and by Increase Mather in his *Brief History* as having committed "Aspostasie" (39). Printer was clearly known and despised by his English neighbors. Even though hundreds of other Praying Indians were participating in raids against English villages, attacking colonists, and waging war between 1675 and 1676, Printer's reversal of roles was extremely threatening to the English, more so than the other mutineers, because he wrote back to the empire from his position of rebellion. Bhabha notes, "What emerges between mimesis and mimicry is a *writing*, a mode of representation, that marginalizes the monumentality of history, quite simply mocks its power to be a model, that power which supposedly makes it imitable" ("Of Mimicry" 125). Through his writing,

---

[23]   See Lepore, 136; Wyss, *Writing Indians*, 42; Amory, *First Impressions*, 41; and James D. Drake, *King Philip's War: Civil War in New England, 1675–1676*, 114, for further scholarship on the possible reasons for Printer's support of Philip.

Printer demonstrates a critical awareness of how colonial narratives of power and order are "scripted" through literacy and writing and how those narratives work to legitimate and include only certain forms of colonial identity—heterosexual, Anglo, Christian, and male. Printer strategically disrupts this established order by un-suppressing his own critically fluent, alternatively literate subjectivity—the "Writerly Indian" within—and writing back to the empire.

Printer's written responses to the colonial powers from his self-revised position as a relapsed "Savage Indian" are two letters, both written on behalf of the Native combatants and both written to engage the English in a cultural exchange with the Indians. While on the surface, these letters subscribe to English expectations for and definitions of literacy—definitions that scholars like Elizabeth Boone, Andrew Newman, and Matt Cohen have challenged—it cannot be overlooked that they also bear traces of indigenous traditions and alternative literacy systems that run counter to rigid Anglo expectations for "literacy."[24] Matt Cohen, for example, has suggested Native orality, writing, and print are intersecting worlds that narrow definitions of literacy (both historic and modern) have obscured. Instead, he suggests a reconceptualization of Native-Anglo encounters that take other communication systems, like "traps, paths, wampum, monuments, medical rituals, and other messaging systems" into account (Cohen 4). Unmasking these alternative forms of self-expression would allow scholars to rethink "theories about the relationships among representation, media, and the social order" (Cohen 5).[25] Such a reconceptualization also exposes the subversive nature of publicly performed literacy because writing, as in the case of James Printer's letters, can create subjectivity out of objecthood for the colonized, a move that challenges and expands the narrow colonial frameworks of identity.

The first letter, or note really, was found tacked to a bridge post outside the town of Medfield, Massachusetts, in 1675 after a raiding party of Algonquians had attacked and burned the settlement. Although the author of the Medfield note is not definitively known and the original note has been lost, many scholars attribute its creation to James Printer because he was one of the few highly literate Indians

---

[24]   See Elizabeth Boone's (and Walter Mignolo's) *Writing Without Words: Alternative Literacies in Mesoamerica and the Andes*; Andrew Newman's *On Records: Delaware Indians, Colonists, and the Media of History and Memory*; and Matt Cohen's *The Networked Wilderness: Communicating in Early New England*.

[25]   Other scholars, like Heidi Bohaker ("Nindoodemag: The Significance of Algonquian Kinship Networks in the Eastern Great Lakes Region, 1600–1701") and Germaine Warkentin ("In Search of 'The Word of the Other': Aboriginal Sign Systems and the History of the Book in Canada"), have also argued that Anglo definitions of text, print, and literacy are inadequate in dealing with Native American graphic expression. Andrew Newman, however, has eschewed such arguments for broadening the definitions of texts and literacy to include nonalphabetic productions, and instead seeks to demonstrate the impoverishment of Anglo-European definitions of writing (which focused on alphabeticity) and how that contributed to the destruction of Native libraries and the dehumanization of Native peoples.

who would have taken part in the attack against Medfield.[26] The note, written in English, reads, "Thou English man hath provoked us to anger & wrath & we care not though we have war with you this 21 years for there are many of us 300 of which hath fought with you at this town[.] we hauve nothing but our lives to loose but thou has many fair houses cattell & much good things" (as qtd. in Lepore 94).[27]

The sharp hostility and mocking tone of the note cannot be overlooked. While it certainly suggests "the pride and insolence of these barbarians" as Daniel Gookin noted after having read the note, it also suggests the keen cultural literacy of the attacking Native Americans who realized the close ties between English identity and property (494–5). The devastating loss of "fair houses cattel and much good things" would leave the English deprived of their most affluent and stable markers of Englishness, leaving them confronted by Indians who, like Printer, could conceivably usurp their English identities through more variable markers, like clothing and literacy, both of which held ranges of acceptable possibilities. The note is intended to strike at the most inherent of weaknesses in the colonial position, the ambivalence of colonial identity. The Native author of this note was no longer the apparently peacefully needy/savagely threatening Indian of the seal image, but rather a culturally sophisticated and educated Native American who could write as well as read English and knew how to manipulate the weaknesses in the colonial system. The message of the note strikes directly at the core fears of the English colonists: vast multitudes of an Indian other who are not only able to adopt Englishness, but also able to corrupt it and undermine its foundational beliefs about identity, leaving the English denuded of their Englishness.

However, the note also evokes a sense of the hostility many Native Americans would have felt after having been subjected to missionary efforts of the Christian English for years. The note indicates that if Native lives were truly valueless without the sanctification of English culture, religion, and lifestyle as they had been taught, then the losses of the war parties were truly insignificant while the English losses of property would be enormous.[28] The writer is turning the very sentiments and beliefs of the English about value against the colonists; if Indian lives are truly worthless in this world as the English claimed, why should the Indians care if they die? This note, while operating within the expectations of colonial discourse, disrupts its authority by undermining and manipulating the terms of that discourse. It no longer simply "mimes" English expectations as drawn out on the various seals of the colony, but twists them to such a degree that

---

[26] See Wyss, *Writing Indians*, 43–4; Lepore, 94–5; and Salisbury, *Sovereignty and Goodness*, 98.

[27] Lepore states that Noah Newman copied the content of the note out in a letter to John Cotton on March 14, 1676. This is the version Lepore utilizes in her analysis (and that I quote here); there are variations of the note, however, that were based on other copies and recopies made by other colonists; see, for example, the variation in Neal Salisbury's *The Sovereignty and Goodness*.

[28] See Lepore, 94–6, and Wyss, *Writing Indians*, 43–4, for extended readings of the Medfield note.

their inherent flaws are painfully evident. The mockery and agency of this note occurs on more than just a single level of "tone"—and it stands in sharp contrast to the flattened, two-dimensional Indians inscribed on the seal. This "real" Native American is complex, intelligent, and very aware of how to corrode the system.

The second letter attributed to James Printer is one written during the 1676 ransom process of Mary Rowlandson and other captives held by the Algonquians. This would have been the second letter in the negotiation process between the English and the Indians for Rowlandson and her fellow captives; the first exchange of letters, initiated by the English, contained the establishment of the "ground rules" and expectations for both sides. The English first indicated the desire to ransom "some English, especially women and children in Captivity" for "payment in goods or wampum or by exchange of prisoners" (Salisbury 133). It also established the need for any response to be made in writing with the "paper pen and incke" provided and that any messengers come bearing "a white flag upon a staffe, visible to be seen … as a flag of truce, … used by civilized nations in time of warre" (Salisbury, *Sovereignty and Goodness* 133). This insistence by the English upon the use of western European conventions for wartime communication, a white flag of truce, paper and pen, is an attempt to reassert control over the Indians and the hostage crisis the English are facing. While the English are at the mercy of the Indians and ultimately assenting to (and even desiring) captive negotiations with "savages" in this letter, there is still an effort to reestablish the dominance of English "civilization," even if it is only rhetorically. Also interesting is the fact that this negotiation note from the English bore the official seal and signature of Governor Leverett (Figure 1.4), which depicts the pleading and "uncivilized" figure of the Native. The ironic placement of this needy, savage, leaf-aproned Indian at the bottom of a letter which tacitly recognizes the civilized, literate, and formidable nature of the Indian captors—even the vulnerable position of the English—underscores the anxiety and ambivalence with which the English viewed their own position in the New World.

The Native response to this opening volley, transcribed by Peter Jethro (Nipmuck), indicates their unwillingness to make concessions to the English. They insist upon two messengers instead of one and call attention to the heavy English losses: "we know your heart grew sorrowful with crying for your lost many many hundred men and all your house and all your land, and woman, child, and cattle, as all your thing that you have lost and on your backside stand" (Salisbury, *Sovereignty and Goodness* 134). Printer's letter was written in response to the English reply to Jethro, which has been lost.

This second letter in this ransom negotiation attributed to Printer reads:

> For the Governor and the Council at Boston
> The Indians, Tom Nepennomp and Peter Tatatiqunea hath brought us letter from you about the English Captives, especially for Mrs. Rolanson; the answer is I am sorrow that I have don much to wrong you and yet I say the falte is lay upon you, for when we began quarrel at first with Plimouth men I did not think that you should have so much truble as now is: therefore I am willing to hear your desire

about the Captives. Therefore we desire you to send Mr. Rolanson and Goodman Kettel: (for their wives) and these Indians Tom and Peter to redeem their wives, they shall come and goe very safely: Whereupon we ask Mrs Rolanson, how much your husband willing to give for you she gave an answer 20 pounds in goodes but John Kittels wife could not tell. And the rest captives may be spoken of hereafter. (as qtd. in Salisbury 136)

This letter speaks to Printer's, as well as the other Native Americans', complex relationship with the English. Placed in a provisional position of power—at least in the captive negotiations—the Native Americans are able to negotiate the terms of ransom for their captives, especially the valuable Mary Rowlandson, because they held all the chips. They wield that power rhetorically in the letter, as they indicate a willingness to "hear your desire about the Captives" and insist upon the terms of release for and value of the captives. However, at the same time, the first-person conciliatory apology and attempt to deflect the blame for the outrages of the war indicate a growing sense of urgency, at least with Printer, the letter's author, to begin mending fences with the English. The tribes were faced with the reality of defeat and retribution after the war. Their food was dwindling, their people were starving, and the English, while suffering humbling losses, were not going to back down. Speaking boldly in the first person, James Printer extends an olive branch to the men he once knew and the society he once called his own—men and a society that could ultimately reabsorb and forgive him or criminalize and execute him.

Printer's shrewd move toward positioning himself as truly sorrowful and yet respectful of the Algonquian position—yet another variation of his performance of Indianness—was undoubtedly a successful technique. Mary Rowlandson was released and reunited with her husband, her 20 pound ransom paid, and the other captives were returned to their families a few weeks later. Printer himself was ultimately granted amnesty for his role during the war, along with other Christian Native Americans who were deemed "innocent" by the English, provided they were willing to demonstrate loyalty to the colonists. This was sometimes accomplished through service in the English Army or by fighting and killing anti-English Indians and presenting their scalps to the Council.[29] Whatever was required of Printer, however, must have been accomplished by him because for nearly all the rest of his life, Printer continued to work for the Cambridge press and the Green family, aiding in the publication of all their Indian texts and proving himself to be a literate and highly skilled typesetter. He eventually followed Bartholomew Green to Boston in the 1690s to continue as a printer and entered into a cooperative project with the younger Green, an Indian Psalter, on which he shares joint imprint credit with Green. This 1709 text, printed in both Indian and English, bears the imprint, "Boston, N.E. Printed by B. Green and J. Printer, for the Honourable

---

[29]   Jill Lepore notes there was a council issued order that demanded Printer prove his loyalty through producing enemy scalps; consequently, she posits that Printer must have done so in order to gain forgiveness. It is unclear, however, what Printer actually did to demonstrate his fidelity. See Lepore, 147–8.

Company for the Propagation of the Gospel in New England, &c." (Thomas 93).[30] It is the only known text to contain Printer's name and is also the last recorded note of his whereabouts.[31] It seems after 1709, Printer and his family subsided into a quiet, unassuming rural life.

Although his most prolific work as a printer/translator was accomplished with the Indian tracts of Eliot and the New England Company, it was his ransom letter to the Boston Council that was Printer's most important work as a printer/ translator. It was his first step toward successful reintegration to English society and the resumption of his role as the "good Indian"—the non-threatening and needy Indian from the seal image. It was also his first textual encounter with Mary Rowlandson.

In the letter Printer, speaking in the communal "we" instead of the earlier "I," notes: "Whereupon we ask Mrs Rolanson, how much your husband willing to give for you she gave an answer 20 pounds in goodes" (Salisbury 136). This is an interesting moment because essentially, Printer is writing Rowlandson into existence as a textual subject. By revealing her behind-the-scenes agency in determining her own value, and perhaps even her desire to give the Indians a fair ransom price, Printer is giving Rowlandson an authority, an identity that has heretofore not existed.[32] While allowing Rowlandson to determine her own ransom may have been reflective of the conciliatory efforts on the Indians' part, it is still a moment of agency on Rowlandson's. And because Printer transcribed it, made it official, he wrote that moment, and consequently her, into textual existence. Rowlandson has emerged in this text as a subjective, rather than objective figure, the author of her own value and redemption.

However, this would not be the last time Printer aided in Rowlandson's textual self-creation. Perhaps most notably and ironically, he even worked as the typesetter for Mary Rowlandson's narrative of her captivity during King Philip's War, *The Sovereignty and Goodness of God*, in 1682. Printer worked for Samuel Green during the time the Cambridge Press produced the second and third editions and,

---

[30] Thomas notes that one of the reasons for prominently featuring Printer's name is that, aside from his knowledge of the languages and skill as an experienced printer, he was well known among the neighboring tribes. Attaching his name to any such work might "excite the greater attention among the Indians, and give it a wider circulation" (93). It is also likely that Printer's entrepreneurial skills and ambitions as an independent printer were motivational factors behind the joint imprint.

[31] Printer also served as the schoolmaster at Hassanamesit for a time around 1698. See Szasz, 179.

[32] In the previous round of ransom letter negotiations transcribed by Peter Jethro, there is a supposed "request" from Rowlandson for "thre [sic] pound of tobacco" (Salisbury 135). However, due to the absence of Rowlandson's signature and her own attempts to cease the use of tobacco pipes as revealed in her narrative, it seems unlikely that Rowlandson was aware of this request or even shown the letter before it was sent. Additionally, Rowlandson angrily denies she made any request for tobacco, and insists it would be a "great mistake" for anyone to think otherwise. See Salisbury, 102. This is not likely a reflection of Rowlandson's agency and textual emergence.

as Neal Salisbury has noted, "Printer's edition is the closest one to Rowlandson's own writing" (Introduction 49). Rowlandson was dependent upon Printer for not only her ransom and return to her former life, but also for her transcendence from that life in the form of her narrative. Printer provided for Rowlandson an opening through which she could emerge as a self-created entity, someone who determines her own worth through her own voice in his ransom letter and then later, tells her own story. This was the moment where Rowlandson received sanctification from Puritan and Indian authority; she was recognized, heeded, and forever written into the history of King Philip's War. And James Printer was her author.

In a further ironic twist, however, while it was Printer who gave Rowlandson a textual identity and wrote her *into* textual existence, she used her newly granted agency to write him *out of* existence in her seminal work by flattening out and erasing his and other Christian Indians' roles in her salvation/re-creation. Rowlandson creates the narrative equivalent of the flattened and two-dimensional Indian from the seal in her *The Sovereignty and Goodness of God*; however, just as the stereotypical and complex images of the seals contain ruptures that hint at the physical reality of the Natives in the New World as well as the accompanying anxieties that held for the colonists, so, too, does Rowlandson's erasure of the Christian Indians hint at the complex ties her own authorial identity had to Indianness.

Mary Rowlandson's Praying Indians

It wasn't until six years after her return from captivity that Mary Rowlandson published her narrative. Although it is unclear as to when exactly Rowlandson began composing, there is evidence to suggest that she began recording her experiences from the captivity soon after her release in 1676, when events and remembrances would have been vivid in her mind.[33] This also would have been when Rowlandson most closely viewed herself in terms of Indianness. As a recent captive who had spent 11 weeks with the Nipmucks, Narragansetts, and Wampanoags who kidnapped her but also showed her kindness and consideration, Rowlandson would have held complicated views about her captors and her own connections to them. Many of these complexities are revealed in Rowlandson's narrative, as she wavers between revulsion for the "merciless Heathen" (Rowlandson 69) who held no respect for English life, property, and beliefs, and moments of compassion, or at least understanding, for certain Indians who share their food or offer her refuge. Rowlandson vacillates between "they" and "we" mentalities in the narrative, indicating her fluctuation between defining herself through contrast—against the Indians—and through comparison—as a temporary member of the Indian group. Either way, Indianness is the pivotal factor in the narrative that allows her to assert her own subjectivity. Indianness, whether she sides with it or against it, is what gives Rowlandson the credibility to say

---

[33]   See Salisbury, 40–41, Derounian-Stodola and Levernier, 98, and Breitwieser, 189–94, for analysis of Rowlandson's authorial timeline.

the things that she does, in the manner that she does—in print. The fact of her captivity and survival makes her one of God's own saints, singled out from the sea of Puritan believers as one who is marked by God for salvation; she is sanctified by the religious and social elite of the time and given their blessing to publish her narrative. Rowlandson's narrative was published in between the texts of two Anglo male authority figures: a preface to the reader from Ter Amicam, thought to be Increase Mather, and the final sermon preached by her husband, Joseph Rowlandson. Both texts lent Rowlandson's narrative an authority and approval that allowed it to be published. However, it is the fact of her textualization of that Indian experience that creates Rowlandson as female authorial subject. Without Indianness and her complex relationship to it, Rowlandson's text could never have been written. Yet, ironically, it was the imagined version of Indianness, not the very real Indians she traveled with and depended upon, that gives rise to her independence. Just as the colonists of Massachusetts Bay relied upon the image of the Native to validate and define their ties to and place within the New World, so, too, did Rowlandson appropriate Indianness to authenticate her own identity.

Rowlandson needed "real" Indians and her captivity among them in order to gain sanctification, an independent authorial identity, and leave to pursue that identity textually; however, what she necessarily had to produce or perpetuate in her text is the imaginary Indian, the flattened out, threatening-yet-needy, "uncivilized-yet-capable-of-civilization" version of Indianness depicted visually in the seal. The use of the imagined Indian from the seal would lend yet another layer of sanctification to her text as she played off known and "official" stereotypes that were recognizable even across the Atlantic and would authenticate in narrative form all of the fears, anxieties, and identity struggles inherent in the visual seal. She could not reproduce without consequences, and perhaps not even understand herself, the "real" Indians that she encountered, Indians who varied in personality, vanity, kindness, wealth, and vices just as the colonists did. Instead, she has to reproduce in her prose the Native on the seal, the one who ambiguously signals the "American" identity through negation of Indian reality and tries so desperately to contain, define, and authenticate that which the colonists themselves had yet to understand and work out. Rowlandson, throughout her narrative, but particularly in her treatment of the Praying Indians, effectively erases and rewrites Indian reality in order to establish her own authorial reality. She must negate the connective elements that bridge, or begin to bridge, Englishness and Indianness—the transculturated Christian Indians—in order to keep the Indians as the utter other. As Kristina Bross notes in *Dry Bones and Indian Sermons*, "Rowlandson understands and represents Indian transculturation as hypocrisy [and] … reinscribes the markers of English-Indian transculturation into the rhetoric of Indian hating" (178). Pamela Lougheed similarly argues that Rowlandson attempts to assign intentional "malice" to the acculturated Indians as not only a justification for English violence, but as a way to reinforce Calvinist beliefs that humans may exercise "intention," but God controls "actions." In this schema, Lougheed posits that for Rowlandson, "God's providence, at least rhetorically, is well preserved" (288). Rowlandson must have a complete opposite against which to define herself and assert her own identity, and Praying Indians like James Printer, although absolutely pivotal to her release, her narrative, and ultimately her publication, must be erased from the equation.[34] She must write them out of existence in order to write herself in.

Rowlandson reserves her most vitriolic passages in *The Sovereignty and Goodness of God* for the Praying Indians. While Rowlandson certainly reveals anger and displeasure with various non-Christian Indians during her captivity, she also mentions moments of kindness and compassion from some of her captors, presenting, if not an unbiased view of the range of "humanity" within the tribe, at least a more balanced one; there were "bad" Indians and some "not-so-bad." For example, in the third remove Rowlandson mentions an Indian who gives her a Bible (76), in the eighth remove she tells of two Indians who comfort and feed her when she is crying (82), and in the ninth remove, there is a squaw who allows Rowlandson to use her cooking utensils and offers her some ground nuts to go with her bear meat (84–5). Clearly, Rowlandson is aware of and responsive to the kindnesses of her captors. However, her portrayal of the Praying Indians is negative and derogatory across the board. In her mind, Praying Indians are the absolute incarnation of duplicity and evil.

In the third remove, Rowlandson relates what has become of all of her children post-capture. Her youngest daughter, Sarah, has just died from the wound she received during the initial attack and been buried by the Indians without Rowlandson's knowledge or permission. Her son, Joseph Jr., has been taken by another group of the raiding party, presumably to another Native town, and his whereabouts are unknown. However, her daughter, Mary, is at the same Native settlement with Rowlandson in a nearby wigwam. The mother and daughter are not given much opportunity to spend time together, though, because as Rowlandson notes, "When I came in sight, she [Mary] would fall a weeping; at which they were provoked, and would not let me come near her, but bade me be gone; which was a heart-cutting word to me" (75). This emotionally wrenching situation for mother and daughter, Rowlandson is clear to reveal, had its origins in the first moment of capture: "[Mary] was about ten years old, & taken from the door at first by a Praying Indian & afterward sold for a gun" (75). While not an overt indictment of the behavior of Praying Indians at this point, it is clear Rowlandson equates her separation from Mary with the greed and violence of Mary's Christian Indian captor, a man who was willing to take children away from their mothers as prisoners only to callously trade them for more implements for war.

In a later instance in the sixteenth remove, the ransom process has begun and the Indians inform Rowlandson that a letter had come to the Indian Sagamores about redemption and she must return to the town by the time the next letter arrives. During the group's return trek, Rowlandson writes that

---

[34] Some of the other scholars (among many) who have examined Rowlandson's text and her treatment of Praying Indians include Hilary Wyss ("Captivity and Conversion"), Andrew Newman ("Captive on the Literacy Frontier"), Neal Salisbury (Introduction to *Sovereignty and Goodness*), and Pat Cesarini ("'What has become of your praying to God?'"), to name just a few.

a company of *Indians* came near to us, near thirty, all on horse-back. My heart skipt within me, thinking they had been *English men* at the first sight of them, for they were dressed in *English* Apparel with Hats, white Neckcloths, and Sashes about their waists, and Ribbonds upon their shoulders; but when they came near, there was a vast difference between the lovely faces of Christians, and the foul looks of these Heathens, which much damped my spirit again. (italics in original, 94)

Rowlandson's intense attention to the physical detail of clothing of the Praying Indians in this instance is worth noting, as is her carefully structured retelling of this encounter. In the written version of this event Rowlandson breaks with the chronology of the original occurrence by clearly identifying the men as "Indians" before she ever reveals to her reader that she first believed they were Englishmen. Her initial excitement and consequent heartbreak upon seeing the group is negated in this retelling of the event, thus voiding for her reader the shock she had originally experienced and preventing his/her deception. Through altering the sequence of events in this passage, Rowlandson is effectively erasing the power held by these Praying Indians. Their ability to not only accurately assume the cultural accoutrements of the English, as evidenced through her precise description of their clothing, even down to the peculiarities of their English accessories, but also their ability to "become" English, at least for that moment in which Rowlandson believed them to be so, are destabilizing events for Rowlandson. If she can be deceived into seeing Indianness as Englishness, then the boundaries of identity are permeable and fluid. She must reassert the definitional distinction between the two identities and reinscribe the Praying Indians as the absolute other to Englishness. Consequently, she declares that once the men come closer, the "foul looks of these Heathens," their non-Christian appearance, distinguishes their true identities. She is quick to note, "[t]here was a vast difference between the lovely faces of Christians" and those of the Praying Indians. The "foulness" of the Indians' faces supersedes any of the other markers of Englishness they may have adopted and deceived Rowlandson with.

Although a key part of her retelling of this experience, it is not the culturally appropriated appearance of this group of Indians that matters for Rowlandson, as Michelle Burnham and Kristina Bross have posited,[35] but rather the difference between Christian and heathen because that is the factor that undermines not only her own Christian exceptionality but also her authorial agency. If truly Christian Indians were to exist in Rowlandson's narrative, or even in her consciousness, her singular position as the sainted Christian in the wilderness would be diminished, her authority to textualize her story would be forfeited. It is the "praying" part

---

[35] Burnham proposes that what may have upset Rowlandson in this encounter is that the English clothes worn by the Indians may have been stripped from English casualties ("Journey Between" 69), while Bross states it was the "newly dislocating experience of Indian bodies inhabiting English clothing (however the clothes were acquired) that makes the moment notable" (*Dry Bones* 181). While I certainly do not disagree with these sharp assessments, I see Rowlandson's alarm as stemming from a different crisis, as stated above.

of these Indians not their "Englishness" that so rankles Rowlandson because, simply put, for her Indians cannot be both Christian and Indian. Christianity and Indianness are irreconcilable essences that cannot coexist because if they do, they begin to undermine the foundations of her own identity as English and Christian.

However, the undeniable, un-erasable presence of the Praying Indians does make its way into Rowlandson's consciousness and narrative. At the beginning of the nineteenth remove when the second ransom letter from the Council is being delivered to the Indian encampment, Rowlandson writes,

> Then came *Tom* and *Peter*, with the second Letter from the Council, about the Captives. Though they were *Indians*, I gat them by the hand, and burst out into tears; my heart was so full that I could not speak to them; but recovering my self, I asked them how my husband did, and all my friends and acquaintance? they said, *They are all very well, but melancholy.* They brought me two Biskets, and a pound of Tobacco. (italics in original, 92)

In this passage, the Tom and Peter Rowlandson refers to are Tom Dublet (also known as Nepanet) and Peter Conway (a.k.a. Tatatiqunea), both Nipmuck Indians who were sympathetic to the English cause, and both Praying Indians. Both men had been confined to Deer Island in Boston Harbor with other English-loyal Massachusett and Nipmuck families during King Philip's War and volunteered to carry messages between the Council and the Native captors.[36] The fact that Rowlandson mentions these Indians by name and in such warm and affectionate terms is very interesting. She clearly recognizes these men as individuals whom she can trust to give her truthful information about her friends and family, much in the same way she recognizes the kindness and honesty of certain individuals among her Indian captors. She is also, as Neal Salisbury has noted, speaking in "strikingly different tones when referring to [these] individual Christian Indians [Tom and Peter] whose actions benefited her" (Salisbury, Introduction 43). However, what is especially notable about this passage is that Rowlandson erases Tom and Peter's Christian identities; she does not get Praying Indians by the hand in this passage, but just "Indians." Whereas the earlier band of English Indians who approached Rowlandson's group were quickly dismissed as Christian imposters by Rowlandson because of their "foul looks," these men are mentioned by name and warmly welcomed by Rowlandson with handshakes and tears. Obviously, Tom and Peter rate higher with Rowlandson than previously encountered Praying Indians because of the nature of their mission—to procure her release—but the fact of their Christianness is not even acknowledged by Rowlandson. She cannot acknowledge it. For if Rowlandson recognizes this gesture of goodness, one that

---

[36]   Tom Dublet alone volunteered to carry the first message at the persuasion of John Hoar, an advocate of Christian Indians and a Concord lawyer. Because previous attempts to find willing volunteers among those Christian Indians interned on Deer Island had not surprisingly failed, Joseph Rowlandson persuaded Hoar to intercede with the Indians on his behalf and Dublet agreed to Hoar's request. When the Nipmuck sachems insisted upon two messengers to transport the letters of redemption, Peter Conway joined Dublet in the second exchange of letters. See Salisbury, 32–5 and 132–7, and Lepore, 145–7.

ultimately leads to her redemption, as originating from Christian Indians, the line between the "us" and "them" becomes so blurred and permeable that the Indians are no longer the absolute other. Rowlandson cannot sustain the momentum of her text and her own authorial agency if she recognizes that there is an "in between"—Indians that are truly Christian and acculturated as Tom and Peter appear to be. Rowlandson must reinscribe the Praying Indian as malevolent; by the end of the nineteenth remove, she has done just that.

As the ransom negotiations are being finalized and Rowlandson sets the 20 pound amount for her own ransom as requested by the Indians, she acknowledges that it was a "Praying Indian that wrote their letter for them" but avoids the actual mention of James Printer's name (Rowlandson 98). From there, however, she launches into a vicious tirade against other Praying Indians who have committed such atrocities as defying Old Testament mandates and personal conscience to eat horse, betraying their fathers into English hands in order to escape punishment themselves, fighting against their own Christian kindred at the Battle of Sudbury, wearing a string of Christian fingers about their necks, and leading a heathen "powaw" before battle (Rowlandson 98). Rowlandson then spends a great deal of time and descriptive effort to detail the proceedings of the Praying Indian-led pow wow, betraying perhaps her own interest in such an event or her keen awareness of her audience's thirst for such gory, titillating information.[37] Either way, her entire diatribe about the atrocities committed by the Praying Indians she encountered is built upon the notion inherent in the colony's seal: the idea of the Indians' stereotypical duality. They can be everything and nothing the colonists want them to be, consequently undermining any chance of the colonists achieving a coherent understanding of themselves. These Praying Indians in particular have successfully passed as both Christian and "civilized," yet they willingly and even gleefully in Rowlandson's estimation, flaunt their "savagery" against the English at every given opportunity. As Kristina Bross observes, by vilifying the Praying Indians in these sensational ways, Rowlandson "signals her perspective on conversion and on the possibility of an Indian spiritual or cultural transformation: it can never be certain and is most likely a façade for cruelty camouflaged by the trappings of conversion" (*Dry Bones* 184). I would additionally argue that Rowlandson is horrified not only by the cruel façade and violence of these Praying Indians' actions, but also by the threat this poses to her own colonial and Christian identity. If they can so easily slip in and out of Englishness/Christianness and do so undetected by the English themselves, then is Englishness/Christianness really the stable identity the colonists claimed it to be? Can Rowlandson herself slip away from her Englishness/Christianness simply by virtue of her exposure and acculturation to Indianness? Therefore, Rowlandson must write over the reality of these historic individuals, Praying Indians such as Tom Dublet, Peter Conway, and James Printer, whose very real existences thrust such questions and anxieties to the forefront, exposing the vulnerabilities of colonial dominance and of Rowlandson's own exceptionality as a Christian and Anglo female author.

---

[37] See Rowlandson, 98.

Rowlandson's Praying Indians cannot be acknowledged by her; they must be downplayed, stereotyped, and removed to the background. Yet their specters are still evident in her text, peeking through the ruptures and slippages inherent within the colonialist discourses of her narrative. Just as Rowlandson's female authorial identity pushes back against and evades the suppression imposed upon it by patriarchal dominance, so, too, does historic Native identity push back against and evade the racist and colonialist frameworks Rowlandson reinforces. These moments of resistance and "push back" as evidenced in both the Massachusetts Bay Colony seals and Rowlandson's narrative are significant because they allow alternative subjectivities and new social identities, such as Anglo-American colonials, women writers, and Native Americans, to emerge from within and expose the circumscribed biopolitics of the colonialist system. However, for those new identities to emerge, as in the case of Rowlandson, intentional appropriation or elimination of another alternative identity, such as that of the Praying Indian, must occur.

Consequently, within her narrative Rowlandson must continually create and revise her "paper Indians" in order to establish and maintain her own agency and authorial identity. It was unimportant that there were contradictions in her narrative depictions of the Praying Indians, just as it did not matter to the colony that its "fixed" seal vacillated among divergent representations of Indianness and the colonial mission. Ultimately, the colonists and Rowlandson were not concerned with the fixity or facticity of the textualized Indians on their seals or in their texts. The importance for the colonists and Rowlandson lay in the agency provided by these Indian constructions, which the colonists could mold to certain expectations and use to confirm their own interpretation New World American identity that they wished to foreground, to fix. The "real Indians" existed only to serve as templates for the construction of a New World English identity, an identity that constantly needed to revision itself in order to maintain its tenuous grasp on stability and authority, an identity that needed to overwrite and ideologically silence Native Americans to assert itself.

Chapter 2
Revising the Indian of the Seal: Anglo Masculinity, Paul Revere's "Sword-in-Hand" Seal, and Ann Eliza Bleecker

Part 1
Iconography: Paul Revere's Seal

On July 19 of 1775, the province of Massachusetts made arrangements for a new official seal. The figure of a nearly nude Indian clutching a bow and arrow and crying out for aid, which had been in and out of use since the colony's inception in 1629, was no longer the image the beleaguered colony wanted to present of itself. However, the royal coat of arms that had been in use in various forms with various English-appointed governors since the revocation of the charter in 1692 was not a proper reflection of the colony's newly revolutionary and independent stance either. An appropriate, official, seal image was needed to signify the severance of any lingering ties with English rule and to set Massachusetts apart from the other colonies as the pacesetter of the patriotic movement. Massachusetts and all of the American colonies had suffered through the American Revenue (or Sugar) Act of 1764, the Stamp Act of 1765, and the Townshend Duties of 1767, which were imposed by Parliament as a means of covering the expenses of quartering English troops on American soil (rather than demobilizing them), after the French and Indian War. On their own, however, Massachusetts residents experienced the fallout from the Boston Massacre in 1770 and the Boston Tea Party in 1773, both of which placed the colony's citizens in direct conflict with Parliamentary rule; Massachusetts was setting itself apart as the "example" of open rebellion in colonial America.

Parliament, with their closure of Boston Harbor and the passing of the restrictive Coercive Acts in March of 1774 in direct response to the Tea Party, wanted to use Massachusetts as a negative example, isolating and punishing the colony in order to illustrate the fate that would await other colonies if they continued to be defiant. As historian Gordon Wood notes, "The British government had long assumed that Boston was the center of the disturbances in America: the collapse of colonial resistance would follow simply from isolating and punishing the port" (252). To the American patriots, however, Massachusetts was an example of the dire situation that awaited all Americans if they failed to resist Parliament's ever-increasing demands for taxation and legislative control. Consequently, the eyes of both nations—America and England—were upon Massachusetts, and the colony needed a symbol reflective of its position at the forefront of the fight for American independence.

Therefore, on that July day in 1775, a committee appointed by the Council presented a seal "somewhat similar to that under the first charter to be established as the seal of the colony for the future" (Middlebrook 8). A sketch of this new seal was presented to Council, and although now lost, the Council's reaction to and revisions for the seal indicate not only the original appearance of the sketch, but also what Council wished to underscore about the new identity of the colony. The Council dictated: "Instead of an Indian holding a Tomahawk and Cap of Liberty, there [is to] be an English American holding a Sword in the Right Hand, and Magna Charta in the Left Hand, with the Words '*Magna Charta*,' imprinted on it" (*Journal of the Honorable House of Representatives*, as qtd. in Greenough 3).[1] Around the figure were to be the words "Ense Petit Placidam Sub Libertate Quietem"—"By the sword we seek peace, but peace only under liberty," which remains the motto of the Commonwealth today.[2] This design was approved on August 7, 1775, and within a few days, the new seal (see Figure 2.1), known as the "Sword-in-Hand" seal, was engraved onto copper plates by Paul Revere and was immediately featured on bills of credit with the words, "*Issued in defence of American Liberty*" printed below it (Middlebrook 8, italics in original).

In this new version of the seal, the Native has been replaced by the native; the bow and the arrow replaced by more "culturally developed" European weapons of Magna Carta and the sword; the leaf or fabric loin cloths and the disheveled and wild hair are similarly replaced by a bicorne hat, smart breeches, a vest, and a topcoat—the uniform of a military officer. The Indian who for so long had defined

---

[1]   Magna Carta, as we know it today, has also been referred to throughout history as "Magna Charta," with the "h," as is seen on the "Sword-in-Hand" seal. I will refer to this document as modern scholars do, as Magna Carta, but will retain traditional spellings when used in other sources. Magna Carta is also correctly referenced without the use of the article "the" as it is actually not a single, static document but a series of evolving documents.

[2]   When the original recommendation was made by the Committee for the new seal to feature an Indian figure holding a cap of liberty and tomahawk, a different motto was also suggested. According to Chester Greenough, "[T]he new seal was intended to bear a shorter motto: 'Petit sub libertate quietem'" (Greenough 4). However, when the Council amended the petition to change the figure from an Indian one to an Anglo-American one, they also specified that on the seal, "previous to the word Petit be Inserted the word Ense and subsequent to it the word placidam" (Greenough 4). The original, shorter motto— "We seek peace under liberty"—obviously lacks the force of the revised statement, which clarifies the colony's desire for peace, but *only* under liberty and their willingness to achieve both through the use of the sword. It is possible the original, shorter motto is simply a misquote. The longer of the two phrases is a quite well-known quote traditionally attributed to Algernon Sidney. The author of *Discourses Concerning Government*, Sidney was a well-known political theorist and very influential thinker of the time, often cited by leaders of the American Revolution. John Adams, for example, wrote, that "revolution principles" are "the principles of Aristotle and Plato, of Livy and Cicero, and Sydney, Harrington and Locke. The Principles of nature and eternal reason. The principles on which government over us stands" (as qtd. in Greenough 5). This motto is still in use on the Great Seal of the Commonwealth of Massachusetts today.

Figure 2.1   Paul Revere, the "Sword-in-Hand" Seal of the Commonwealth
of Massachusetts (1775–1780). Courtesy of the
Massachusetts Archives.

the Massachusetts Colony, and was even the Committee's instinctive first choice
for the basis of the new seal (as indicated by the Council's response to the sketch),
has been removed from the official symbol of the province. Indianness can no
longer be the identifying mark of New World or Massachusetts exceptionality and
burgeoning independence. On the cusp of the Revolution, the colony must present
an image of equality to the world and especially to England. The Indian, while for
so long the "standout" image in the Massachusetts region where "[n]early every
seaboard settlement … derived its living from the sea" and therefore employed
seals with maritime design elements including anchors and codfish, was also
an image of difference and "inferiority" (Middlebrook 6–7). As discussed in
Chapter 1, the Massachusetts Bay colonists embraced the indigenity represented
by the Indian figure of the seal. Simultaneously, however, they also struggled to

contain their own dis-ease caused by their close proximity to Indianness. In short, the very Indians that lent exceptionality to the Massachusetts Bay and its New World errand into the wilderness also underscored the colonial fears of "devolving" into that very Indianness. The Indian on the earlier seals, consequently, wavered between an image of uniqueness and authority and an admission of colonial frailty. With the onset of a war with England, such an image must be remade and re-visioned to erase any signs of weakness and self-doubt.

In the same vein, earlier seal images that fluctuated between feminine and masculine versions of colonial identity, between visions of "savage" female sexuality and feminized Indian manhood, must be remade into a more constant, dominant image with which the world, and particularly England, could grapple—that of a white male. Therefore, the new seal image becomes one that showcases—or attempts to showcase—Anglo-American masculinity in its most physically and politically threatening form: a uniformed and armed officer carrying the guarantee of his inalienable rights as an Englishman, a copy of Magna Carta. But for all of its seemingly "direct" symbolism and clarity, what emerges when viewing this seal, however, are ambivalences akin more to the earlier Indian seals than an assertion of a confident, stable, and authoritative identity of a newly forming republic. In fact, I would argue the figure depicted on this seal does not represent the citizenry of Massachusetts any more accurately than the Indians on the earlier seals do.

Although it is overwhelmingly more similar to the earliest seals of the Massachusetts Colony than different, the "Sword-in-Hand" seal does have some notable alterations from its forbears. This newer seal, as a whole, is much less cluttered than previous versions. The central figure of this image is not backed by trees and uncultivated earth nor is he contained by dual rows of leafy, orderly garlands as his Indian predecessors had been. The Anglo soldier at the center of this seal stands alone against a blank background, his figure filling the entire space of the seal's center area with only the slightest shading around his feet to ground him and prevent him from being unmoored in the blank space of the seal. Nature, as a whole, is entirely absent from this image; there are no leaves, sheaves of wheat, trees, or weapons constructed of natural elements. Instead, this man is surrounded by the advancements of civilization: forged metal weapons, machine printed documents, fashionable clothing, Latin phrases, and a declaration of his guaranteed rights as a citizen. This was undoubtedly a conscious choice by the designers of this version of the seal to underscore the "civilized" and "rational" character of this figure rather than a bodily, indigenous connection to the American landscape or the natural world. Whereas earlier images of the seal were attempts to establish American colonial exceptionality through the use of the Indian and indigenous landscape, this image is clearly meant to establish parity with England and national pride within the residents of the newly forming republic. Regardless of these seemingly divergent surface messages of this and previous seals, both iterations of it underscore the foundational myth enabling the colonial project in the New World: Indians are of nature and inferior; Anglo colonists transcend nature and are superior.

Additionally, this seal is round instead of elliptical as the previous Indian seals had always been, and it is offset by a single beaded ring that separates the concentric layers of the image. In all, it is visually cleaner and more simplistic than earlier seals, even utilizing a pared-down designation for the colony—*Sigillum Coloniae Massachusettensis 1775*—in the outermost ring, and an unfurled banner that states the colony's new motto in Latin ("By the sword we seek peace, but peace only under liberty") in an inner ring. Overall, more emphasis is placed on the written word in this version of the seal than in previous renderings, with words and phrases dominating the visual space and conveying meaning while the image of the soldier with his upturned saber reinscribes that meaning. Civilization, literacy, and urbane enlightenment are established by the presence of the colony's name and motto in Latin, and the representation of Magna Carta literally spelled out on the seal. Clearly, this seal is attempting to put a great deal of distance between previous official representations of Massachusetts that relied on the natural world and the racialized, sexualized Other and the new image the colony wished to project.

The most striking and noteworthy difference between this image and earlier seals, however, is the fact that the Anglo-American man of this image is silent; no banner pleading for aid (or demanding independence) unfurls from his mouth. He is stoically mute, allowing his raised saber, Magna Carta, and the Latin motto to do his speaking for him—as if the meaning of these symbols is singularly clear and interpretable. Whereas the previous Indian figures on the seal were visualized as speaking, declaring a subjectivity and voice—even if only to plead for domination—this figure is confoundingly silent, ultimately rendering his message and meaning just as conflicted and confused as that of the speaking Indians of earlier seals. Just as the "Come over and help us" plea from the Indians revealed latent anxieties about colonial identity and the place of the colonists in the New World, the silence (and, as I will discuss later, the accoutering) of Revere's "Sword-in-Hand" figure is reflective of the colony's now conflicted sense of loyalty, independence, and cultural identity at the moment of independence from Britain. However, rather than being impenetrable and unquestionable, the silence of this masculine figure on the seal of the colony at the core of the revolutionary movement—Massachusetts—proves to be enabling and empowering. It was within this silence that Anglo-American women writers, like Ann Eliza Bleecker, could see an opening, an opportunity, to re-script the nationalist discourses from a distinctly female and domestic perspective. The absence of a masculine voice and the conflicting, even contradictory, messages conveyed by this seal, which the eyes of both England and America were riveted upon, provide a space through which female writers like Bleecker could give voice to the inverse of this image: the private, female citizen. These authors could shape and give meaning to this ambiguous and silent figure—much as the earlier Indian figures could be manipulated by authors like Mary Rowlandson—articulating and advocating for the Anglo feminine, domestic concerns that this seal image (and its forbears) omits. The masculine silence and dissonant imagery on the "Sword-in-Hand" seal provides a crack through which feminine voice can emerge.

Rejecting the Indian, Rewriting Anglo Masculinity

Although now clearly "whitewashed," masculinized, and with a few marked visual differences from the previous Indian seals, the "Sword-in-Hand" figure of the seal still contains the vestiges of Indianness of its forbears (Figures 1.1–1.6). Rather than boldly declaring a culturally and politically independent "American" identity, the new Massachusetts seal is instead a restatement of former conceptions of Indianness; it presents an Anglo-American man in the form, stance, and armament of the Indians that preceded him. He is the Indian, only in a more "civilized"—and notably silent—form. Whereas the Indian before him openly pleaded for colonial domination, the lone Anglo-American male figure stands silently in the center of the new seal image, holding a sword, actually a saber, in his right hand with its point upward and grasping a scrolled Magna Carta, slightly unrolled, in his left. He is armed and prepared for "combat," just as the Indian in the original seal was, only now this figure carries Anglo-specific weapons of resistance, although they are in the same position as the Indian's weaponry before him. The saber is in the same hand, the right, and in the same position—extended outward from the body in a right angle—as the Indian's arrow was in previous seals. While the tip of the saber is now pointed upward whereas the Indian's arrow pointed downward in a show of peace, the position of the arm holding the weapon is identical. The figure also stands fully facing the viewer, his knees slightly bent with his toes turned outward and his arms bent at the elbows, slightly extended away from his body, just as his Indian predecessors were pictured. This awkward pose that offered such an unnatural and ambivalent representation of Indianness in the earliest seals as simultaneously aggressive and passive is now reenacted in the stance of the Anglo-American figure. Is his crouched position one of defense, recoiling to ward off an onslaught from the Crown? Or is he the aggressor, pointing his saber skyward in a bold declaration of Massachusetts's intent to take the offensive in defiance of England? Is this figure defining himself as subject to Englishness—a "victim" reacting to it—or is he defining himself against Englishness—an American patriot completely separate from it? His intentions, like the Indians' before him, are unclear.

This Anglo-American man of the "Sword-in-Hand" seal has essentially been "remade" in the image of his Indian forbear, the very Indian that caused so much anxiety in the formation of the colonial self. The Indian, at once evoking colonial repulsion and desire, was an ambivalent image that for all of its perceived and intended fixity relayed more about the complexities of New World identity than it did to stabilize it. Now, the image of Anglo-American masculinity that dominates the seal essentially reinscribes the same conflicted sense of identity that had as its genesis the colonial encounters with Indianness. While the Indianness has been ostensibly "removed" from the focus of this seal, vestiges of its ambivalence remain and serve to underscore the still malleable and conflicted nature of American identity on the cusp of the Revolution.

The colonists of Massachusetts were clearly grappling with their relationship to and understanding of "Englishness" at the onset of the Revolutionary War.

It was unclear if they were subjects to the crown with inalienable rights and wanted to remain this way or if they were independent from the crown and citizens of their own nation. The slightly unfurled copy of Magna Carta in the figure's left hand only adds to this ambivalence. Long known as the "symbol of the 'Rights of Englishmen,'" Magna Carta is arguably the basis for the rule of constitutional law throughout the modern world and was most certainly the basis for colonial protest against England at the outset of the Revolution (Young 326). First issued in 1215 on the plains of Runnymede when English Barons confronted a despotic King John about his overzealous financial policies, the document required the king to limit his ability to raise funds, to respect certain legal procedures, and to accept that his will could be bound by law.[3] Because Magna Carta was perceived as the guarantor of "common law" over sovereign law, many patriotic American citizens and leaders looked to it when asserting their rightful liberty from English Parliament and King George III. Specifically, they looked to the words of Sir Edmund Coke, a seventeenth-century attorney general to Queen Elizabeth who used Magna Carta as a way to combat the oppressive maneuvers of the Stuart kings. According to Coke in a 1628 address to Parliament, "Magna Carta ... will have no sovereign" (U.S. National Archives).[4] But would the colonists?

The document, after all, is a contract between the "freemen" of England and their king. It is an assertion of an equitable relationship with the king, one in which the rights of English citizens were guaranteed to be recognized by the sovereign power. However, at the time when Paul Revere engraved the image of the "Sword-in-Hand" seal, American Patriots desired not an equitable relationship with their king, but an entirely separate and independent identity altogether. Many colonists wanted freedom and separation from the English crown and Parliamentary rule. Americans had been in open rebellion since the Coercive Acts of 1774 and "[w]hatever royal authority was left in the colonies [was] dissolved" (Wood 248). By the spring and summer of 1775, fighting had broken out in Massachusetts with the Battle of Concord and Paul Revere's famous ride to warn John Hancock in

---

   [3]   Interestingly, the "original" document issued and signed on June 15, 1215, was called the "Articles of the Barons" and is now lost; however, the document was redrawn with some wording and formality changes and officially reissued on June 19, 1215, as Magna Carta. One of the significant changes that would affect future generations was the change of the wording from "any baron" in the original document to "any freeman" in the final, authorized version of the Magna Carta. Although barons and freemen were both statistically small proportions of the population in 1215, over time, the term "any freeman" grew to include all English and was consequently a very significant change.

   [4]   Coke's four volume *Institutes of the Laws of England* was "widely read by American law students[.] [Y]oung colonists such as John Adams, Thomas Jefferson, and James Madison learned of the spirit of the charter [Magna Carta] and the common law—or at least Coke's interpretation of them" from these texts (U.S. National Archives). Therefore, with Coke's powerful influence on American legal thought and his own strong support of Magna Carta, it is not surprising that on the cusp of the Revolution, many colonists would turn to Coke and Magna Carta for justification.

April and the Battle of Bunker Hill in June, so by July when the Council passed the orders for a new seal to be inscribed, the idea of remaining under Parliamentary control and subject to the crown must have been inconceivable for many. So while the use of Magna Carta in the image certainly champions the ideas of rights for all men and the limitations of the crown, it also, perhaps unwittingly, reinforces the authority of the Crown and the colonists' conflicted and still dependent relationship to it. The newly inscribed seal image fluctuates uneasily between an independent American identity and an English subject identity, and when the accoutrements of the Anglo-American figure is considered, this dis-ease is even more apparent.

Wearing breeches gathered at the knee, calf-length gaiters, a single-breasted frock coat with the more practical shorter skirts worn open to expose the waistcoat beneath, and a bicorne, or cocked, hat, this figure is the picture of military sensibility. He is uniformed, armed, and ready to defend his rights as defined by Magna Carta wielded in his left hand. Yet his military attire is confusing in this context. It is unclear whether this man is a Continental or British soldier. Just as the Indians of previous seals were portrayed in ambivalent positions and in a conflicted relationship with the viewer, so, too, is this figure sending similarly mixed signals because of his impeccable military appearance and the context into which his image was thrust.

Although many of the myths of America's revolutionary origins champion the idea of a colonial population unequivocally supportive of the Patriot cause, it is a well-known fact that not all Americans supported the idea of a revolution. Some Americans supported the Crown even after the start of the conflict; it has been estimated that "loyalists may have numbered close to half a million, or 20 percent of white Americans" (Wood 285). Further, Gordon Wood notes that as many as "20,000 of them [Loyalists] fought for the crown in the regiments of His Majesty's army, and thousands of others served in local loyalist militia bodies" (285). David Maas has observed that some loyalists "decided to hide underground by masking their true feelings. The number of Tories who remained in Massachusetts throughout the war was higher than most patriotic citizens were willing to admit" (106). Other Americans simply tried to avoid involvement with either side in the struggle. Some recent European emigrants, pacifists, and otherwise apolitical men simply wanted to avoid a conflict with the British Army, which was a "well-trained professional force, having at one point in 1778 nearly 50,000 troops in North America alone; and more than 30,000 hired German mercenaries" (Wood 261). Conversely, the Continental Army, which basically began from scratch, consisted at times "of less than 5,000 troops, supplemented by state militia units of varying sizes … [with] inexperienced, amateur officers serv[ing] as American military leaders" (Wood 262). The idea of a conflict between two such disproportionately numbered and experienced sides must have been inconceivable to many Americans, and abhorrent to those who were in support of the crown.

Additionally, there was some ambivalence among American patriots as to why the Revolution was even being waged. Gordon Wood notes that throughout most of the imperial crisis,

American patriot leaders insisted they were rebelling not against the principles
of the English constitution, but on behalf of them … By emphasizing that it
was the letter and spirit of the English constitution that justified their resistance,
Americans could easily believe that they were simply preserving what
Englishmen had valued from the beginning of their history. (257)

However, many of the principles held dear by the Americans were actually
"revolution principles" that were beyond the mainstream of English thought. Some
colonists supported the "country opposition" espoused by English intellectuals
like Jonathan Swift and Alexander Pope, which lamented the commercialization
of English life and the networks of influence controlled by the luxurious courtly
classes. Americans, who viewed themselves as more unaffected in character than
their sophisticated English counterparts, understood the relevance of these "grass
roots" rumblings and had even invoked these ideas off and on in colonial assemblies
during the first half of the century. Now, however, on the cusp of the Revolution,
such ideas "not only prepared the colonists intellectually for resistance, but also
offered them a powerful justification of their many differences from a decayed and
corrupted mother country" (Wood 258).

Such ideas leave the colonists in an ambivalent relationship with that mother
country, though. Are they her children and subject to her law but merely want their
constitutional rights to be heard and their voices counted? Or are they divorcing
themselves from the crown, rejecting not only the English way of life but also
its royal power? Further, what about the citizens who fall into neither camp,
those who just want to maintain the status quo and have no desire whatsoever to
rebel or voice complaints? Colonists of all these varying degrees of "Britishness"
occupied American soil. Consequently, American identity during the onset of the
Revolution was clearly a confused and diffuse matter for the colonists. Depicting
that identity as static and cohesive in a symbol, like the Massachusetts Colony
seal, would be nearly impossible. No single image, no matter how distinctively
marked, would carry the same meaning for the various Anglo-Americans who
would view it. Revere's "Sword-in-Hand" seal with its uncertain message and
indistinct audience is especially marked by this ambivalence.

Additionally, because British troops so vastly outnumbered American forces,
it would be far more likely that colonists of any political leaning would have
encountered well-uniformed and armed British troops that more closely matched
the figure on the seal than a Continental soldier who looked the same way.
The colonial militia, described by the Revolutionary-era British General John
Burgoyne as "untrained rabble," was often without uniforms or any uniformity
of dress throughout most of the Revolution (qtd. in Wood 252). As Captain Oscar
Long has noted in his overview of American Army uniforms between 1774 and
1895, "At Lexington, as well as at Concord … not an officer or soldier of the
Continental troops engaged was in uniform, but were in the plain ordinary dress
of citizens" (2). Once George Washington was elected General and Commander-
in-Chief of the American Army in 1775, an order was issued that different colored
cockades would be used in the hats of the various ranks in order to distinguish "the

commissioned officer from the non-commissioned, and the non-commissioned from the privates" due to the fact that "the Continental Army have, unfortunately, no uniforms" (as qtd. in Long 2).

By November of 1775, Congress resolved "that the clothing for the Army should be paid for by stoppages from the men's pay" and that the clothing "be dyed brown and the distinctions of regiments made in the facings" of the waistcoats (Long 2). However, due to scarcity of cloth and difficulty of distribution, many soldiers remained without uniforms even after this order. In July of 1776 Washington consequently "encouraged … [for] those who would have been unprovided with uniforms, the use of hunting shirts, with long breeches made of the same cloth" (Long 2). Even at Valley Forge in the winter of 1777–1778, American troops were still a motley crew of mismatched uniforms and equipment. Inspector General Baron de Steuben even noted that during his inspection of the troops he "saw officers at the grand parade at Valley Forge mounting guard in every sort of dressing gown, made of an old blanket or woolen bed-cover" and that officers had "every color and make" of coats (as qtd. in Long 3). Although some well-heeled Continental troops and officers, like Washington, undoubtedly had the financial ability to outfit themselves in military finery befitting their positions and their post, many other Continentals would have worn actual British uniforms that had been issued to them during the earlier colonial wars when they served as volunteer regiments. For example, during "the early stages of the French-Indian Wars expeditions of colonial volunteers were mounted to seize French forts or build British ones" (Windrow and Embleton 13). Such recruits would have often been given the "[t]ypical British infantry private's coat," although "[c]olonial units probably wore coats … without the decorations" (Windrow and Embleton 12). Some Continental troops, therefore, would have literally donned British "red coats," perhaps with altered facings and decorations, during the Revolutionary War. How, then, can the impeccably uniformed figure on the seal have reflected the Continental reality? The uniformed soldier of the seal could just as easily signify a member of the American or British forces because of the inconsistent attire of the Continental soldiers, the varying allegiances of colonial citizens, and the differing levels of literacy of viewers. Once disseminated into the heterogeneous public of the colony on official broadsides or bills of credit, this seal image becomes one of diffuse and multiple meanings, particularly to audiences with varying degrees of literacy. It is not the static and stable image the design committee and House undoubtedly intended it to be, but rather an unintentionally similar and ambivalent remake of the previous Indian seals. The Indian may have been visually removed from this Revolutionary-era image, but his (or her) spectral presence and instability remains.

Beyond the confusion of national identity represented in the "Sword-in-Hand" seal is a conflict of class. Not only does the Anglo-American man vacillate between remnants of Indianness from previous seals and British and American identity, he also wavers between distinctions of social class. The idea that the Revolution was, at its heart, a "class war" has been posited by scholars such as J. Franklin Jameson in the early twentieth century. Jameson posits:

it seems clear that in most states the strength of the revolutionary party lay most largely in the plain people, as distinguished from the aristocracy. It lay not in the mob or rabble, for American society was overwhelmingly rural and not urban ... but in the peasantry, substantial and energetic though poor, in the small farmers and frontiersmen. And so, although there were men of great possessions like George Washington and Charles Carroll of Carrollton who contributed a conservative element, in the main we must expect to see our social changes tending in the direction of leveling democracy. (25)

Although this interpretation has been largely abandoned by more recent historians who tend to emphasize the ideological unity of the American colonists rather than their class differences, Jameson's observations about class disparity during the Revolution are worthy of note. Class differences did exist in early America and were at the core of many of the issues that led to the conflict with England. Many Americans despised the extravagant, courtly lifestyles of their English counterparts, championing their own brand of "country opposition" and frill-free sensibilities. The most incendiary pamphlet of the Revolutionary era, Thomas Paine's *Common Sense*, not only dismissed King George III as a "brute" and called for American independence, but also reached out to "new readers among the artisan- and tavern-centered worlds of the cities" (Wood 254).[5] Paine eschewed fancy Latin quotations and references to erudite literary sources in favor of coarse imagery and Biblical references in order to reach his "common man" audiences. America not only wanted to be free of England's political tyranny, but also wanted political equality among its citizens. For too long, America had been the poorer, country cousin to England and no longer desired to simply reintegrate social stratification into the newly forming republic. Consequently, whether or not the Revolution was fought as a "class war," issues of class certainly underpinned many facets of the conflict, and because of his complete and stylish uniform, the figure pictured on the "Sword-in-Hand" seal is most decidedly a member of the higher classes.

He is outfitted in a full, proper military uniform from his knee-length breeches and gaiters, which were heavy coverings of cloth or leather that protected the leg from the foot to the knee, to his waistcoat and military frock coat, complete with a contrasting color facing along the collar and lapels. Additionally, the coat features the more elegant cut and style of the day with features like lowered "shoulder seams, reduce[ed] fullness of the skirts, and curv[ed] ... fronts [of the facings]," as well as a series of buttons that run down each lapel, which traditionally displayed the regimental numbers or symbols on military uniforms of the day (Mollo 48). This is no cast-off civilian coat or hastily "made from scraps," homespun cloth uniform. It is clearly a well-made and official Army costume that conforms to General Washington's orders that the uniforms of the Continental Army consist of "blue coats, waistcoats and breeches" with "the facings for certain states [to] be

---

[5] Paine's *Common Sense* was first published in January 1776 and went through some 25 editions in 1776 (Wood 254).

of different colors" (Long 4).[6] However, such complete and professional uniforms were almost unilaterally reserved for officers. As John Mollo has noted in his text, *Military Fashion*, in the early to mid-eighteenth century, "The provincial militia were supplied with weapons and equipment only. The men wore their own clothes and only the officers had any semblance of uniform" (67). Further, Mollo notes that, in the case of Washington, it was his officers who were "smartly turned out in blue with red facings, laced waistcoats and hats" (67). People who witnessed Washington's troops noted that the "ordinary soldiers [had] no uniforms nor [did] they affect any regularity" (Mollo 67). The Anglo-American man of the seal, then, is no "ordinary" Continental soldier; his uniform identifies him as a privileged officer, a man of some esteem. He is not representative of the typical American militiaman.

The figure of the seal also grasps a sword, or saber, to be more accurate. Sabers, which are a form of a sword that are typically curved and have only one cutting edge, were often carried by Continental troops during the Revolution. Specifically, the figure appears to be grasping a short saber, which was the "fighting style of sword worn by many officers [and] had a light cut-and-thrust blade (straight or curved) of about 30 inches, with a guard on the hilt" (Neumann 217).[7] The figure's saber also appears to have the "simple separated guard with a knuckle-bow and one branch on either side" as is "most common" on this particular style of short saber (Peterson 273). George Neumann in his *The History of Weapons of the American Revolution* further notes that the short saber was "one of the most popular styles [of sword], especially during the second half of the [eighteenth] century" (240). Harold Peterson observes that these short sabers were,

---

[6]   Once Congress passed a resolution in 1779 that required a uniformity of costume among the troops, Washington passed the above-mentioned general order "prescribing the uniform in general terms, to be furnished as soon as the state of public supplies would permit" (Long 3). Although this decree comes years after the Massachusetts "Sword-in-Hand" seal would have been engraved, the basic appearance of the uniform described by Washington was identical to those uniforms of other nations, including Britain, which had been in use for many years. The main difference in Continental troop uniforms was to be in the color choice—blue. Washington was basically making official the style and type of uniform that had already been in use, albeit sporadically, among Continental troops for years. Therefore, this order essentially confirms the uniform style pictured on the "Sword-in-Hand" seal.

[7]   Based on the position and extension of the saber blade in the image—from the figure's rib cage to about his temple/tip of his head—the blade of his saber would measure approximately 30 inches, categorizing this edged weapon as a short saber. Other Revolutionary-era swords and sabers, such as the hunting sword, naval cutlass, horseman's saber, and small sword (to name just a few) typically had blades of different lengths; in my research, the short saber was the only edged weapon I found to be curved, of this approximate length, and in wide use during this time period. For further reading, see Neumann, Harold Peterson (*Arms and Armor in Colonial America, 1526–1783*), and Moore (*Weapons of the American Revolution*).

next to the small sword ... the most widely used type. Both mounted and foot officers carried such [sabers]. Indeed, they were almost mandatory for the mounted officer who expected to become personally involved in a hand-to-hand conflict, for none of the other types were practical for use on horseback. (273)

Clearly then, it is a short saber raised in defiance/agitation by the Anglo-American man of the seal, as it was the weapon that was "indispensable for mounted officers" (Peterson 126).

But what about the average militiaman? What about those men who volunteered to fill infantry positions without officers' commissions or prestigious appointments? Would they have carried swords like the man in the seal? Not likely. As Alfred Hopkins, Curator of the Morristown National Historical Park, has noted, swords and sabers were worn "principally by officers, [and] for the most part ... carried by the gentry of the time" (1). The reason for this, according to Harold Peterson in his *Arms and Armor in Colonial America*, is that by the time of the Revolution most colonies required the barest of armament requirements for local militias and those requirements typically followed the British pattern. When British infantry privates, for example, began abandoning swords during the first part of the eighteenth century, leaving the "sergeants alone among enlisted men [to] retai[n] the traditional weapon," American militias soon followed suit (257). Peterson notes that in 1705, for example, Virginia required militia members to have a sword, but that by "1738 either a bayonet or sword was acceptable; and in 1755 the sword was omitted for all but corporals and sergeants and the bayonet became mandatory" (257). Many other colonies, per the recommendation of Congress, required their militias to arm themselves with "a sword *or* hatchet in addition to the bayonet" by 1775 (Peterson 257, emphasis mine). Peterson further observes only "non-commissioned officers of both state and Continental troops were required to wear swords when obtainable throughout the war" (Peterson 258). As a consequence, the sword was slowly working its way out of the hands of the "common" foot soldier and into the hands of officers and the cavalrymen. It was becoming a weapon for the elite and the higher-ranking soldiers rather than the "everyman" weapon it had been in the past.[8] The Anglo-American figure on

---

[8]   Harold Peterson has noted that of all the edged weapons, the one that was in most widespread usage throughout the entire period of American colonization was the sword. He states, "All men on military duty whether they carried a firearm or not were required to have a sword. Since all able-bodied men in a colony were normally called upon for such a duty, this meant that all had to be familiar with the use of that weapon" (69). He further comments that when Captain John Smith left Virginia in 1608, Smith "reported that there were on hand in the colony more swords than men and that in 1618 a Committee for Smythes Hundred in Virginia recommended that 40 swords and daggers be provided for 35 men expecting to come from England" (as qtd. in Peterson 69). Swords and edged weapons, therefore, were the armament of choice of all classes of men, not merely the gentry.

Undoubtedly, there would have been swords in the hands of militiamen and foot soldiers during the Revolution; I am not attempting to argue against this point. As Warren Moore has

the seal, therefore, is clearly not a reflection of the "average" Massachusetts, or even American, fighting man or citizen. He is an amalgamation of elitist New World fantasy and blatant Old World prejudices. Even though the man on the seal is meant to represent Massachusetts, the vanguard in the patriotic fight against British oppression, he instead depicts the privileged few in American society: white, wealthy men of English ancestry. And while this image would certainly present a formidable, dashing American identity to the rest of the world, as it was no doubt intended to do, it was not any more of an accurate depiction of Massachusetts citizenry than the Indians on the earlier seals.

Consequently, the "reality" of revolutionary-era Massachusetts peeps through the polished, elitist veneer of Revere's "Sword-in-Hand" seal. Just as the Indianness from previous seals is still apparent behind the "white-washed" image of the well-accoutered cavalryman in the seal, so, too, is the tension between colonial identifications of "Englishness" and "Americanness." The colonists' own uncertainty about their communal identity as an entity independent from England is unwittingly portrayed through the ambivalent nature of the image. The unclear signifiers, such as the soldier's uniform and his presentation of Magna Carta, as well as his awkward stance, make comprehension of his wavering image dependent upon the situation in which it is viewed and the circumstances of the viewer. Persons of different means, allegiances, literacies, and even genders would view this declaration of Massachusetts's unity through vastly different lenses. Once disseminated on Continental bills or other government documents, the "Sword-in-Hand" seal, rather than stabilizing a communal Massachusetts identity, instead produces countless variations and interpretations of that identity due to the cracks inherent in its construction.

The Indian Returns

Clearly, these cracks and confusion were a serious issue for the residents of Massachusetts because within five years of the "Sword-in-Hand" seal's design, it was replaced with an updated version of the original silver seal from 1629. In November of 1780, when Massachusetts became a state, "one of the first acts of the legislature was the establishment of a new seal" (Cummings 11). By December of that same year, Council Records report that Nathan Cushing was ordered to

> Prepare a Seal for the Commonwealth of Massachusetts who reported a Device
> for a Seal for Said Commonwealth as follows viz. a Sapphire, an Indian dressed

---

noted, "Americans used almost anything they could lay their hands on. At the beginning of the Revolution the American colonials were asked to bring along swords as well as shoulder arms. As the war continued, the United States gradually acquired a quantity of swords to issue its soldiers" (128). However, I am trying to assert that, as these Revolutionary-era weapons experts have claimed, officers and the higher classes would have "carried a greater variety of … swords during the period under consideration" than civilians or militiamen of lower classes (Peterson 268).

in his Shirt; Moggosins, belted proper, in his right Hand a Bow Topaz, in his left an Arrow, its point towards the Base; of the second, on the Dexter side of the Indian's head, a Star; Pearl, for one of the United States of America. (as qtd. in Cummings 12–13; see Figure 2.2)[9]

The Indian has returned to the seal. Now, however, he is unequivocally and permanently male and doggedly silent—just as his Anglo-American forbear from the "Sword-in-Hand" seal had been. However, now, unlike earlier Indian seals, there is no more ambivalence about this figure's gender and no curled banner emerging from his mouth. This new Indian is silent, stoic, masculine—a more stable representation of Massachusetts identity post-separation with England, perhaps. Or perhaps not. For years, this revised version of the Indian seal existed in multiple, inconsistent forms when used by various state agencies and prepared by various engravers because there was only a casual description of how the seal should look. Consequently, the figure's skin tone, clothing, stance, and even the framing containing him differed quite noticeably from seal image to seal image; this "stable" image was still unmoored and open to personal interpretation and representation until 1885, when its appearance was officially prescribed by legislature into the standardized form which is still in use today. The Indian was once again, and now always would be, a constant in Massachusetts Commonwealth iconography.

However, even in the standardized and newly consistent version of 1885, the Indian of the seal is no less ambivalent than any of his predecessors; this revised Indian figure still contains the spectral presence of the original, pleading Indian from the first seal. The discourses of colonialism, identity formation, gender, and race still circulate within the seal despite the figure's silence and consistent appearance even today, and those discourses distinctly exclude white womanhood and the domestic sphere. However, due to the stoic silence of these differently raced but similarly masculine seal images and their overwhelming ambivalence, there remains a gap through which feminine agency can assert itself by providing the dialogue to accompany these potent images. A feminine voice can be scripted to accompany these fluctuating representations of race and masculinity that not only asserts feminine agency, but also exposes the historic realities and hardships faced by women and the domestic sphere during the nation-defining moment of the Revolution. Ann Eliza Bleecker in her Revolutionary-era Indian captivity narrative, *The History of Maria Kittle*, does just that. By deploying the trappings of the feminine sphere in the uniquely feminine genre of the captivity narrative, Bleecker aggressively addresses these seal images of Indian and Anglo-American masculinity and writes the feminine into national rhetoric in a bold and significant way.

---

[9] The entry describing the seal goes on to read: "Crest. On a Wreath a Dexter Arm cloathed and ruffled proper, grasping a Broad Sword, the Pummel and Hilt Topaz with this Motto…ENSE PETIT PLACIDAM SUB LIBERTATE QUIETEM—And around the Seal SIGILLUM REIPUBLICAE MASSACHUSETTENSIS" (as qtd. in Cummings 13).

Figure 2.2   The revised Indian Seal of the Commonwealth of Massachusetts (1780–1885). Courtesy of the Massachusetts Archives.

Part 2
Narrative: Ann Eliza Bleecker and Maria Kittle

The Revolutionary War was a difficult time for Ann Eliza Bleecker, to say the least. The daughter of successful Dutch merchants and the wife of a lawyer turned gentleman farmer, Bleecker lived most of her life prior to the war in plentiful security, first in New York City and then on her husband's pastoral Tomhanick estate north of Albany, New York. She gave birth to two daughters, Margaretta and Abella, and spent her time surrounded by her beloved mother and sisters, managing her home and writing poetry, political essays, and short fiction which she shared with family and friends with the full support and encouragement of her husband. Bleecker enjoyed a pampered and idyllic domestic lifestyle—the prescribed and ultimate ambition of upper-middle class Anglo womanhood—until the British troops of General John Burgoyne and the realities of the American Revolution invaded her beloved domain in 1777.

In a memoir of her mother, included in *The Posthumous Works of Ann Eliza Bleecker in Prose and Verse* (1793)—a collection that contained works by both mother and daughter, most notably *The History of Maria Kittle*—Margaretta Bleecker Faugeres details her mother's war-related experiences. Faugeres notes that in August of 1777, General Burgoyne's army advanced toward the Bleeckers' Tomhanick, New York, estate on their way toward Lake Champlain, "burning and murdering all before them" (v). The violent advance of the British—who undoubtedly resembled the masculine, uniformed image on the seal of the Massachusetts Commonwealth—and their Indian allies forced Bleecker to flee on foot from her home with her two young daughters, Abella, who was still an infant, and Margaretta, who was four, while her husband was away procuring temporary lodgings for the family. After being reunited with her husband, Bleecker's infant daughter died of dysentery while the family was attempting to reach the safe haven of Albany, New York, by water. Bleecker's mother, who had evacuated the Tomhanick residence earlier with Bleecker's sister, Catharine, died soon after the extended family was reunited. Catharine then died on the family's return journey home to Tomhanick after their exile of four months. Then, in 1781 after their return to Tomhanick, Bleecker's husband John was seized by "a raiding party of Tories, British regulars, and Hessians (one bearing a tomahawk)" while he and two servants were harvesting the family's crops, but he was liberated by Connecticut troops six days later (Ellison, "Race" 452). In a letter to a friend after the incident dated May 8, 1783, Bleecker notes that shortly after this experience with John, "I fell into premature labour, and was delivered of a dead child. Since that, I have been declining" (Faugeres 178). The war and its collateral damage had entirely ravaged Bleecker's family and sense of domestic tranquility. Over the course of a few short months, Ann Eliza Bleecker had lost two children (one to a miscarriage), her mother, her sister, her health, and almost her husband to a war-time raiding party. However, perhaps even more importantly for Bleecker, she had lost the sanctity, security, and Anglo female identity provided by her family and home—a home that would never be the same for her after the war.

Bleecker, like many women during the Revolution, endured the distinctly gendered degradations and violences that accompany war: the attack and invasion of her home; the necessity of fleeing with young children on her hip; the absence of masculine protection; and the inevitable loss of children. Her experiences with the Revolution would have been nothing like what she would have seen depicted upon the Revere's "Sword-in-Hand" seal of the Massachusetts Commonwealth—a contemporary image. Bleecker, as a woman and mother, would not have felt the sense of authority and safety the uniformed officer armed with a sword portrayed. In fact, she may have recoiled at its uncanny resemblance to the British troops who caused her to flee her home and later captured her husband. She would not have reveled in the individual rights and protections guaranteed by Magna Carta in the soldier's hand. Bleecker also certainly wouldn't find any semblance of herself in the Indian seals that would have replaced Revere's "Sword-in-Hand" seal. She would have seen nothing of herself and her status as an Anglo woman, wife, and mother depicted in either of these versions of Revolutionary/early republican American identity. As an experienced writer, she did, however, see an opportunity to write the experiences of Anglo womanhood and the domestic realm into the historical consciousness of the new nation that was forming around her by adopting the genre of the captivity narrative, which was not only an acceptable and common genre for women writers, but also, because of its emphasis on the invasion and destruction of the domestic sphere, validated feminine authorship.

Captivity narratives, which often "depend on a central and sympathetic figure of a captive woman" and, indeed, often feature the authorial voice and perspective of white, middle-class womanhood, have always been inherently political (Burnham 2). Just as Mary Rowlandson's inaugural captivity narrative attempts to negate the presence of Praying Indians and reinscribe her own Anglo-female subjectivity, the captivity genre in general seeks to discipline, dominate, and restructure the uncolonized inhabitants of the New World by deploying the racial, cultural, and gendered frameworks of the colonizers. It also relies heavily on the stereotyped, savage image of the Indian who, often in the absence of white masculinity, abducts and menaces white women, the primary victims and survivors of captivity. As such, these narratives are intimately connected to the process of nation building and the construction of a nation's identity. By turning to the genre of the captivity narrative and then melding the historical fact of the captivity of Maria Kittle during the French and Indian Wars with her own observations and experiences gleaned during the American Revolution, Bleecker constructs a narrative that foregrounds not only the experiences of white women but also the failures of white men during moments of historical, national crises and gives them a distinctly feminine voice. However, in order to write feminine gendered agency and reality into the national rhetoric, Bleecker must necessarily critique and subvert the masculine discourses, both Indian and Anglo-American that dominate and terrorize white womanhood. She must aggressively censure white patriarchy and write out Indian reality in *The History of Maria Kittle*, in a similar fashion to Rowlandson, while simultaneously writing herself and her domestic experiences in. In short, she takes to task the two Revolutionary-era versions of the Massachusetts Bay Colony/Commonwealth's seal—the male Anglo soldier and the revised Indian man—and supplies a differently gendered dialogue to fill the ambivalent silences these images leave behind.[10]

Set during the French and Indian Wars, *The History* relates the fictionalized experiences of the very real Maria Kittle, a wife and mother of two young children

---

[10]   Ann Eliza Bleecker and her textual subject, Maria Kittle, both resided in New York and not in Massachusetts where they would have been directly under the authority of the Commonwealth and its seal. However, Bleecker would have been highly aware of the cultural assumptions perpetuated by images like the Revere "Sword-in-Hand" seal and would have been responding to those dynamics. The discourses about race, gender, and national identity that these seals attempt to proclaim and stabilize are, as I will argue, exactly what Bleecker is attempting to revise.

who is captured and taken from her home in upstate New York by a band of neighboring Indians with whom she had previously been friendly. The attack occurs, much like Rowlandson's and in predictable captivity fashion, when Maria's husband is away procuring wagons for evacuation and she is left at home alone with her children and several members of her extended family, including a heavily pregnant sister-in-law, Comelia Kittle, and her hapless, yet unnamed husband. The Indians descend upon the Kittle home, killing Maria's in-laws and her own infant son in the most brutal fashion, and then setting the house ablaze with Maria's young daughter inside. Maria, along with her brother-in-law Henry (who is the only other survivor from the raid on the home), is then marched to Montreal, Canada, where she is fortuitously adopted into a supportive female community. Introduced into this circle of sympathetic French and similarly displaced English women by Mrs. D___, an English woman who accommodates and employs her, Maria finds herself surrounded by women who commiserate with her trials and losses as a woman and mother. For two years the women forge lasting friendships, sharing their stories of grief and captivity and offering sympathetic support to one another. Then, almost inexplicably, Maria's husband, who has been serving in the Army in an almost suicidal capacity because of his grief, finally reunites with her in an emotional denouement that at long last "redeems" Maria from her captivity and brings the narrative to its close.

With its overly sentimentalized diction, surplus of affecting scenes, and obvious ties to the conventions of the sentimental fiction of the day, *The History* has long been viewed as a purely fictionalized tale of captivity, as "one of America's first novels" (Derounian-Stodola and Levernier 186), and as "a novel of sensibility" (Castiglia 131).[11] Sharon M. Harris in her *Executing Race* argues, however, that "the narrative is not fiction or at least is not a wholly imaginative production" as has been the conventional (mis)understanding of *The History* for years (100). Bleecker, as would most families in the Schaghticoke region around Albany, would have been familiar with the Kittle family massacre and captivity, which was "one of the most notorious incidents during King George's War" and, subsequently, a well-known part of Dutch and English lore in the region (Harris, *Executing Race* 101). Superimposed upon the historical foundation of Maria Kittle's captivity are glimpses of Bleecker's own life and experiences as woman, wife, and mother during the Revolutionary War some 20 years later. Like Maria Kittle and even Mary Rowlandson before her, Ann Eliza Bleecker also faced the domestic displacement and familial destruction of war as well as the realization of the vulnerabilities of a woman—any woman—living during a war—any war.

---

[11]   Additionally, most scholarly attention has been devoted to Bleecker's overtly political and pastoral poetry rather than this text; see Ellison ("Race and Sensibility in the Early Republic: Ann Eliza Bleecker and Sarah Wentworth Morton" and *Cato's Tears*), Harris (*Executing Race*), Kutchen ("The 'Vulgar Thread of the Canvas': Revolution and the Picturesque in Ann Eliza Bleecker, Crevecoeur, and Charles Brockden Brown"), and Giffen ("'Till Grief Melodious Grow': The Poems and Letters of Ann Eliza Bleecker"). The scholars who have attended *The History*, even briefly, include Castiglia (*Bound and Determined*), Ellison, Burnham (*Captivity and Sentiment*), and Harris.

From the very beginning of *The History of Maria Kittle,* Ann Eliza Bleecker places her authorial voice and her own historical moment as the organizing frames of the text. Subtitled *In a Letter to Miss Ten Eyck,* dated "Tomhanick, December, 1779," and begun with the salutation "Dear Susan," *The History* from its very opening positions Bleecker as an active participant—albeit as a narrator—in the events of Kittle's captivity and return (3).[12] Structured as a letter to Bleecker's beloved half-sister Susan, and ostensibly based on Bleecker's knowledge of "the unfortunate adventures of one of [her] neighbours, who died yesterday," *The History* becomes a female-centered nexus of moments of historical crises, a palimpsest of women's lives, voices, and specters (Bleecker 3). The disparate elements of time, place, and experience that separate the two women, Kittle and Bleecker, from each other, and even further separate Susan Ten Eyck from them both, become melded into one narrative experience that highlights the vulnerability of women and their domestic domain during any war. By placing Kittle's story of maternal and domestic losses into the framework of Bleecker's own fixed place in time and history—Tomhanick, New York, during the heart of the Revolution in 1779—and into the context of a letter shared between feeling, compassionate sisters, Bleecker creates a circuit of women readers, writers and factual personages united by the horrors of war. And through the production and publication of *The History,* she also writes that circuit into the historical and national consciousness of the fledgling republic that worked to erase its gendered existence.

Bleecker's Indians

The power of the Native American figure in the American colonial mind, as I have argued previously, was potent and fraught with anxiety. At once signaling an indigenous identity that could be appropriated and claimed by the European colonists as their mark of certainty and belonging in the New World, and simultaneously functioning as a symbol of ungovernable difference that both highlighted and threatened European "superiority" and stability, the Indian was a fraught figure for Bleecker.[13] While certainly racist and stereotypical in her

---

[12]   For my analysis, I have chosen to reference the edition of *The History* that appears in Sharon M. Harris's *Women's Early Historical Narratives* (2003) because of its ready availability and ease of access; however, when citing Margaretta Faugeres's biography of her mother, I have used the original 1793 version of the text because this biographical material is typically not reproduced in later editions of *The History.*

[13]   Sharon M. Harris has noted that Bleecker in her writing often transferred her maternal guilt from the death of her youngest daughter, Abella, and the Revolutionary War's chaotic disruption of her idyllic life onto "a series of constructions of 'savages' who attack and destroy innocent lives" in her poetry and earliest writings rather than the actual sources of her suffering (*Executing Race* 94). Harris goes so far as to argue Bleecker's racialism is actually a "hatred of Native Americans" and that "The most complex and revealing representation of [her] sentimentalized vision of the Dutch American settlers coupled with her racist attitudes toward Native Americans occurs in *The History of Maria*

depictions of the Indian in her narrative, Bleecker is also reliant upon that figure, both for her protagonist's survival and her own authorial identity, much in the way Mary Rowlandson is reliant upon her Praying Indians for both survival and authorial identity. It is in the figure of the imagined Indian—the colonist-created specter of loathing and desire from the seal—that Bleecker found her ground, her point of departure from which she could launch her gendered revision of the nation. The Indian, imagined rather than real, served both as a veil and a justification for her female characters' "inappropriate" actions and by contrast, the male characters' failures and errors. The Indian, with his "disorderly" and "savage" body and his incursion into the "civilized" realm of the feminine, allowed for and even excused the non-traditional, disorderly behavior of Bleecker's characters, giving her the opportunity to posit an alternative gender vision, one that revised and revalued women and their sphere and wrote them into historic specificity. The ambiguity of the Indian in the colonizer's mind allowed for ambiguity in the interactions of the colonizers with him. Acts of colonial/Euro-American feminine agency that would ordinarily be deemed unacceptable, become excusable, if not logical, when the figure of the Indian is brought into contact with white womanhood.

However, beyond merely bringing Indianness into collision with white, feminine domesticity, Bleecker suggestively and aggressively genders that Indianness as male. In earlier colonial depictions of Indians, such as the images on the earliest Bay Colony seals and Mary Rowlandson's captivity narrative discussed in Chapter 1, gender was a much more fluid or unimportant category. The Indians of the earlier seals could smoothly transition among being male, female, or some blended composite of the two genders and still affirm the gendered, cultural, intellectual, and religious paradigms that underpinned white colonial identity. And in Mary Rowlandson's narrative, in which most of the Indians she had contact with were male, gender was not the primary signifier for her; Indianness and its relationship to Anglo-Christianity were. For Rowlandson and the Bay Colony seal designers, the inclusion of feminine or masculine characteristics when describing Indianness varied depending upon the historical moment in which the text was contrived and the purpose that it served. What mattered to them was whether or not that Indianness reaffirmed—or attempted to reaffirm—Anglo, Christian superiority.

This is not the case for Bleecker and her text; gender matters for her in a very significant way because her focus is on the gendered realm of the domestic. She needs to demonstrate that not only Indianness, but also Anglo masculinity, work to negate and damage white womanhood, often in very similar ways. While in traditional colonialist fantasy, it was the male Indian who threatened and ravaged white womanhood and her domestic realm through captivity or violent attack, in reality, it was often white masculinity that failed in its role of protecting and

---

Kittle" (*Executing Race* 98). While I do not doubt that Bleecker held racist views, I believe her appropriation and use of the Indian figure in *The History* is more complex and fraught than simple hatred.

fostering the feminine realm of the domestic, as was the case with both Bleecker and her subject, Maria Kittle (and even Mary Rowlandson), who were attacked while their husbands were absent. It is also, Bleecker pointedly suggests, white patriarchy—not Indianness—that refuses to value and include white womanhood in discourses informing the newly forming nation and American identity. However, Bleecker must carefully launch her criticisms of white patriarchy through a strategic use of male Indianness. In Bleecker's narrative, Indianness functions as a veil for both the insurgent actions of her female characters and Bleecker's own pointed critiques of white masculinity. By masculinizing Indianness, and then bringing white womanhood into contact with it in an assertive, productive way, Bleecker is able to inscribe the feminine and the domestic with a new agency and even begin the visualization of a differently gendered nation.

Empowering the Domestic

One of the most interesting authorial moves Bleecker makes in *The History* is her decision not only to bring the domestic sphere into direct contact and conflict with the political/public sphere, but also to do so within the confines of the domestic realm. Rather than move her female characters outside of their domestic realm and into the "savage" wilderness where the traditional constraints of gendered codes of behavior and household responsibilities are removed (or at least displaced to an Indian setting and system) as in the traditional captivity format like Mary Rowlandson's narrative, Bleecker instead injects the external political, historical, and racial conflicts into the domestic scene.[14] She makes the familial and domestic the locus for nation-defining moments in her narrative, positing this domain as the point from which the nation should ultimately rebuild itself. Because nearly all of the moments of crisis and conflict that occur in *The History* occur within the dominion of white, European womanhood—the home and its surrounding grounds—Bleecker inscribes this realm with paramount significance, not only entering into the complex and multifaceted discourses governing nationalism in the early republic but also offering a radical critique of patriarchal hegemony.[15] Bleecker boldly re-scripts and disrupts the images of militaristic Anglo and Indian masculinity as portrayed on the Massachusetts seals of the Revolutionary era by confronting them with their inverse.

---

[14]   See Derounian-Stodola and Levernier (*The Indian Captivity Narrative*), VanDerBeets (*The Indian Captivity Narrative: An American Genre*), and Vaughan (*Narratives of North American Indian Captivity*) for further discussion of the captivity formula.

[15]   Many scholars have argued against the ideas of "separate spheres" and a single, "official" discourse governing nationalism in early republican and Victorian America as I do here. In addition to Cathy Davidson (*Revolution and the Word*), Shirley Samuels (*Romances of the Republic*), and Linda Kerber ("Separate Spheres, Female World, Women's Place: The Rhetoric of Women's History") noted above, see also Carroll Smith-Rosenberg (*Disorderly Conduct*), David Waldstreicher (*In the Midst of Perpetual Fetes*), and Julia Stern (*The Plight of Feeling*).

Only a small portion of the text of *The History* occurs out in the wilderness during Maria's forced removal from her home to Montreal, Canada. However, even when she arrives in Canada, Maria is almost immediately placed into another domestic scene, the home of the good Mrs. D___, an Englishwoman living in Montreal. By focusing so intently upon the realities of a woman's existence and the circumscribed territory and cultural responsibilities that define them, Bleecker is able to place the habitat and work of women at the forefront of her narrative. Furthermore, as she brings the domestic and all it entails, even stereotypically, into focus and into contact with the public, masculine realm, she can interrogate the gendered hierarchies already in place, and more importantly, revalue and reiterate the role of women and the domestic in the various national dialogues.

Because feminine authority was restricted to the province of the home, including its surrounding property and any children or servants who occupied that sphere, Bleecker takes great pains to assign this sphere and its inhabitants weighty significance. She makes certain to imbue Maria with transcendent female authority through the exceptional nature of her family, particularly her daughter, Anna. Anna, a child who was "the lovelier resemblance of her lovely mother" provides further validation of the domestic and its female head (Bleecker 4). Bleecker writes:

> The Indians, in particular, were extremely fond of the smiling Anna; whenever they found a young fawn, or caught a brood of wood-ducks, or surprised the young beaver in their daily excursions through the forests, they presented them with pleasure to her; they brought her the earliest strawberries, the scarlet plumb, and other delicate wild fruits in painted baskets. (4–5)

Stereotypically portrayed with their rustic painted baskets and "uncivilized" gifts of wild animals and fruits, the Indians in this passage validate not only the goodness and open-mindedness of the Kittles in their familiar relationship with their Native neighbors, but also the relevance of motherhood through their approval of Maria's infant daughter. If the Indians can see the precocity and value of Anna—and act in an accordingly worshipful manner—then she must, indeed, be a precious child, and her parents, or more specifically her mother in whose image Anna is made, have produced a being that literally bridges the gap between nations, cultures, and races. Motherhood and infancy, specifically white motherhood and infancy, Bleecker is suggesting here, are such powerful states of being that even the "wild savages" of the forest can be brought under their thrall and in such a way that is compatible with and beneficial to white colonial society. It is almost as if colonial motherhood and childhood have a civilizing and neutralizing effect upon the Indians, something that has heretofore not been achieved with any great regularity or success with male-dominated processes such as proselytizing, treaties, and martial law.

Although these same Indians will later function in the text as the threats to and destroyers of Kittle's motherhood, in this instance, they serve to validate it. It is their recognition of Anna's superior graces that substantiates the Kittles', and more particularly Maria's, identities as colonial parents in the New World. These doting parents' hearts "delight to see their beloved one so universally caressed" because the caressing of Anna by the natives serves to demarcate their own identities as non-native indigenes (Bleecker 5). As parents, the Kittles are extensions of their child and the Indians' recognition of the difference and exceptionality of that child reflects back onto them. This new generation of colonist in the New World wilderness has clearly not devolved into "savagery" (or else the Indians would take no notice of young Anna because she would be just like them); therefore, the parents obviously have not degenerated either or they would be incapable of producing such a remarkable child. Furthermore, the fact of the Indians' acceptance of Anna and by extension her parents, places the Kittle family as natural, native members of the landscape. Through their attentions and considerations to Anna and her family, the Indians have essentially "adopted" them, authenticating the Kittles' rightful place in the American wilderness—as native (not *N*ative) Americans. The Kittles are simultaneously validated as "different from" but also "part of" the native land and people around them by their Indian neighbors. They have been recognized, through the obeisance given to Anna by the Indians, as rightful owners and rulers of the land.

These Indians who bring Anna treasures and offer adoration at the Kittle home operate in much the same fashion as Rowlandson's Indians before them. They serve to validate white motherhood and womanhood as positions of power within the colonialist system just as Rowlandson's Indians served to underscore her Christian exceptionality; however, to produce such corroborative Indians, Bleecker necessarily relegates Indianness to a flattened out and stereotypical fantasy that can only stand to define and highlight white domesticity. The Indians of *The History* are not attempts by Bleecker at an authentic portrayal of Indian reality, but rather updated versions of previous colonial imagination that she uses to reinscribe the value of Anglo femininity and her domestic realm.

Bleecker further accentuates the domestic scene of the Kittle home by foregrounding the generative power of the Kittle women within the home through images of nursing babies and pregnant bodies. Bleecker reports that after 11 years of marriage and no signs of a second pregnancy, Mr. Kittle "silently wished for a son, and his desires were at length gratified; [Maria] was delivered of a charming boy, who was named, after him, William" (5). However, soon after the birth of William, Maria and her family find themselves facing the grim realities of the French and Indian War. The Indians from the region around Schochticook, where the Kittles reside, are beginning to make raids into the colonial settlements and committing "the most horrid depredations on the English frontiers" (Bleecker 5), so Mr. Kittle decides for safety purposes to bring his brothers and their wives, one of whom is hugely pregnant, to reside with them for the duration of the war. However, no sooner do the relatives arrive than "the enemy made further incursions into the country, burning the villages and scalping the inhabitants, neither respecting age or sex" (Bleecker 5).

In this set-up, Bleecker is clearly invoking the topos/threat of captivity and the duality of Indian nature. At once threatening and dangerous and at once friendly and neighborly, but ultimately unknowable, these Indians are the same ones of the Massachusetts seal and Mary Rowlandson's captivity who plague colonial identity, serving to define it through difference at some moments and by mirroring it back as the "almost but not quite" at others. Additionally, the emphasis of the heightened maternal state of the entire Kittle household is especially noteworthy. Maria has just delivered her second child, a boy, who at eight months is an extension of his mother, still nursing and sleeping in Maria's chambers. William is not yet a "separate" individual from his mother and is dependent upon her in every way, highlighting Maria's important function as a literal "Republican mother" who is still physically nourishing the next generation of male leadership. Anna, Maria's eldest child who is now 11 years old, functions as a miniaturized version of her mother. Tending to her infant brother, doting upon her father, and serving as a mediator between her family/home and the Native others, young Anna is already performing her future role as a potential woman under the guidance and tutelage of her mother.

There is also the heavily pregnant Comelia, the wife of one of Mr. Kittle's brothers, in the home. The advanced and precarious nature of her situation serves not only to heighten the immediacy of the Kittle family's evacuation, but also to invoke the sentimentality and horror of the captivity tradition. As Michelle Burnham has noted, "Captivity narratives nearly always begin with the moment of Indian attack, and the descriptions of these attacks incessantly focus the reader's attention on the abduction or death of infants ... Clearly, this stylized scenario was both politically effective and potently affective" (50). However, it was not a purely fictionalized scenario; Laurel Ulrich states that "[f]ully one fifth of adult female captives from northern New England were either pregnant or newly delivered of a child" (205). Comelia, with her productive, potent belly as her one outstanding characteristic, becomes, at least on the surface, representative of the metaphoric woman, "the strength or virtue of the nation incarnate, its fecund first matriarch, ... a role which excludes her from the sphere of public national life" (Boehmer 6). In fact, Maria, Anna, and Comelia, by virtue of their confinement to the home and range of domestic duties, all exemplify the deeply rooted notions of women as "apolitical [and] isolated with their children in a world of pure emotion, far removed from the welter of politics and social struggle" (Orleck 3). Each one epitomizes a different point on the prescribed continuum of a woman's existence—pre-maternity, maternity, and active motherhood; unfortunately for the Kittle women, however, all of these stages of motherhood are effectively extinguished as the political, masculine world of war and nationalism invade the sanctity of the domestic. During the raid of the Indians against the home, both of Maria's children are killed, Comelia and her unborn baby are slain, and Maria is marched away to Canada, childless.

Bleecker uses the presence of these maternal bodies in all their forms, and their inevitable and drastic losses, to not only highlight their necessary generative powers in the production and maintenance of a nation, but also to disrupt the gendered paradigms which underpin that nation. By framing the narrative with her own history and telling about the maternal, lived experiences and vulnerabilities of women—recording a feminine "geography" so to speak—Bleecker is further challenging the nation's understanding of itself through "territorial claims, through the reclamation of the past and the canonisation of [female] heroes" (Boehmer 11). Not only by depicting women in their most stereotypical and gendered role, as mothers, but also by demonstrating how that maternity interacts and collides with the political realities of a nation still defining itself, Bleecker exposes the female, domestic inverse of the of martial, Anglo-American masculinity and its Indian counterpart depicted on the Massachusetts seals, re-scripting the national picture in a bold way. Bleecker is revising and foregrounding the institution of motherhood, in essence, enacting "motherist" politics in the pages of *The History* through which she suggests that maternity, beyond merely defining a woman by her proximity to it, affects the stability and perpetuation of nationalism, as well as the history of a nation in profound and very political ways (Orleck 5).

Border Crossings: The Domestic Ruptures the Political

Once Bleecker posits the re-visionary idea of the validity and potency of the domestic/maternal, she moves directly into having that sphere intersect with the masculine, political sphere. As the extended Kittle family makes preparations for their departure from Tomhanick due to the encroaching battles, a group of neighboring Indians who "always seemed well affected to the English" approaches the home (Bleecker 5). An older Indian, speaking on behalf of the others, "desired the family to compose themselves, assuring them they should be cautioned against any approaching danger. To enforce his argument, he presents Maria with a belt interwoven with silk and beads" (Bleecker 5). As she takes the token offering, the Indian also offers Maria this promise: "There, receive my token of friendship: we go to dig up the hatchet, to sink i' in the heads of your enemies; we shall guard this wood with a wall of fire—you shall be safe" (Bleecker 5). Maria, now with "a warm glow of hope deep[ening] in [her] cheeks," orders wine to be brought to the "friendly savages" to signify her acceptance of the proffered deal (Bleecker 5).

However, lest she be too hasty in bestowing her faith in the word of an Indian, Maria seeks additional reassurance from the Indians. She expresses her concerns that necessity or "neglect of promise" may cause the tribe to abandon her family, even after this promise was made. The elder of the group, after having given a token of sincerity before, now makes a more solemn, verbal oath to relieve Maria of her concerns: "Neglect of my promise! … No, Maria, I am a true man; I shoot the arrow up to the Great Captain every new moon: depend upon it, I will trample down briars round your dwelling, that you do not hurt your feet" (Bleecker 6).

This brief speech, although a mix of racist stereotype, caricature, and romantic subservience with its Christianized rendition of Native belief and "Noble Savage" sentimentality, placates Maria. "[W]ith a sort of exultation," she returns to her home to relate the news to her husband who, it turns out, had absented himself from the meeting, "having formed some suspicion of the sincerity of their friendship and not being willing to be duped by the dissimulation" (Bleecker 6). She boastfully tells him, "[O]ur fears may again subside: Oh my dear! My happiness is trebled into rapture, by seeing you and my sweet babes out of danger" (Bleecker 6).

In this vignette, Bleecker masterfully disrupts the male-dominant hierarchical structure of the family unit and consequently, the nation. It is the lead female character—a wife and mother—who ventures outside to not only face the "savage" threat of the Indians, but also to negotiate with them for the safety of her family and succeed at it. The dialogue and descriptors chosen by Bleecker to characterize Maria clearly indicate her subjective agency as well; she returns "exultant" to share the news of her victory because she has conducted—"seen"—her entire family, including her husband, out of danger on her own. Maria has stepped into the authoritative, masculine role in this instance, going out to meet a high-ranking representative of another nation and then not only accepting, but also granting the symbolic gifts that serve to bind the alliance, even insisting on a restatement of the terms of the deal before she acquiesces. She has, in effect, served as an international diplomat but on a singularly domestic level; the deal with the head of another nation is made to protect her specific home and family within the confines of her very own yard, but during an international, nation-defining crisis—the French and Indian War. This alliance between nations, an opportunity to share information and defenses in a wartime situation, is made and confirmed by Maria and without the presence or sanctification of a male authority figure. Even more interesting is the fact that Bleecker chooses not to mediate the absence of a male authority at the Indian conference by providing any extenuating circumstances that could have physically prevented Mr. Kittle's presence at the meeting; she makes it clear that he simply chooses not to be in attendance. Bleecker is clearly interrogating naturalized beliefs of the legitimacy of masculine political and domestic leadership and positing the possibility of feminine leadership.

When the Kittle family home is later attacked by Maria's "friendly Indians," the same ones who swore to protect her only the evening before, Bleecker further disrupts the masculinized power relations of nation through an intense moment of recognition and mis-recognition. As the Indians storm the home in a violent attack, Bleecker writes:

> Maria soon recognized her old friend that presented her with the belt, through the loads of shells and feathers that disguised him. This was not time, however, to irritate him, by reminding him of his promise; yet guessing her thoughts, he anticipated her remonstrance. 'Maria,' said he, 'be not afraid, I have promised to protect you; you shall live and dance with us around the fire at Canada: but you have one small incumbrance, which, if not removed, will much impede your progress thither.' So saying he seized her laughing babe by the wrists, and forcibly endeavoured to draw him from her arms. (11)

In this moment, Maria and her attacker are both recognized for who they are, or at least were the night before: independent parties engaging in a contractual exchange. Not only does Maria recognize the Indian, despite his costume, as the legal entity who gave her his word, which she expects him to keep—after all she is tempted to scold him and call to mind their deal—but he also recognizes her, both as "Mrs. Kittle," the acting head of this household, and as his partner in the deal. She is expecting and deserving of not only their deal being kept, but also an explanation of what is going on, and he gives it to her. He intends to keep his end of the deal, it turns out, and take Maria away to Canada where she will be safe; however, he intends to do so at the cost of her family and children and home.

Undeniably, this passage smacks of racist and sexualized stereotypes with the threat of the dark other desiring the white woman for a possible sexual relationship, and its rendering of the Indian, much like Said's Oriental, as an "inveterate[e] lia[r], … 'lethargic and suspicious,' and in everything oppose[d] [to] the clarity, directness, and nobility of the Anglo-Saxon race" (Said 39). Bleecker has produced an Indian that, in the words of Gerald Vizenor in his influential work *Manifest Manners*, is an "occidental invention" (11), a "simulation" of Indianness that enacts "the absence of the tribal real," (4) and provides for the colonial audience a "vicious encounte[r] with the antisel[f] of civilization, the invented savage" (7). She has, in short, reproduced the flattened out Indian images of the Bay Colony seal and Mary Rowlandson's narrative; she has also reproduced their inherent anxiety and ambivalence concerning colonial identity. The Indian's presence in this scene, like his precursors' on the seal and in Rowlandson's captivity, is one of both resemblance and menace. Because he keeps his word to Maria, offers her no unwanted sexual advances, and transports her safely to Canada to a supportive, female community, his presence becomes one of resemblance to colonial sensibility rather than one of utter difference; yet his wholesale destruction of white domesticity and family, underscores his "savage" otherness. Similarly, he at once serves to validate Maria and her rightful place in the domain of politics and history, but his Indianness undermines any authority his actions may bestow upon her. His existence in the narrative, although providing a rupture through which Bleecker can assert feminine agency, ultimately highlights a fracture in the colonial certainty of absolute difference and reveals the limitations of colonial domination. Consequently, Maria's Indian "friend" drops out of textual existence after this point in the narrative. Designed by Bleecker as a tool for validating the legitimacy of the domestic and the feminine and for critiquing the failures of Anglo patriarchy, this Indian "friend" quickly becomes a figure of ambivalence and anxiety (a figure of "almost but not quite") and must be erased from the narrative (Bhabha, "Of Mimicry" 129). Much like Rowlandson's Christian Indians who threatened her own authorial status as a Christian exemplar in the wilderness, Bleecker's male Indian also threatens her own authorial status, as well as her heroine's, as being capable of political agency because he, too, exercises it within the text. After all, how exceptional is a white woman, author, or character, who rises above her subjugated place to enter the historic and political realms as an illustrative prototype when a duplicitous, murdering Indian can do it, too? Perhaps most importantly, though, Bleecker's Indian "friend" must be erased because in his most threatening moments he challenges the naturalized belief in the authority and superiority of colonial manhood by enacting standards of feminine protection and valuation of which his white counterparts are incapable. Such a move, while certainly working to destabilize and critique white patriarchy, also potentially posits an Indian "superiority" over white womanhood. Bleecker must do away with, or "sacrifice," her male Indian character in order to maintain feminine agency, because, as Rey Chow notes, sacrifice is "mimesis' conceptual double or conjoined twin" (82).[16] In authorial moves such as these, Bleecker is successfully providing subversive dialogue for the silent, masculine images of the Revolutionary-era Massachusetts seals—both Anglo and Indian. It is a dialogue that clearly records the absence of Anglo masculinity and erases the potential disruption of the Indian while bringing white womanhood to the foreground.

Men Behaving Badly, Women Behaving Boldly: A Study in Contrast

One of the most intriguing aspects of Bleecker's narrative is her extended contrast of male and female characters' behavior in moments of familial and national crisis, and her triangulation of that contrast with Indianness. Most captivity narratives recount the experiences from a singular perspective—that of a single gender, single captive, and single race. Bleecker's *The History of Maria Kittle* distances itself from this formula, however, in that it juxtaposes the differing reactions of men and women in the same or similar situations throughout the entire narrative and positions those reactions in close proximity to Indianness. Men and women both face brutal assaults, the loss of family and children, and the physical hardships of captivity in detail in *The History*, and while Bleecker is certainly writing about these experiences through the gendered filter of womanhood, both hers and Maria's, she is still attempting to provide an extended view of both genders in the circumstances surrounding Indian captivity and in contact with Indians themselves. In doing so, Bleecker creates an opportunity not only to represent both genders, but also to critique them, particularly the white male perspective, when they are confronted with the legitimizing-yet-threatening Indianness of colonial

---

[16] Interestingly, there is one encounter between Maria and a female Indian. It is after Maria and Henry have been stripped of their English clothes and are facing their last stop at an Indian settlement before they reach Montreal. As the captives are canoed across a river, Maria tells Henry, "Here, my brother! ... I shall find some of my own sex, to whom simple Nature, no doubt, has taught humanity; this is the first precept she inculcates in the female mind, and this they generally retain through life, in spite of every evil propensity" (Bleecker 22). Upon reaching shore, however, the hopeful Maria encounters "the fair, tawny villagers" who attack her and Henry with "clubs and a shower of stones, accompanying their strokes with the most virulent language" (Bleecker 22). Among the group is an old, deformed squaw who "with the rage of Tisiphone, flew to Maria, aiming a pine-knot at her head, and would certainly have given the wretched mourner her quietus has she not been opposed by the savage that guarded Mrs. Kittle" (Bleecker 22–3). The guard, after scolding the woman, must finally pull the cudgel from the woman's hand and force her to the ground where she is left to "howl and yell at leisure" (Bleecker 23). I argue that this encounter, although differently gendered than the others, is still working to racialize the domestic and foreground the agency of white womanhood. Maria has expectations of meeting up and possibly bonding with other "civilized," domesticated women; instead, however, she is greeted with furious, savage violence at the hands of female Indian others. Clearly, Bleecker is suggesting not only the competency of white womanhood, but also its exceptionality.

imagination, and then offer alternative visions of how they are viewed in terms of nationhood and the family.

On the morning before Maria's Indian "friends" descend upon the Kittle home, Mr. Kittle and his brother, Peter, set off on a pre-planned but ill-advised hunting trip in order not to "intimidate the neighbours by cloistering [them]selves up with women and children" (Bleecker 6). The two men are on their return home at the end of the day when they end up exchanging fire with a pair of Indians who had tracked the Kittle brothers from the sound of Peter's gunfire at an unsuspecting doe.[17] Peter is immediately shot by the Indians, forcing Maria's husband to fight back, killing both Indian attackers. He loads his brother's body onto his horse and returns home in an understandably agitated state. Once there, Mr. Kittle laments to Maria, "[M]y angel! The very savages that solemnly engaged to protect us have deprived him of life" and that he believes they attacked "no doubt … from some private pique" (Bleecker 8–9).

These are interesting comments from Mr. Kittle, both in terms of their admonitory tone toward Maria, their stereotypical portrayal of Indians, and their complete disjuncture from the historical moment in which the Kittles reside. Through his invocation of the "very savages" that had visited Maria the previous night, Mr. Kittle is not only casting aspersion upon the duplicitous nature of these specific Indians (it couldn't have been any others), but he is also implicating Maria in the death of his brother, intimating that her gullibility and her deference to the Indians during their visit were at the root of this attack. He also dismissively nullifies the importance and validity of Maria's pact with the Indians; clearly, her negotiation skills and word were not highly valued by the Indians because they violated the agreement almost immediately and in the most violent of ways. The word of a woman, apparently much like that of an Indian, at least in Mr. Kittle's eyes, is not something of weight and consequence.

Even more significant is Mr. Kittle's denial of the war-torn environment in which he and his family live. By claiming the same Indians who formed an alliance with Maria are the ones who attacked him and his brother due to some trivial offense, Mr. Kittle is not only erasing the existence of the various tribes with differing allegiances (not to mention appearances, languages and customs) in his region, but he is also diminishing the war around them to nothing more than a personal affront between neighbors. Maria's treaty and the Indians' willingness to enter into it to form an allegiance between nations becomes nothing more than a misguided and

---

[17]   Peter spots a "fat doe walking securely on the beach" and shoots it, as he and his brother had vowed not to return home without killing anything (Bleecker 7). Bleecker comments that "This seeming success was, however, the origin of their calamities; for immediately after, two savages appeared," pointedly connecting the two men's competitive and rash sport hunt with the preceding attack and deaths (Bleecker 7). Sharon M. Harris notes that it is a pregnant doe that Peter kills, which foreshadows "the many mother/child deaths in the narrative. It also recalls the shift in 'To Miss Ten Eyck' from the human mother/child to the doe and her child" (*Executing Race* 104). Bleecker does not definitely state if the doe was in fact pregnant in her narrative.

broken promise made between petty and feuding neighbors instead of a potential political alliance. Further, the fact that the Indians willingly recognize Maria's feminine agency and deal with her directly and successfully concerning matters of military intelligence—things Mr. Kittle summarily dismisses—highlights the circumscribed racist and masculinist beliefs of Mr. Kittle and positions the Indian other as a legitimizing force in Bleecker's feminist revision. When read in this manner, Mr. Kittle's oblivion to the realities around him and his antithetical position to Indianness become a powerful critique of the kind of misuse of white, masculine agency, or lack thereof, which Bleecker is aggressively pursuing.

Once he has brought his brother's body home and explained everything to Maria, Mr. Kittle prepares to set off once again, this time to procure wagons so he can evacuate his family from the area. The evacuation has already been suspended once by Mr. Kittle because after the Indians' warning and promise of protection to Maria the night before, he determined that "to be suspicious might be suddenly fatal"; therefore, the family should delay their departure for a few days even though he placed no confidence in the word of an Indian (Bleecker 6). Now, however, Mr. Kittle is ready to swing the evacuation plan into action, leaving his family unprotected, despite the fact that he just engaged in a deadly firefight in the near vicinity of his home, a site that even he himself now describes as a "hostile place" (Bleecker 9). Maria begs her husband not to leave her and their children, even chastising him, "Is it not enough ... that you have escaped one danger, but must you be so very eager to encounter others?" (Bleecker 9). Young Anna also begs her papa not to go: "Oh papa! Do not leave us; if any accident should happen to you, mamma will die of grief, and what will become of poor Anna and Billy? Who will care for me? Who will teach me when my papa, my mamma's papa is gone?" (Bleecker 9). However, Mr. Kittle, in a manly show of bravado (or obtuseness), tells Anna, "[T]here is no danger!" and after kissing his wife and babies, promptly departs, promising to return in an hour (Bleecker 10).

Both Maria and Anna in this instance are pointedly interrogating the logic and sanity of Mr. Kittle's behavior. Maria sharply critiques his rash actions that earlier in the day cost his brother his life and served as the opening volley, the "origin of calamities," that brings the Kittle family and home into the war sooner rather than later and quite possibly is the entire reason the Indians later attack: to revenge what they view as an assault stemming from war-based allegiances. Anna similarly questions her father's plans to abandon the family. In the self-absorbed way of children, Anna wonders who will care for and teach her and her younger brother once "her mamma's papa is gone." These female characters confront Mr. Kittle with very real concerns over the most basic of necessities that are stereotypically the province of the male authority figure in a family: the guarantee of physical presence/governance, protection, and the provision of necessities, including educational guidance. It is the women who are thinking in logical terms of preservation, both of the sanctity of the family unit and the safety of its head and protector, not the actual head and protector himself. He, on the other hand, is behaving in self-destructive and impulsive ways, a pattern that

Mr. Kittle is doomed to repeat for the remainder of the text. After the destruction of his family and home, he becomes reduced to a state of emotional instability and confusion, suffering from a lingering illness for six weeks and then throwing himself into a suicidal enlistment in the Army. He never once seeks answers about the attack, attempts to rebuild a domestic scene, or considers that anyone in his family could have survived or been captured. Mr. Kittle's culturally defined role as masculine provider and protector is completely forfeited and forgotten by him. Even when he does have a moment of proactive agency late in the text and decides that his brother Henry just might be alive and determines to search for him, Mr. Kittle's masculine priorities are still entirely out of the prescribed, hierarchical order. Rather than seeking his wife (or her female substitute) so that he could repopulate the devastated republic and rebuild the familial sphere, Mr. Kittle throws himself into a search for his brother, which, even if successful, would be a sterile and fruitless reunion that would rupture not only the structure of the conventional, male-governed family unit, but also the patriarchal structure of the nation, which is built upon the microcosm of the family. Instead of attempting to preserve or reconstruct his family (and by proxy, the nation)—which is his defined role as its masculine head—Mr. Kittle's behavior becomes just as destructive for the nation as the assailing Indians' had been against his own family. Bleecker has essentially created a speaking, narrative version of the Anglo-American soldier on the "Sword-in-Hand" seal through the character of Mr. Kittle. Her version, however, simply exposes the flaws and failures of white masculinity rather than perpetuating an ambivalent and static impression of its potency. When Mr. Kittle does reunite with Maria in Canada after two long years, it is quite by accident, and only after he has reunited with his brother Henry first. The family dynamic and the drive to sustain it are subverted by Mr. Kittle's disordered masculine mind and lack of focus.

In a similar episode that highlights the starkly contrasting gendered perceptions of the domestic, Comelia Kittle, the wife of one of Mr. Kittle's brothers who is never named, has to beg her "rash, rash, unfortunate husband" not to open the door to the Indian attackers when they raid the home (Bleecker 10). Hugely pregnant, Comelia falls to her knees, beseeching her husband, "O pity me! Have mercy on yourself, on me, on my child!" as he numbly heads toward the door having given all up for lost (Bleecker 10). Her final plea for mercy, as Christopher Castiglia aptly observes, is "made not to the Indians, but of her nominal 'protector'" (126). Comelia's husband's half-hearted response is just as bewildering and irresponsible as his brother's earlier response is to Maria and Anna when he is leaving to procure evacuation supplies; he says to Comelia, "Alas! My love … what can we do? Let us be resigned to the will of God" (Bleecker 11). Mr. Comelia then, upon opening the door to the war party, promptly receives "a fatal bullet in his bosom, and [falls] backward writhing in agonies of death" (Bleecker 11). Unfortunately, Comelia herself and her unborn baby also pay for her husband's reckless behavior. Indians storm into the Kittle home and after scalping her husband, one advances on Comelia, cleaving her forehead with his tomahawk and then, "not yet satisfied with blood; he deformed her lovely body with deep gashes; and, tearing her unborn babe away, dashed it to pieces against the stone wall; with many additional circumstances of infernal cruelty" (Bleecker 11). Cruelties, Bleecker suggests, which are tied to, if not caused by, white masculine misguidance and ineptitude.

Enabling this critique of masculine "governance" of the domestic sphere are Bleecker's Indians. Without the presence of these "savage" others who throw the hierarchy and stability of the domestic sphere into fractured disarray, Bleecker would be unable to offer her revisions of those structures. As the Indians invade, scatter, and destroy the Kittle home and massacre the family, previously held regulations about gendered participation in the public arena are suspended, and extraordinary behaviors and usurpations of those roles, particularly by women, are excused. In the (seemingly) understandable absence or failure of white male authority in the face of the disorder and violence of Indianness, white female authority and agency can emerge and offer an alternative vision of the preservation and guidance of the familial, domestic domain, and by proxy the nation.

Notably, Bleecker does not stop her critique of white patriarchy at the boundary of the domestic realm. Beyond merely examining how fathers and husbands manage and/or mismanage their own families and homes within the confines of those homes, Bleecker also scrutinizes that same masculinity in a broader context that transcends the domestic; she critiques white, adult manhood as it functions in a far more public, masculine realm: the Indian wilderness. Bleecker depicts white manhood in direct contact and conflict with Indianness, as well as in stark contrast to white womanhood in the same environs, in order to rupture and revise the masculine standards that undergird colonial society. Consequently, she is able not only to politicize and historicize femininity as it participates in nation-defining events, but also to bring her narrative of masculine critique into national focus.

For example, Bleecker devotes much narrative attention to Maria's brother-in-law Henry, the only other member of the Kittle family taken captive along with Maria. Henry is another male figure who behaves in as questionable a manner as his brothers and other male protectors do. While he is not as blatantly neglectful or rash as the unnamed Mr. Comelia and Maria's husband are, Henry still exhibits traits that bring the whole conception of masculine protection and leadership into question, especially when it is directly confronted with the threat of Indianness and contrasted with Maria's femininity. As the captivity and the march to Canada progress, Henry again displays questionable behaviors in terms of his prescribed masculine role. Always careful to please the Indians and smilingly obey their commands, Henry becomes, in effect, the model prisoner; however, because of the perceived inferiority, degeneracy, and "savagery" of his captors, Henry's supplication to the Indians (while carefully justified or at least explained by Bleecker) becomes a critique of his own manhood and national allegiances.[18]

---

[18] Certainly, the willing compliance of Maria's brother-in-law Henry during his captivity with the Indians can be viewed as a strategic method of survival and subversion. As noted by Zabelle Stodola and James Levernier, most "tortures were reserved for adult male captives ... Because captives were tortured primarily to avenge the death of Indian warriors, adult men were generally considered the appropriate object of

On the morning after their captivity, when Henry and Maria are caught conversing in English over Maria's refusal to eat the Indians' food, Bleecker notes, "the savages were inquisitive to know the subject of [the conversation], [and] at the same time enjoin[ed] them both never to utter a syllable in their presence except in their own uncouth dialect" (Bleecker 18). Maria says nothing to this demand, but Henry immediately relates the gist of his and Maria's conversation to their captors with some minor changes. He, of course, omits the sentimental overtones of his entreaty that blatantly appealed to Maria's roles as wife and mother, and excludes Maria's refusal to take nourishment from "bloody hands yet dropping with murder" (Bleecker 17). However, he also turns Maria's refusal of food due to anger and grief into one of taste. Henry proclaims to the Indians, "his sister, objecting to their method of preparing food, had desired him to prevail with them to indulge her in dressing her meals herself" (Bleecker 18). Maria's reasons for not eating, described by Bleecker as stemming from "the dignity of conscious merit in distress," are reduced by Henry to superficial issues of culinary preference (Bleecker 17). Further, Henry's quick response to the Indians, and in their own tongue as requested, is also an attempt to place Maria back into her domestic place even in the disorder of the wilderness.

By requesting from his captors the permission for Maria to prepare her own food, Henry is struggling to reassert his masculine dominance over not only Maria, but the Indians as well. He has already been emasculated and deposed from his position of authority through the very act of his captivity and the destruction of hierarchical white domesticity; consequently, Henry tries to restore some semblance of "civilized" order by re-domesticating Maria and requesting that the Indians adhere to that order. As author, however, Bleecker subverts this attempt by white masculinity to reaffirm itself by already declaring it subject to Indianness; Henry's immediate and submissive response to the Indians' demands, particularly in the face of Maria's noncompliance and silence, clearly indicate his subjugation to the Indian, and ultimately his subservience to Maria. When the Indians do grant Henry's supposed request from Maria and bring a brood of wood pigeons for her, it is Henry who "cleaned and broiled them on sticks, with an officious solicitude to please his sister" (Bleecker 18). Henry is clearly functioning in a feminized and domestic role here. This particular instance is also reminiscent of Mary Rowlandson's attention to Indian food and its preparation within her captivity narrative as a means of foregrounding or preserving her own Anglo femininity and domesticity. Rowlandson, for example, notes that while at first she could barely "get down their [Indians'] filthy trash," she eventually, due to hunger and some level of acculturation, found the Indians' "strange" foods "sweet and savory to

---

Indian vengeance" (3). Therefore, Henry could conceivably be working as much to ensure his own survival as well as that of Maria through his careful, obsequious actions toward his captors. However, as I will argue, because of the close proximity of Henry's acquiescent actions and Maria's contrary ones, Bleecker is clearly critiquing Henry's faltering responsibilities in his masculine role rather than positing an alternative mode of survival.

[her] taste" (Rowlandson 79).[19] Just as Rowlandson utilizes her "disgust" over and reluctant acceptance of Indian food as a means of reasserting her difference from and superiority over her captors, so, too, does Bleecker utilize food and its preparation as a means of making white masculinity subject to, or domesticated by, Indianness.

Later, Henry's "eager to please" manner again receives careful attention from Bleecker. As the captives are approaching their final destination in Canada, they are stripped of their English clothes and "attired each with remnants of old blankets" (Bleecker 20). Maria expostulates with her captors, but realizing she is getting nowhere with them, finally retires to some brush to arrange her blanket the best she can and to "indulg[e] herself in the luxury of sorrow" (Bleecker 20). Henry, however, reacts quite differently. Bleecker writes:

> Henry, sensible that [the Indians] expected more fortitude from him, and that if he sunk under his adverse fortune he should be worse treated, affected to be cheerful; he assisted them in catching salmon, with which the lake abounds; an incredible quantity of wild fowl frequenting the lake also, he laid snares for those of the lesser sort (not being allowed fire-arms), and succeeded so well that his dexterity was highly commended, and in night coming on they regaled themselves on the fruits of their industry. (Bleecker 20–21)

Although in this passage Bleecker depicts Henry in a manner that showcases his masculine abilities in hunting, providing, and assisting his captors, she also suggests that Henry is seeking the praise and recognition of the Indians. His efforts to be cheerful and supportive of his captors' activities—in effect helping them to provide for their own domestic, familial needs—produces a rupture in the paradigm of white manhood and its relationship to nationhood. As one of the designated providers for and leaders of the fledgling American nation and on a smaller scale, his own family, Henry, as a white male, should be serving the interests and needs of his own nation. Instead, however, he is working diligently to meet the domestic needs of another nation, that of the Indian other, and striving cheerfully to meet their cultural expectations of manhood. Henry is no longer operating within the accepted and expected gendered and raced paradigms of colonial America; instead, he has entirely and willingly inverted them.

Bleecker is clearly suggesting, through the actions of male characters like Henry and Mr. Kittle that the naturalized colonial system of patriarchy is perhaps flawed and subject to not only history and its complex progression, but also to the various cultural lenses through which it might be viewed. White masculine patriarchy is clearly not enacted and deployed in universally unchanging forms;

---

[19] Rowlandson additionally addresses issues of hunger, food, and food preparation in the seventh, eighth, ninth, fourteenth, and seventeenth removes of her narrative. See, for example, Mary Carruth ("Between Abjection and Redemption: Mary Rowlandson's Subversive Corporeality") and Jordan Stein ("Mary Rowlandson's Hunger and the Historiography of Sexuality") for further discussion of Rowlandson and food.

there are varying degrees of "manhood" that emerge and subside depending on the situation, the cultural environment, and the aptitude of the man wielding it—including Indians. Bleecker is clearly suggesting that not all men are capable of appropriately managing the wholesale power over the domestic that is invested in them; however, some women just might be. Once the masculine realm makes its incursion into the domestic/feminine realm and leaves it fractured, vulnerable, and without patriarchal attendance, Bleecker authorizes an active feminine response that does not need masculine validation, and consequently can act independently to preserve the sanctity of the home, family, and ultimately the nation.

Women's Voices: Speaking and Writing the Domestic History of a Nation

In her own life, Bleecker sought for many years after the Revolutionary War to recreate the supportive women's community she shared with her younger half-sister Susan and her mother Margareta at her beloved Tomhanick estate. It was something she was never able to realize due to the fractured nature of her family after the war; however, that did not prohibit her from attempting to recreate it within the pages of *The History*. The final passages of Maria's narrative are played out in Canada, where Maria has spent the two years of her captivity ensconced in a women's group, visiting, working, and chronicling her life with her sympathetic "sister[s] in affliction" (Bleecker 27). Much of the time spent with the women, who include French Canadians as well as English captives like Maria, is stereotypically feminine and homey, devoted to the exchange of gifts and womanly sentiment. It is also, once again, restricted entirely to the confines of the domestic realm. Bleecker, however, infuses the gatherings of this feminine community and its discussions with topics of national and political concern, once again articulating the potential role of women in nation building. The women, although appropriately positioned within their prescribed domestic environment, and appropriately desirous of their former married and maternal identities, participate in a uniquely female-centered nation within a larger nation. They compose another circuit of empowered women writers/narrators and readers/auditors that are united across cultural, experiential, and historical boundaries much like the circuit Bleecker constructed at the onset of her narrative between herself, her sister Susan, and her female audience. These women within the confines of their group are able to discuss at length the horrors and casualties of war, their experiences as women during and after the war, and even their own understandings of what caused the war. In a telling moment in the final pages of *The History*, one of the French women, Madame De R., after hearing Mrs. Willis's tale of misfortune, expostulates, "Would to Heaven … that brutal nations were extinct, for never—never can the united humanity of *France* and *Britain* compensate for the horrid cruelties of their savage allies" (Bleecker 32, italics in original). Such an exclamation clearly articulates the awareness of these women of not only the international scope of the war being fought literally in their own back yards, but also the great threat posed by that war to European "humanity" and domesticity. However, the authority to vocalize such sentiments comes not from the lived wartime experiences of these women, but from the Indians, reviled and misappropriated, who have "savagely" intruded into their feminine realm.

Without this execration of the "brutal" Indian nations and the recognition of European humanity, neither Madame De R. nor any of these captive women would be able to voice their histories and opinions. The Indian's displacement and destruction of the domestic order—in short, his spectral presence in the narrative—allows Bleecker to voice her critique of the gendered nation from the sanctioned position of feminine outrage. It is the white male protector figures within the text that deny or restrict those voices. Nowhere does Bleecker more powerfully illustrate this than at the end of *The History*, because, once reunited with her husband and vocalizing a brief lament over their shared domestic loss, Maria is silenced, as are the other women of her group. *The History*, which has previously been filled with women's stories of and concerns with the domestic and its role within the larger nation, is now filled with Mr. Kittle's relation of his own masculine experiences during his lengthy (and ill-conceived) separation from his wife. Although Maria is obviously present during the reunion and the telling of Mr. Kittle's account, even relating her own experiences to her husband, it is done so indirectly. Bleecker never directly quotes Maria's words after the initial reunion with her husband.[20] She and the rest of the women in her support group fall silent, subsumed once again by the patriarchal versions of the war around them and that history patriarchy is making. Mr. Kittle's voice takes over and brings the narrative to its close, effectively reassigning Maria and the other women to their places of subordination within the domestic realm.

However, because Bleecker has so effectively critiqued the masculine agency of white manhood, especially Mr. Kittle's, and aggressively foregrounded feminine agency throughout the text of *The History*, this conclusion rings hollow and leaves a gaping hole where the reader recognizes a feminine voice should be. The reunion of this husband and wife certainly completes the anticipated story arc; the captive is "redeemed" and returned to her former, domesticated life as the traditional captivity formula demands. However, in the wake of Bleecker's aggressive assertion of a differently gendered nation and her exposure of the wholesale destruction of the domestic realm, the reader is left wondering what there is for Maria to return to. Her home has been destroyed, her children murdered, and the masculine authority that was designated to protect and foster her domestic existence has been rendered ineffectual time and again. Consequently, the silence on the parts of Maria and her formerly outspoken group, rather than indicating an acquiescent submission to masculinity once that presence (finally) reemerges,

---

[20]   Maria's last words are spoken after she sinks into her husband's bosom upon his first arrival. She exclaims, "Alas! how can your beggared wife give you a proper reception? She cannot restore your prattling babes to your arms—she comes alone! Alas! her presence will only serve to remind you of the treasures—the filial delights you have lost!" (Bleecker 33). While this passage certainly places Maria firmly within the maternal/domestic spheres, I would argue it also shows aggressive agency in her desire to restore the sanctity of her family on her own and then present it, fully realized, to her husband. Maria does not look to her husband for aid or assistance in this effort (and has not for the entire narrative); she is utterly dependent upon herself in these ventures, and is lamenting her inability to do so.

instead signifies a grudging unwillingness to reenter into that subordinate feminine role, a refusal to validate the gendered, and necessarily masculine, voice of the nation. However, even within that final narrative silence, Bleecker has constructed a narrative that not only confronts the masculine imagery of nation-building as envisioned on the Revolutionary-era seals of the Commonwealth of Massachusetts, but also foregrounds the experiences of women in moments of historical, national crises—even though to do so, she must silence Native reality in the same ways patriarchal and colonialist discourses work to silence women. By writing her Indians out of the picture once their usefulness has been mined for her authorial female agency, Bleecker is able to empower the feminine, domestic world of her narrative with agency and a distinctly feminine voice: her own.

Chapter 3
Transculturated, "Mixed-Blooded" Womanhood:
Pocahontas and *The Female American*

Part 1
Iconography: Picturing Pocahontas

The Pocahontas narrative is a potent one for Americans, even today. The story of the young "Indian princess" who selflessly risked her own life to save Captain John Smith from execution and then married another Englishman, John Rolfe, to secure good relations between her people, the Powhatans, and the English, is known (to varying degrees of accuracy) by almost every American citizen. She has been called "America's Joan of Arc because of her saintlike virtue and her courage to risk death for a noble cause" (Rasmussen and Tilton 7), and has been widely credited with "saving Jamestown from destruction and preserving the North American continent for future English colonization" (Abrams 3).[1] However, it was her marriage to John Rolfe—her rejection of her "pagan" past and acceptance of English religion, society, and culture—that, perhaps, is the most significant part of her legend, at least in terms of the colonial project. As the feminist scholar Annette Kolodny has noted, this marriage served "in some symbolic sense, as a kind of objective correlative for the possibility of Europeans actually possessing the charms inherent in the virgin continent" (5). It was an accepted and necessary union that allowed Anglo-Europeans to lay claim to Indianness as well as the cultural and geographical markers of Indianness; it was also the genesis of a uniquely "American" family tree. Americans reach back to Pocahontas, the ubiquitous "Indian grandmother" of America, to lay claim to an "authentic" autochthonous identity.[2] Author Frances Mossiker notes, "A long line

---

[1]   There have been many excellent scholarly studies of both the historic life and the mythos of Pocahontas. See, for example, Helen Rountree's *Pocahontas' People* and *Pocahontas, Powhatan, Opechancanough* or Philip Barbour's *Pocahontas and Her World* for historical/anthropological examinations of Pocahontas and her people. See Rasmussen and Tilton's *Pocahontas: Her Life and Legend*, Ann Uhry Abrams's *The Pilgrims and Pocahontas*, and Robert Tilton's *Pocahontas: Evolution of an American Narrative* for readings of the cultural and artistic legend surrounding Pocahontas and her story.

[2]   Native American historian Vine Deloria Jr. notes of this "Indian-grandmother complex," "It doesn't take much insight into racial attitudes to understand the real meaning of [it] … A male ancestor has too much the aura of a savage warrior, the unknown primitive, the instinctive animal to make him a respectable member of the family tree. But a young Indian princess? Ah, there was royalty for the taking" (11).

of proud Virginians claims consanguinity or affinity with Pocahontas: Jeffersons, Lees, Randolphs, Marshalls, along with other lesser lights—to the number of two million, if the calculations of twentieth-century genealogists are accurate" (319). However, the trope of this acculturated Indian princess, who through her marriage to Anglo-America gives literal and figurative birth to a unique American identity, problematically reasserts the authority of an Anglo-colonialist identity at the expense and foreclosure of a Native one.

As we have seen in earlier chapters, a transculturated Indian figure was a troubling one for Anglo-European colonists. Whether such a figure originated from colonial imagination and anxiety, as did the Indians of the Massachusetts Bay Colony seals and Ann Eliza Bleecker's captivity narrative, or existed as a threatening, cross-cultural reality as James Printer and other Praying Indians did, an Indian who "crossed over" into European culture and custom was problematic. Such a "mimic man/woman" would reflect the gaps and fissures in colonial discourse through his/her continual production of an identity that was not quite like the colonizer's—Bhabha's *"almost the same, but not quite"*—which would in turn underscore the inherent weakness in colonial discourse: namely, its uncertainty in exercising control and dominance over the behavior of the colonized ("Of Mimicry" 123, italics in original). This blurred copy of the colonizer, what Bhabha calls a "partial presence," "articulate[d] those disturbances of cultural, racial and historical difference that menace the narcissistic demand of colonial authority" by simultaneously resembling it and mocking it ("Of Mimicry" 126). Consequently, the adoption of an Anglo-European/American cultural identity by an Indian, while a necessary part of the process of colonization, was still profoundly disturbing for New World residents struggling to maintain their dominant role in colonial discourse and to establish their own uniquely American identity. Therefore, the later Anglo-American narrative, historic, and artistic retellings of the story that commemorate Pocahontas's life and marriage are very clear about the unidirectional flow of this significant event of acculturation. Pocahontas imbibed Anglo-Europeanness; Anglo-Europeans did not internalize her Indianness. Any evidence that suggested Indianness was being absorbed into and recognized by Anglo-Europeans was erased or muted, pushed from colonial consciousness in order to preserve the fantasy of a "pure" American origin.

But the fact of the matter is that Anglo-European identities were changed by their contact with Indianness. Even when Indianness was moving toward and adopting the "superior" ways of the Anglo-European colonists—when acculturation flowed unidirectionally as colonial consciousness desired and demanded—alterations were occurring in the supposedly unchangeable, essential Anglo-European core identity. By admitting Indianness into the "civilized" ways of English society, that very civility was being transformed and diversified. Acculturated Indians were proving that the perceived superior essence of Anglo-European identity was neither superior nor essential. While Indians of both genders could (and did) successfully appropriate Anglo-Europeanness, changing its unchangeable nature by their very presence within the system, Indian women faced a more complex process of acculturation. In Anglo-European society, women were *feme coverts*, literally "covered" and protected by the men in their lives, first by fathers and brothers, then by husbands, in terms of identity, property ownership, and the law. As Cathy Davidson has noted:

> [A] wife's status as a *feme covert* effectively rendered her legally invisible ... [A] married woman typically lost her property upon marriage. She lost her legal right to make a will or to inherit property beyond the one-third widow's rights ... [B]y law and legal precedent, a married woman's signature had no weight on legal documents and she had no individual legal identity. (118)

Of course, as Davidson and scholars such as Linda Kerber, Carroll Smith-Rosenberg, Julia A. Stern, and others have noted, the system of coverture, while restrictive of women's lives in early and Revolutionary America, was not absolute. There was room for "disorderly conduct" (to use Smith-Rosenberg's term) and women quite often attacked the system of coverture to their advantage, exposing "the conflict between motherhood and citizenship [and] ... the world of domesticity and the world of politics" that the system seemingly belied (Basch 232). However, for the most part, coverture was a social, legal, and political reality for Anglo-European women in America. It also was a means through which Indian women could be much less problematically, and less threateningly, absorbed into colonial society than their male counterparts. Indian women who married and/or lived among Anglo-European men as servants or slaves would be summarily subjected to the same patriarchal system that disallowed feminine forms of agency and identity independent of their male guardians. The Indian woman would become not only Anglicized through her acculturation, but she would also become enthralled by white masculinity. Just as Pocahontas "fell in love with" and became subservient to white manhood, first with John Smith and later with John Rolfe—at least in the constructed narratives of Anglo-American fantasy—so too would other Indian and "mixed-blood" women. They would abandon all vestiges of Indianness and succumb to Anglo-ness, at least hypothetically.

Of course in reality, such acculturations were never so smooth or unimpeded. Indian women who acculturated, such as Pocahontas, did not/could not/would not entirely leave their Indianness behind. It remained with them as a mark of an alternative identity, one that resisted the ideological closure of the Anglo-colonialist, patriarchal system. Pocahontas, as I will discuss later in Chapter 4, likely maintained many of her ties to her Powhatan ancestry and relatives, even leaving the indelible stamp of her Indian pedigree on future generations of Americans through her son, Thomas.

Pocahontas Redux: The Simon Van de Passe Engraving

Pocahontas was a figure who, at least in the imagination of Anglo-America, recognized the worth and validity of English identity and rescinded the "savage" identity of her birth to become a Christian, an Englishman's wife, and the mother of a "mixed-blooded" son, beginning a line of descent that is the only "imperial" family tree in the New World. The only life image known to exist of Pocahontas, an engraving made by a young Dutch-German artist named Simon Van de Passe in 1616, vividly illustrates her cultural duality. Made from a sketch obtained from an actual sitting with Pocahontas near the end of her ill-fated visit to England, the engraving is a complex image of an Indian and Anglo mixed identity. It is an image that visually engages the larger discussions about race, gender, nationalism, and American identity that the iconographic images and Anglo women writers of this study sought to engage and untangle in their texts (see Figure 3.1).

When preparing for the portrait sitting with Van de Passe, Pocahontas and her handlers, a group undoubtedly consisting of her husband and perhaps other members or representatives of the Virginia Company who desired (and footed the bill for) this engraving, would have carefully chosen each item of dress, each accessory, to be depicted in this portrait. As Karen Robertson has noted, "Pocahontas' transformation into a Christian woman is signaled by her abandonment of what the English saw as the lewd clothing of the savage ... The familiar coverings of Englishwomen's dress not only signal her abandonment of heathen ways but facilitate the marking of her rank" (568).

Certainly not wanting Pocahontas to appear as anything less than an ideal "success story" of colonization, and as nothing less than an Indian emperor's daughter, she was accoutered according to Elizabethan and Jacobean standards. However, within those rigid standards of dress and visible identity are contradictions, ruptures in the logic of "self" and "other," that become exposed when an "other" is fashioned into the "self." The Anglo-European desire was to "reform" and "civilize" the Indian other, to turn them into copies of themselves, and to use the original "difference" of the Indian other to affirm the Anglo-European center. However, that center becomes de-centered when the difference of the other, the periphery, rather than being negated through acculturation, becomes the centralized focus, as in the case of the Pocahontas engraving. Such ruptures expose not only the uncertainty of colonial dominance, but the permeability and instability of the nascent Anglo-American identity. Pocahontas "became" an English lady of the court in this engraving, yet her Indianness alters that identity, changing her Anglo accessories into signifiers of Indian identity rather than Anglo-European "superiority." It is her Indianness that decides the meaning of this image rather than the Anglo-European signifiers.

As an image, the Van de Passe engraving of Pocahontas is perhaps as well-known as another famous graven Indian—the Indian from the Massachusetts Bay Colony Seal. Like the seal, the engraving of Pocahontas was meant not only to capture an image that commemorated the success of the colonial enterprise—conversion of the Indians—but also to raise money to continue the work of colonization. Although the Massachusetts Bay seal was perhaps more overt in its pleas ("Come over and help us!" is pretty direct), the image of Pocahontas was still an attempt to inspire interest and garner funds for the still struggling Virginia colony. As Camilla Townsend points out, the Virginia Company at this time

> was involved in various lawsuits. It had sued various investors who had promised
> certain sums of money but then failed to deliver after reading some of the more

Figure 3.1   Simon Van de Passe. Engraving, *Matoaka als Rebecca*, 1616.
Courtesy of the Virginia Historical Society.

dire reports coming back from Virginia. The organization's financial situation would remain shaky until the general public became convinced that Virginia was truly a land of promise. Naturally, tobacco shipments would be critical, but to raise a significant crop the company first needed to convince potential settlers and investors that the Indians were not bloodthirsty savages. (140)

Pocahontas and her Indian retinue would certainly make this point while they were actively present in London, but in order to preserve the memory of her visit and the message it entailed, a permanent record, an image, of her visit would need to be made available to the public. Such an image that could then be sold, displayed, and reproduced at will, much like the printer's cuts of the Bay Colony seal, would be a more permanent reminder that could be continuously revised and revived at different times to invoke the great transformation of the Indian princess and the success of the Virginia Colony. Consequently, just like the Massachusetts Bay Colony Seal, the single engraved image of Pocahontas created by Simon Van de Passe exists in multiple forms and resurfaces at various times throughout history.

The earliest copies of this life image of Pocahontas appeared, as intended by the Virginia Company, on "piece[s] of memorabilia that could be distributed" to commemorate Lady Rebecca's sojourn in England and celebrate the colonial progress in the New World (Townsend 151), but its first textual publication occurred, according to Ann Uhry Abrams, in the 1618 edition of the *Baziliologia: A Book of Kings* (52). John Smith later included the original engraving in his *The Generall Historie* in 1624, alongside a similarly styled engraving of himself, also by Van de Passe, undoubtedly as a calculated attempt to capitalize on the renown of Pocahontas and his ties to her. Later, variations of this striking image of the acculturated Indian princess surfaced in the late eighteenth century in another engraving, *Matoaka als Rebecca*, by an artist known only as "W. Richardson" which was styled after the original Van de Passe engraving, although it depicts Pocahontas as slightly less "Indian" with softer features and lighter skin (see Figure 3.2). In the mid-eighteenth century an oil painting in the style of Van de Passe's engraving, known as the *Booton Hall Portrait*, also appeared. This depiction, much like Richardson's, aggressively Anglicized Pocahontas by lightening her skin, softening her features, and even giving her lovely—albeit unrealistic—auburn-hued hair.[3] There have even been twentieth-century variations of this engraving, such as Mary Ellen Howe's 1994 portrait, *Pocahontas*, which she hoped would resurrect the true appearance of Pocahontas by combining research into the facial structure and skin tones of modern Virginian Indians and Van de Passe's work from nearly four centuries before (see Figure 3.3).

---

[3]   Interestingly, Grace Steele Woodward (*Pocahontas*) has suggested that the auburn hair depicted in the *Booton Hall Portrait* of Pocahontas, rather than being a "white-washing" of her Indianness, is instead, "a reddish-colored wig of the style popular among high-born Englishwomen of the day" (177). I disagree with this assessment because, as I discuss later, the hat Pocahontas has chosen to wear marks her as distinctly "middle-class"; therefore, she would most likely not don a wig that identified her as "high-born" or a fashionable Englishwoman.

Figure 3.2   W. Richardson. Engraving, *Matoaka als Rebecca*, late 18th
century. Courtesy of the Virginia Historical Society.

Figure 3.3   Mary Ellen Howe. *Pocahontas*, 1994. Courtesy of Mary Ellen
Howe through the Virginia Historical Society.

Clearly then, this singular image of Pocahontas from 1616 is a potent one, not
only because of its stature as the only acknowledged life image of Pocahontas,
but also because of its depiction of an "Indian princess" as an "English lady," and
its simultaneous and disruptive suggestion that an "English lady" can be Indian.
The melding of identities in this image, the fusion of supposedly "diametrically
opposed" cultures, races, and sensibilities is what endows it with an ominous,

threatening power that necessitates revision and repetition. Underlying the surface intention of the engraving—to preserve Pocahontas in her beautifully acculturated "glory"—is the veiled threat of Pocahontas's usurpation of English identity, a disruption that modern artists like Howe embrace. In the Van de Passe engraving, however, Pocahontas has not only become "English" for all intents and purposes as these images suggest, but she has irrevocably changed what it means to be "English" simply by the virtue of her Indianness. Englishness and Indianness are fluid, these images seem to suggest; they inform and shape one another as identities. They are not binaristic extremes on the identity continuum. Consequently, the Van de Passe engraving of Pocahontas has been repetitively remade, re-recorded with varying degrees of Englishness, formality, and aesthetic detail in attempts to regulate its suggestive power as a marker—and disruption—of both English and Indian identity. Just as the Massachusetts Bay Colony seal (discussed in chapters 1 and 2) necessarily had to be replicated at various times in the colony's history to reinscribe Indianness as separate from, yet necessary to, the forming Anglo-American identity, so too must Van de Passe's image, with its fraught portrayal of an Indian "English" woman, be anxiously revised and reinterpreted in an attempt to contain the Indianness within it.

Attention to Detail: Van de Passe's Masterpiece

On the surface, the engraving by Simon Van de Passe appears to be quite typical of its genre (Figure 3.1). The subject is a young woman, certainly of no more than about 19 years of age, although listed as 21 in Latin directly beneath her image;[4] interestingly, the artist was himself young, about the same age as his subject. Perhaps his youth and inexperience explains some of the clumsy proportions of the figure and the strangely crooked fingers of the subject's right hand. The image is framed by an oval ring containing the Latin words, "Matoaka Als Rebecca Filia Potentiss Princ Powhatani Imp Virginiae"— "Matoaka, alias Rebecca, daughter of the most powerful prince of the Powhatan Empire of Virginia"—and the center features a close-up image of the young woman—from about the waist up—whose body and face fill the oval. The young woman's eyes stare directly, almost challengingly, out at the viewer rather than being diverted in a show of coy, submissive femininity, and her posture is stiff, full of straight-backed pride and discipline.[5] She is decked out in Jacobean finery with layers of luxurious, expensive fabrics, in a dress that Millia Davenport notes is "a development of the Spanish coat-dress spreading wide

---

[4] In *Pocahontas and the Powhatan Dilemma*, Camilla Townsend notes that the use of the age of 21 instead of Pocahontas's actual 19 years on the portrait stems from "Virginia Company officials [who] would have wanted to hide that, as they needed to present a convert who was a consenting adult in order to make their point effectively" (151–2). See Townsend for further discussion as to Pocahontas's actual age during her various encounters with the English.

[5] See Robertson ("Pocahontas at the Masque") and Townsend for a more detailed reading of Pocahontas's posture and facial expression.

to show the underbodice and skirt" (507). The visible short sleeve of Pocahontas's outer gown is, according to seventeenth-century fashion, "slit down the inseam, and caught with a rosette, where it is cut off above the elbow" and is fastened over a fashionably slashed sleeve of her long-sleeved dress beneath it (Davenport 507). Both dress and outer gown are complemented by her ruff and cuffs, which are of fine reticella lace. The entire outfit is accessorized by a stately beaver hat and ostrich feather fan.[6] Beneath the portrait is an expanded inscription echoing the Latin words in the frame of the engraving: "Matoaks als Rebecka, daughter to the mighty Prince Powhatan, Emperour of Attanoughskomouck als Virginia converted and baptized in the Christian faith and wife to the wor[ff] Mr. John Rolff." Karen Robertson notes that this second inscription, through its dissemination of Pocahontas's secret familial name, Matoaka, "asserts English verbal dominance through their possession and exposure. The makers of the portrait define her status and label her as property: daughter of a king, trophy of conversion, and, finally, wife of an Englishman" (570–71).[7] Pocahontas becomes an exemplar of the success of the colonial project in this image; she is a converted Indian princess, encased in all of the finery of English tradition: erudite Latin headings, fine clothing, and symbolic accessories. It is significant that she is never once identified as the mother of Thomas Rolfe in this miniature biography, even though that is the role that ultimately allowed her illustrious Native lineage to be claimed by countless Anglo-Americans. Here in the engraving she is only daughter, wife, and convert.

The engraving also reveals a tension between "Matoaka" and "Lady Rebecca," between Indianness and Englishness. Even though she is clearly depicted as culturally "English," in this image, Pocahontas's Indianness, her "almost but not quite" status as an acculturated woman, is still undeniably visible because she is clearly raced as an Indian. Her Indianness is the "sign that *remains* ... an externalization and an exhibition in the aftermath of [the] process of sacrifice" (Chow, italics in original, 90). Although in later depictions of this image, such as W. Richardson's version (Figure 3.2), Pocahontas is portrayed with lighter skin and hair and more Anglicized features, in Van de Passe's version she is decidedly indigenous. Dark, thick hair pulled back from her face is visible beneath the beaver hat and heavy, dark brows frame equally dark, almond-shaped eyes, but, as Helen Rountree suggests, Van de Passe was unfortunately "no expert at depicting an Amerind face with epicanthic folds over the eyes" (*Pocahontas, Powhatan* 180). Also, Pocahontas's skin is heavily etched by the artist in this rendition, reflecting not only her darker, "tawny" complexion, but also through shading, her high cheekbones—which is "the" stereotypical mark of Indianness in Anglo-American

---

    [6]   See Robertson for a brief reading of Pocahontas's wardrobe in this image.

    [7]   See Robertson's excellent work for further discussion on Pocahontas's "containment" through the various rhetorical and visual strategies of patriarchy in the Van de Passe engraving as well as other, male-authored sources. See, too, Camilla Townsend who extends Robertson's work by noting that although Pocahontas is, indeed, "contained" by the second inscription on the Van de Passe engraving, there is evidence of "distinct decisions that were made by Pocahontas," such as the use of the name Matoaka and the Indian word "Attanoughskomouck," peeping through (152).

imagination, even today. Especially interesting, however, is the rather square, dimpled chin and slightly pronounced upper lip ascribed to Pocahontas in this engraving. While such fine details serve, of course, as marks of Pocahontas's unique and individual appearance, they also serve as indelible physical ties to Pocahontas's Native heritage.

When Virginia artist Mary Ellen Howe set out to paint as accurate a representation as possible of Pocahontas's likeness using historical and anthropological research as well as Van de Passe's engraving (Figure 3.3), she found that the same overbite, dimpled chin, and high cheekbones were similar to the facial structures of modern Virginia Indians ("Pocahontas Revealed").[8] Pocahontas's "Indianness," therefore, is professed by more than just her "tawny" skin and black hair in the Van de Passe engraving. She literally, structurally embodies traits of her Virginian tribal ancestry. Even in later depictions of the engraving, such as the 1793 engraving done in imitation of Van de Passe's (Figure 3.2), when Pocahontas has been aggressively "whitened" or made softer and more Anglicized in her appearance, the overbite and slightly dimpled chin remain. Her ties to the Pamunkey, Mattaponi, and Rappahannock tribes of Virginia persist in these later, revised images through her facial structure even when the more obvious signs of it—skin and hair color—were excised and ideologically silenced ("Pocahontas Revealed").

Accessory Messages: The Imprint of Pocahontas

Pocahontas's accessories in the Van de Passe engraving are also remarkable in terms of their disruptive undercurrents. There are signs that indicate her choices for clothing and accessories were politically and personally motivated. For example, the beaver hat she wears in the high copotain style was "once only worn by men, [but] had recently been adopted by some women. Queen Anne [even] wore one" (Townsend 152). Although copotain hats during the early seventeenth century were made of both felt and beaver, R. Turner Wilcox in her *The Mode in Hats and Headdress* notes that Pocahontas's hat in the Van de Passe engraving is beaver with a "galloon band" (130). Wilcox further comments:

> The American Colonies exported great hogsheads of beaver pelts to England
> and Holland to be made into hats ... The great vogue of the beaver hat naturally
> caused a serious depletion in the number of beaver in this country [America] ...
> Beaver was most costly, in fact any good hat was costly in those days, valuable
> enough to be left among bequests in a will. (113)

---

[8]   Mary Ellen Howe studied the complexions of living Virginia Indians from the Mattaponi, Rappahannock, and Pamunkey tribes (descendants of the larger "Powhatan" grouping) in order to bring the most accurate coloring to her depiction of Pocahontas. As Pocahontas's sitting for this engraving would have been during the winter of 1616, Howe even took into consideration the lightening of skin tone that would have naturally occurred due to less exposure to the sun and more time spent indoors (interview). My deepest gratitude goes to Ms. Howe for these valuable insights into the six painstaking years of research that went into her beautiful reproduction of this image.

Pocahontas's hat, therefore, was undoubtedly made of beaver and a clear attempt to assign her high status within Anglo-American society. Historian and artist Mary Ellen Howe further asserts that the beaver hat was definitely white, as she depicts in her 1994 rendition of the image, and that the elaborate hat band was attached to the hat itself by a series of gold, hexagonal buttons, something she discovered when she enlarged Van de Passe's image in order to begin her own research (interview).[9]

Because of its masculine associations, women who chose to defy convention and wear a copotain-style hat, however, were often criticized as unfeminine, and when they opted to wear one in a portrait, were recognized as obviously middle-class. As Karen Robertson has noted, "Aristocratic women did not usually wear hats for indoor portraits, although middle-class women did. Pocahontas's fan and ruff suggest indoor dress, not hunting or outdoor clothing" (573). The choice of this particular style of hat for Pocahontas is also worthy of note. A copotain, or capotain, is a conical, high-crowned, small-brimmed hat that was a fashionable hat in the sixteenth century; however, historians note that by the mid-seventeenth century, it was the style worn by supporters of the Puritan faction in England and was more commonly known as the "Pilgrim hat." Although the choice of this hat was somewhat Puritanical—"Puritans and Pilgrims favored the high crown with wide brim uncocked and a simple ribbon held in place by a small silver buckle" (Wilcox 114)—many "adopted the Cavalier fashion with jeweled bands and ostrich [plumes]," or *aigrette*, worn off to one side, as Pocahontas has done in the engraving (Wilcox 114). Wilcox further notes that the feminine version of the copotain, "when worn either for travel or hunting, was a replica of the masculine headpiece in felt, beaver or velvet" (121). All of this reveals that although Pocahontas's beaver copotain was the height of fashion, the choice to wear it with indoor clothing for a portrait sitting was highly unusual, to say the least, and would have been singularly conspicuous to all who viewed this engraving.

Donning a hat, but particularly this style of hat, for her portrait sitting can be argued to be the choice of Pocahontas and not her husband's or handlers' because of the multiple, divergent messages it sends. Pocahontas could be attempting to indicate that she is no ignorant, "backwoods" Indian unaware of fashion trends in England, nor is she afraid to buck convention by being one of the earlier women to defy feminine fashion standards and try out a new style. By deciding to be immortalized in such a fashion-forward and somewhat scandalous accessory, Pocahontas is potentially leaving her personal "mark" on the portrait. The fact that a high copotain hat would have carried distinctly masculine connotations suggests she wished to avoid being viewed in terms of stereotypical Anglo-American femininity; she would not be thought of as dainty or feeble, but strong and daring. Further, the fact that middle-class women were the ones to pose in hats—not the elite—indicates that she held no illusions about who she really was as the wife of

---

[9]   Howe notes that the Virginia Historical Society holds one of these tiny, gold, hexagonal hat band buttons in their collections, previously believing it to be from Pocahontas's dress in the Van de Passe image rather than her hat (interview).

John Rolfe, a middle-class man from a struggling Virginia colony. At the same time, though, the fact that the hat is in beaver, an expensive and elite material, and features fashionable aigrette and fancy band separates her from the fundamental Puritans who would have chosen this particular style of hat but would have worn it plainly dressed. Clearly, the choice of this particular hat is one that Pocahontas's husband and handlers, who were anxious to tout her status as New World royalty and recently acquired position as a fully acculturated English lady, would not necessarily have condoned. The competing messages it sends are too divergent, too risky, for goals they wanted to accomplish with Pocahontas's English tour and engraving. Pocahontas's seemingly straightforward choice to cover her head with a hat in her portrait, upon deeper investigation, turns out to be hugely significant because it not only underscores her awareness of the nuances of seventeenth-century English popular culture, but also her potential defiance of them. She was unwilling to fit the mold prescribed for her by Anglo-American society as a genteel lady of the court, an acculturated Indian princess. She instead disrupts and counters that identity with one of her own composition: that of a very savvy young woman very much in control of her own image and confident in her own identity.

Pocahontas makes a similarly complex statement with another accessory she wears in the engraving: her pearl earrings. The earrings feature a teardrop shaped pearl dangling from a hoop worn in the lobe of her ear. This is not an unusual choice of jewelry because pearls were a fashionable and expensive item of personal embellishment popular in Elizabethan times. Many well-heeled women wore them as necklaces, pendants, brooches, and earrings, especially since they signified wealth and status. In fact, Queen Elizabeth I of England "was not only draped in pearl necklaces, but she had so many pearls stitched to her dresses that she was literally upholstered in pearls" (Loring 9). Because the process of producing man-made pearls, a process called "essence d'orient" that involved manipulating the luster of fish scales, was not developed until 1656, natural pearls were quite costly and reserved for the elite classes of Europe during the early part of the seventeenth century, when the Van de Passe engraving was made. Consequently, women of the highest social classes adorned themselves with costly pearls as a sign of their status. Additionally, since pearls were known for their lustrous glow and prized for their white, creamy colors, they came to represent modesty, chastity, and purity, even becoming a key jewelry item for brides to wear on their wedding day and as embellishments for their bridal gowns. Pearls were even significant gifts to young brides to signify their "purity" before marriage as well as their future modesty as married women. The pearl earrings worn by Pocahontas in her portrait, therefore, seem to be an appropriate adornment for Lady Rebecca, the privileged daughter of an Indian "emperor" and the chaste wife of an up-and-coming colonial man.

However, these earrings may also have been worn, as Camilla Townsend has noted, as "a sign [Pocahontas] is from the New World and specifically Virginia ... Virginia had been seen as a rich source of pearls from the beginning of the colonization project" (152). In fact, the entire New World was often called the "Land of Pearls" after Christopher Columbus's discovery of a seemingly endless supply of pearls off the coast of Venezuela in 1498 (Loring 41). As John

Loring has noted, "It is estimated that between 1513 and 1540 over thirteen tons of Cubagua pearls were taken to Europe by the Spanish," yet "[f]rom the Gulf of Mexico to the Gulf of Lower California, from the Mississippi River to the Ohio River, from Wisconsin, Tennessee, Texas, and Arkansas to New Jersey" American waters produced wide varieties of fresh and saltwater pearls as well (Loring 41–2).

Indians were an especially important source for these pearls in the early days of colonization. Thomas Harriot, for example, relates in his *A Briefe and True Report of the New Found Land of Virginia* that one of his companions, "a man of skill in such matters," had obtained about 5,000 pearls from the Indians and made "a fair chain, which for their [the pearls'] likeness and uniformity in roundness were very fair and rare, and had therefore been presented to her majesty" (Harriot 11). Colonizers had long taken note of Indians wearing pearls and using pearls for trade. John Smith notes that the Powhatan Indians paid their tributes to Powhatan in "skinnes, beades, copper, pearle, deare, turkies, wild beasts, and corne" ("Map of Virginia" 1:174). Even the dead among the Virginia Indians were sent into the afterlife with pearls. For example, Smith writes that Powhatan had a storehouse of his personal treasures, such as "skinnes, copper, pearle, and beades, which he storeth up against the time of his death and burial" ("Map of Virginia" 1:173). Powhatan also, according to Smith, gave Sir Thomas Dale a "greate bracelet, and a chaine of pearle, [through] an ancient Orator" ("The Proceedings" 1:249). Helen Rountree observes that such voluntary exchanges of strings of pearls were most likely attempts to make peace with the English after previous exchanges of belts of wampum and clothing became less effective. In fact, Rountree notes, "The English demanded such a chain as a sign of peace from the Nansemonds in September 1608, after which Indian 'royalty' voluntarily used chains of pearls in appeasing angry English visitors" (125). In lore surrounding Pocahontas, a pearl necklace was the supposed gift Powhatan sent to his daughter upon her marriage to John Rolfe. Clearly then, the pearl earrings in Pocahontas's ears in the Van de Passe engraving signify more than simple European wealth and status. They mark Pocahontas as not only of Virginian provenance, but also as an Indian. She is not an "English" lady posing in pearls, the markers of courtly, Jacobean finery; she is instead wearing the jewelry of her ancestors and tribe, visibly marking herself as "Indian."

She is also signaling her peaceful mission to England as an emissary for the Virginia Company as well as her recognition of the political nature of her visit. Pearls had also been used between the English and the Powhatans as a token of the peaceful intent of either side when sending messengers back and forth. In fact, as Helen Rountree has noted, "In 1614, a chain of pearls was agreed upon as a badge of safe conduct for messengers between Powhatan and the English" (125). The earrings, in this context, serve not only as items that confirm the wealth and abundance of her ancestral home and peoples rather than the English court for which she is dressed and posed, but also as stark reminders of the peaceful exchanges her people have had with the English colonists. Perhaps this is Pocahontas's way of requesting "safe conduct" for herself and her retinue from her

English audience; she may not feel safe among the English who have "saved" her from "savagery." Perhaps it is her way of reminding the English of the lengthy and peaceful relationship they have shared with her tribe in the New World; she may fear her people and their cooperation with the English have been forgotten. In the ears of Pocahontas, these earrings become a critique of colonialism and corrode the goal of the colonial project—fully acculturated converts; clearly, Pocahontas has not been fully acculturated. The earrings undermine the assumed "facticity" of her identity as an English lady and have an unstable and shifting meaning in this image. In other words, pearl jewelry does not always automatically identify the wearer as a member of the European elite. When coupled with darker skin and Indian features, as well as an Indian identity, those same symbols signify something quite different, something foreign and perhaps even threatening to established hegemony. This complex message contained in her earrings would have been both recognizable and disruptive to those who viewed her image.

The ostrich feather fan held awkwardly in long, slender fingers in the Van de Passe engraving also sends a similarly "mixed" message to the portrait's viewers. The fan is composed of three ostrich feathers with a fancy engraved clasp at the base of the feathers that connects them to the handle, a delicate wand, grasped in Pocahontas's fingers. This style of rigid fan did not fold or expand as the more common folding fans did and, because of the ostrich feathers, was not intended to serve the practical purpose of moving air. The fluffy, wispy nature of the ostrich feathers and the narrow width of the fan itself mark it as a merely decorative item. Fans of this nature "came from Italy ... in the time of Henry the Eighth, [and] were ... used by both men and women" (Egerton 109). However, such fans were distinctive symbols of luxury and wealth. In the sixteenth and seventeenth centuries, luxury items from South Africa such as silks, carpets, ceramics, glassware, and animal products like lion and leopard hides and ostrich plumes were incorporated into European courtly culture. Consequently, fans of this period were often of considerable value. The Countess of Wilton, Mary Margaret Stanley Egerton, notes that the most costly of these fans "were made of ostrich-feathers, fastened into handles composed of gold, silver, or ivory, curiously worked ... The bright-coloured feathers from the peacock's tail, too, were frequently formed into the same ornament" (109–10). One fan of this particular style was even "presented to Elizabeth, the handle of which was studded with diamonds" (Egerton 109).

In the Van de Passe engraving, Pocahontas appears to be holding just such a fan, its chain barely visible against the richly embroidered material of her dress and over gown. Further, ostrich feathers in heraldic symbolism were associated with willing obedience and serenity, and in English society, three ostrich feathers surrounded by a crown have been the crest of the Prince of Wales, the heir to the British throne, since 1301. The crest of the Prince of Wales consists of three silver (or white) feathers rising through a gold coronet of alternate crosses and fleurs-de-lis. The motto "Ich Dien" (I serve) is on a dark blue ribbon beneath the coronet. Pocahontas's fan in the Van de Passe engraving closely resembles this badge of English royalty, and although it undoubtedly was not intended to usurp or mimic the symbolic power of the Prince of Wales's crest, it resonates with it, nonetheless. This similarity is especially interesting considering that the detailed description of Pocahontas's identity beneath the engraving labeling her as "daughter of the mighty Prince Powhatan Emperour of Attanoughskomouck als Virginia." Certainly, the insinuation that Pocahontas, like the Prince of Wales, is heir to the throne of a nation cannot be overlooked.[10] Beyond simply implying a royal connection, ostrich feathers were also reserved for the aristocratic of society, especially the pure white plumes, as in Pocahontas's fan, which occur in nature only on mature male birds. Such an exquisite and fashionable fan marked Pocahontas in this image as one of the elite of society—a true "Indian princess" in an English court. This fan is a striking contrast to her decidedly "middle class" choice of head gear, creating a tension between that further complicates Pocahontas's already complex and fluid identity. Is she a fine lady of the court or the unashamedly middle-class wife of a tobacco farmer?

Simultaneously, however, the elegant feathers clutched by Pocahontas call stark attention to her identity as an Indian. Feathers were (and still are), for non-Native audiences, one of the main visual markers of Indianness. Earlier images of Indians from the Virginia Colony, such as the drawing of Eiakintomino in St. James's Park used to advertise a fundraising lottery for the Company just two years before Pocahontas's portrait, relied heavily on animal skins, bows and arrows, and feathered headdresses to relay the subject's otherness (see Figure 3.4).[11]

Pocahontas's portrait seems to be entirely different from images such as these with her high-class accoutrements and elegant clothing that entirely covers her body. However, due to the ambivalence of some of the items within the image, such as her hat, her pearl earrings and, more importantly, her feather fan, Pocahontas's Indianness is still clearly, almost defiantly, reiterated for the viewer. In this engraving, she is still a "feathered Indian" of sorts, and whether through intent or happenstance, that irony cannot be denied. Because of the significance of her identity as an acculturated Indian, as the crowning accomplishment of the colonizing work in the New World, the stock markers of Anglo-European aristocracy, such as the ostrich feather fan, become doubtful and unstable when placed on her person. These markers become mutable and inconstant depending on the environment in which they appear, and they no longer signify a single, established meaning. The ostrich feather fan that would typically symbolize affluence and class when held by an Anglo-American person, now also hints at "savagery" and Indianness, the antithesis of civilization, when held by "Matoaks

---

[10]   The description of Pocahontas as the daughter of the emperor of a nation was a problematic assertion for the English, at best. Ratifying the imperial power and status of Powhatan in this way, while aggrandizing the English achievement of converting his daughter, also threatened to delegitimize English dealings with the Indians, because the English were recognizing them as an equal, civilized nation, and casting themselves as invaders. See Robertson for further discussion of this.

[11]   Eiakintomino was one of two Indians featured on a Virginia Company lottery broadside in 1615–1616.

Figure 3.4   *Eiakintomino in St. James Park*, 1614, as pictured in Michael Van
Meer's *Album Amicorum*. Courtesy of the Special Collections,
Edinburgh University Library.

als Rebecca." Rather than existing in this engraving as either Matoaka *or* Rebecca,
or Matoaka *as* Rebecca, Pocahontas is Matoaka *and* Rebecca, embodying both her
Indian identity and her newly acquired English one simultaneously. The Indian
cannot be separated from the acculturated English woman on display in this
portrait because the acculturated English woman is an Indian. The two identities
are inextricably bound together, two halves of a singularly mixed identity, and the
Van de Passe engraving unwittingly demonstrates this.

Although it was commissioned as a visual testimony of not only the success of
the Virginia Company in the New World, but also the stabilizing and transformative
powers of English identity, the Van de Passe engraving instead posits ambivalence.
It becomes, like the seals of the Massachusetts colony, a text at odds with itself that
presents a wavering uncertainty about Anglo-European/American identity rather
than any semblance of certainty. It represents the fissures and cracks in the dominant
discourses of colonial and early republican America where Anglo female authors
could begin to insert and assert their own identities. Through the appropriation of
a culturally mixed identity, as well as the concept of "mixed-bloodedness," and
the deployment of the particularly potent narrative of the Princess Pocahontas,
these women writers could disrupt and revise dominant ideologies to include
white womanhood, and white female authorship, in significant and meaningful
ways. Women authors could rewrite the master narratives governing race, gender,
and Anglo-American national identity through the fictional portrayal of female

characters that resisted categorization and enclosure within the established binaries of colonial discourse, much as Pocahontas did in the Van de Passe engraving. *The Female American*, published in 1767, takes up this resistant trope of acculturated female Indianness and provocatively extends it by coupling a culturally mixed identity with one of "mixed blood." By introducing a very Pocahontas-like central character who is culturally and biologically both Indian and English, and obscuring authorial identity through anonymous publication, *The Female American* is able to posit radical possibilities for not only female authorship but also for racial and gendered multiplicity within the American identity. However, as with other texts I've examined thus far, this resistance to ideological closure for Anglo-female identity is achieved unabashedly at the expense of Native American identity.

Part 2
Narrative: *The Female American*

Pocahontas, her image, and her narrative have certainly been useful and popular tools in the endeavor to create a distinctly Anglo-American identity for hundreds of years now, and although there are moments of disconnect and ambivalence in that master narrative of colonization, as evidenced in the Van de Passe engraving, her life and image have continued to be enduring ones. Because of her acculturated identity and willing acceptance of "civilization," she became the ideal colonial convert and "mimic man/woman" that Anglo-Americans could (and still do) embrace as an example of "ideal" Indianness. However, Native Americans who held biological claim to both European and Native ancestry—not just claims of assimilation—were far more threatening to colonial hegemony.

On a certain level, such figures, although existing as realities in the New World since the earliest English settlements in America, were far too menacing to be recognized and preserved as part of the developing American identity. In Anglo-American imagination, the "mixed-blood" was the embodiment of the erasure of the distinction between "civilized" and "savage," colonizer and colonized, the very binaries that inscribed colonial identity as dominant and "superior."[12] A "mixed-blood" Indian represented the very real possibility of the loss of the colonists' mastery and dominance, not only because the Indian had now become, at least in part, Anglo-American, but also because she or he would represent what the colonists perceived as the corruption of their own racial purity. Whiteness was now "tainted" with Indianness. Additionally, in the figure of the "mixed-blood," the original colonial fear of degenerating into Indianness, of there being

---

[12]   Here and throughout the next chapter, I use the term "mixed-blood" intentionally alongside more common and widely accepted designations like "biracial." The term "mixed-blood" is less deterministic than other terms for culturally diverse ancestry and, more importantly, calls stark attention to the constructedness of Anglo-American and Native American identity within colonialist discourses, which is key to my argument. See the Introduction, especially footnote 8, where I discuss this choice in detail.

no hierarchical separation between the superior "us" and the inferior "them," was realized. However, instead of whiteness becoming "savage" and losing its privilege and civility, Indianness becomes "white" through the presence of the "mixed-blood," who potentially could gain all of the rights, protections, and benefits of Anglo identity, which was a much more menacing possibility to colonialist discourses—especially if the "mixed-blood" was a privileged male, a discussion I take up in Chapter 4. As a consequence, "mixed-blood" or biracial male Indians were necessarily erased from or recast within the binaristic master narratives of colonization that were attempting to calcify an Anglo-American New World identity, obscuring their existence.

A woman of "mixed blood," however, is quite another story. Because of the numerous cultural, social, and legal discourses governing the feminine gender of any race, a mixed-race woman seems on the surface to be more containable than her male counterpart. She is veiled in a way that a biracial male is not. She can be married off. She can be silenced through religion. She can be denied an authorial voice because of her gender. Consequently, she can remain in Anglo-American imagination in order to be colonized. However, her biracial position allows her to navigate among these many discourses of containment and subvert them. Even in texts authored by white Anglo-Americans, the "mixed-blood" woman can circulate beyond the grasp of colonial discourse and authorial control. Her biracial identity and her gender create textual slippages and ruptures that breach Anglo-American authority in ways that male characters simply cannot.

Author and theorist Gerald Vizenor argues that beyond being trapped in a binary system, the bifurcated, hybrid figure of the "mixed-blood" is an emblem of survival, despite unsuccessful Anglo-American attempts to contain or erase it. Although not speaking directly to the place of womanhood and "mixed-bloodedness," Vizenor's ideas are intriguing when considered in terms of the nexus of race and gender. Vizenor writes, "The crossblood, or mixedblood, is a new metaphor, a transitive contradancer between communal tribal cultures and those material and urban pretensions that counter conservative traditions. The crossblood wavers in myths and autobiographies; we move between reservations and cities, the stories of the crane with a trickster signature" (Interior 263).

The "mixed-blood" identity, in fact, is similar to that of the trickster figure for Vizenor; for him, the biracial Indian reflects the "necessary and productive tension found in the metaphor of the mixedblood position" (Murray 29). As David Murray notes, the "mixed-blood" for Vizenor "acts as a supplement, both in *adding to*, but also in *replacing* the idea of a pure tribal Indian identity based on blood and lineage, and it is this shifting and ultimately undecidable relation of the two terms which ... reflects Vizenor's enterprise" (21, italics in original). I would further add that a "mixed-blooded" identity *adds to* and *replaces* not only the idea of a pure Indian identity, but also that of a pure Anglo-American identity. A person of "mixed blood" resists and subverts any notion of racial purity and posits instead a more fluid, permeable conception of race with their elusive "trickster signatures." When buttressed with a feminine history that is both potent and historically grounded through a Pocahontas-like narrative, such a female "mixed-blood" figure becomes even more uncontainable and disruptive. And when that figure is deployed through an anonymously published work of fiction in which the only "author" is the central female character herself, a "mixed-blooded" woman with Pocahontas-like origins, the result is a radical text that is transgressive of the raced and gendered discourses that undergird colonialism.

Fictionalizing History, Transgressing Race and Gender

First published anonymously in 1767 in London, *The Female American; or, The Adventures of Unca Eliza Winkfield*, was purportedly the autobiography of Unca Eliza Winkfield, a "mixed-blooded" New World woman.[13] It is the story of the granddaughter of both Edward Maria Winkfield (or Wingfield as it is more commonly spelled), a founding father of the Virginia colony, and a powerful Indian chief of the region, a Powhatan-like figure who captures and then ultimately allows the English-born William to become a husband to his favorite daughter, the Indian princess Unca; the happy couple ultimately becomes the parents of Unca Eliza. The heroine/narrator who is born out of this star-crossed and very Pocahontas-like union is a uniquely biracial, bicultural, bilingual character.

Unca Eliza's real adventures begin when, as an adult, she is attempting to return to England after visiting her father in Virginia and her scheming ship's captain strands her on a desert island in the Atlantic for refusing to marry (and sign over her great wealth to) his son. Unca Eliza survives on her own in the island wilderness because of her pluck and the fortunate discovery of some instructions in a diary left by a hermit who inhabited the island before her. By the novel's end, Unca Eliza has not only survived her exile and increased her already substantial fortune, but also even managed to convert the local Indians on a neighboring island to Christianity. She ultimately chooses to stay with "her" Indians, as she calls them, ministering to them for the rest of her life, instead of returning to England when her cousin and future husband finally arrives to redeem her. Most of Unca Eliza's textual adventures, which are strongly indebted to Defoe's *Robinson Crusoe*, occur within the confines of the deserted island where, for the most part, she is entirely alone. Beyond the grasp of the racist, gendered hegemonies of Anglo-America, Unca Eliza's identity is showcased as uniquely mixed-raced, mixed-culture, and even mixed-gendered; it is potent and full of possibilities.

Unca Eliza is raised on her father's English plantation as a part of English society and educated in England through adulthood, but she is also taught Indian customs, language, and skills, and even allowed to dress in a motley amalgamation of English and Indian inspired clothing. So while certainly acculturated to English ways, Unca Eliza is still quite "Indian" in her habits, appearance, and behaviors. Additionally, even though she is seemingly "enclosed" and reined in by patriarchy as a woman, many of her actions challenge and disrupt gendered paradigms.

---

[13]   For my work with *The Female American*, I have chosen to use Michelle Burnham's and James Freitas's readily available second edition of the text, which closely follows the original London edition published in 1767.

As a consequence, hers is an identity white women authors could appropriate and utilize to deploy biracial femininity in their texts with more force and radical possibility than they ever could with a male version of this identity. Whereas a biracial male figure would ultimately threaten to reinforce patriarchy with his masculine presence, a biracial woman can shatter the discourses of patriarchy that governed both gender and race, leaving in their place discourses of multiplicity and possibility instead of binary containment. In short, a "mixed-blooded" female character like Unca Eliza Winkfield can function as the ultimate trickster figure.

The critics who have devoted attention to this text have focused almost exclusively on the anonymous author's gendered transgressions through Unca Eliza's character. Often focusing on the masterful usurpation and re-visioning of the Robinson Crusoe narrative by the author, these analyses have as their central concern the destabilization of the hegemonic discourses regulating gender and how Unca Eliza subverts them.[14] However, Unca Eliza's "mixed-blood" status is a destabilizing force that must also be recognized; her bicultural, biracial identity is an extremely significant factor that enables and complements her many gendered transgressions. This critique of gender and patriarchy could not, in fact, occur without the heroine's "mixed-bloodedness." It is Unca Eliza's "almost but not quite" identity as a person of two distinct and supposedly diametrically opposed races, her literal in-between status, that works alongside her destabilizing gender identity to make the text radically transgressive of the discourses of colonialism and, more specifically, patriarchy. While Unca Eliza certainly transgresses many gendered boundaries in true "female adventure narrative" fashion, it is her status as a mixed-race figure coupled with her status as a gender-bending woman that the anonymous author celebrates and utilizes. Unca Eliza's gender, on the surface, enters the text as a mechanism by which the dominant discourses of patriarchy can attempt to assert racial surety over Unca Eliza by reinscribing her dialectical role as a woman. However, her "mixed-blood" identity makes such gendered

---

[14]   See Burnham's and Freitas's insightful analysis of *The Female American* in the introduction to the second edition of the text, Roxann Wheeler's *The Complexion of Race*, and Betty Joseph's essay "Re-playing Crusoe/Pocahontas: Circum-Atlantic Stagings in *The Female American*" for this gendered analysis. Additionally, Scarlet Bowen ("*Via Media*: Transatlantic Anglicanism in *The Female American*") has examined the narrative for its use of "Anglican theories and structures of mediation" as a means of justifying Unca Eliza's "efforts to missionize among other Native Americans" (189). Kristianne Kalata Vaccaro ("'Recollection ... Sets My Busy Imagination to Work': Transatlantic Self-Narration, Performance, and Reception in *The Female American*") has looked at the ways in which the narrative's "twofold engagement with performance ... explores the vexed relationship between performer and audience, ultimately pointing to the ways in which religious and political beliefs are performed to manipulate audiences into perceiving them as absolute truths" (128). Mary Helen McMurran ("Realism and the Unreal in *The Female American*") has also discussed the novel in the context of oracles and eighteenth-century beliefs, and Matthew Reilly ("'No Eye has Seen or Ear Heard': Arabic Sources for Quaker Subjectivity in Unca Eliza Winkfield's *The Female American*") has compared the novel to the twelfth-century Arabic text *Hayy Ibn Yaqzan* and its later translation by George Keith.

certainty an impossibility. Because of the disruptive nature of her "mixed-blood" identity and her castaway status beyond the confines of mainstream society, Unca Eliza ends up not only defying classification within the racial binary, but also complicating the patriarchal terms that define and regulate New World womanhood. She becomes the locus for a critique of the colonial and patriarchal discourses governing not only race and identity, but also intermarriage, cultural assimilation, religious conversion, and especially the terms of female authorship in Anglo-America.

Female Authorship: Unca Eliza Winkfield

Although the author of *The Female American* has never been identified as either male or female, it is a text that is almost universally spoken of in terms of its feminist foci and feminine voice. With its strong resemblance to Daniel Defoe's *Robinson Crusoe*, the narrative belongs to a genre of female adventure fiction that has been dubbed by Jeanine Blackwell as "female Robinsonades," narratives that place a woman in the circumstances of Defoe's hero (qtd. in Burnham and Freitas 19). Literary scholar Laura Stevens even states the narrative is "intertextual to the point of competitiveness" with *Robinson Crusoe* ("Reading" 151). *The Female American* is also a text that deals quite pointedly with the issue of the female authorial voice. From the very title page of the 1767 London edition, the text boldly announces that both the focus and the voice of the text will be feminine (see Figure 3.5).

Fully entitled *The Female American; or the Extraordinary Adventures of Unca Eliza Winkfield. Compiled by Herself*, the female-centered nature of the text is decidedly apparent. Not only is the story within the cover going to be about a specific type of American—the *female* American—but it is also going to be authored and "compiled" by that actual person herself. Such distinctions, while seemingly minor, clearly place the authorial voice of Unca Eliza in control of the text's production. She assumes agency in the act of gathering, arranging, and telling her own story herself, a far cry from the narratives of "mixed-blood" men like Thomas Rolfe and Charles Hobomok Conant (discussed in Chapter 4), who both stepped quietly into historical and fictional record.

Further, the biracial name of the text's heroine is prominently featured on the title page in font that is just as large as the word *Adventures* of the title, giving the biracial heroine of the tale at least as much weight as the genre in which the text is fashioned. Clearly, her identity is intended to be as much of a textual draw as the adventures she embarks upon. Each portion of the name, *Unca Eliza Winkfield*, also signifies upon a distinct aspect of the heroine's complex identity: she is Indian, she is a woman, she is a direct descendant of the founding fathers of America. In this continuation of the Pocahontas narrative, the heroine is not simply "Rebecca" or "Matoaka," but both simultaneously. Additionally, her name "Unca" is, as Betty Joseph has observed, "a feminized version of an important player in American colonial history. 'Uncas' was chief of the Mohicans when the tribe joined the Puritan settlers in a war against a fellow tribe (the Pequots) in the 1630s" (320). Unca Eliza is clearly not going to function in a purely feminized or

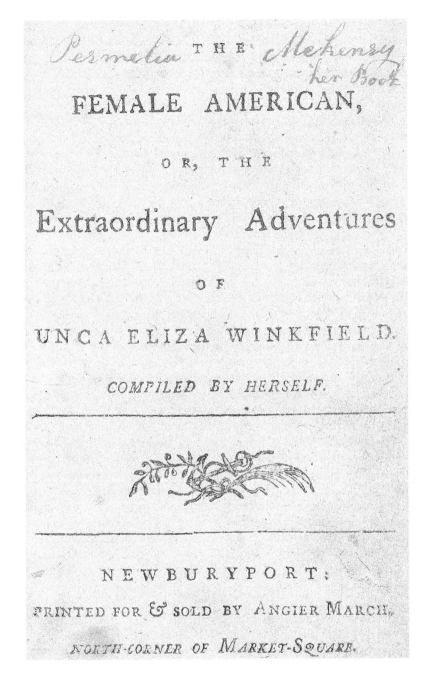

Figure 3.5   Title page of Newburyport edition of *The Female American*, circa
1800. Courtesy of the Yale Collection of American Literature,
Beinecke Rare Book and Manuscript Library.

colonized role. All of these elements, while working to add interest and sensation to the text itself, also work to establish the femininity, the uniquely "mixed-blood" and mixed-gender identity, and the historical authority of the female narrator. Such titling calls attention to Unca Eliza's race and biological ancestry as being key points of the narrative to follow. Her Indian identity and notable heritage are just as important as, if not more so than, her womanhood, which is undoubtedly going to be tempered with masculine attributes based on her name.

Following the title page of the London edition appears an advertisement signed by "The Editor" in which a "worn out old manuscript" technique is invoked.[15] The Editor begins the brief statement by noting that the following "extraordinary History will prove either acceptable or not to the reader; in either case, it ought to be a matter of indifference to him from what quarter or by what means, he receives it" (*Female* 43). However, he or she continues, "if curiosity demands a satisfaction of this kind, all that he can receive is this, that I found it among the papers of my late father" (*Female* 43). By deeming the narrative a "history" and stating that it was found, presumably as is, among the papers of a deceased patriarchal figure, the author/editor is establishing the credibility and authenticity of what is to follow. The writer is summoning up the voice of the noble Virginia colony founders, facilitated by the presence of an editorial voice and the patriarchal preservation of the text, only to disrupt and overwrite them with a female one. However, the preserved voice and text are those of a "mixed-blood" woman daring to appropriate a very masculine task—telling her own story in her own voice; *The Female American* does not need the mediation granted by a veneer (or voice) of masculinity. This text is the direct compilation of a woman and related in a woman's voice. And although *The Female American* is "sanctified" by the masculine authority of the editor's "stamp of approval"[16]—the editor states he/she found the text "both pleasing and instructive"—and preserved through the ages by a father-figure, it still provides a feminine voice that needs no direct mediation, that does not need to be veiled by a masculine voice-over (*Female* 43). Unca Eliza's double ties to an originary American identity, both Indian and English, grant her the authority to speak without masculine arbitration. However, her femininity still positions her, at least theoretically, under the guardianship and containment of a masculine authority whose presence can be seen through the editor and the fatherly figure who preserved the manuscript. Unca Eliza's "mixed-bloodedness," though, eclipses these points of patriarchy,

---

[15]   Burnham and Freitas note that in the later reprints of the text, both in New England, this advertisement is signed by "The Author" rather than by "The Editor" (43).

[16]   Although I do allow for the possibility that the editor could very well be a woman, or even a contrived creation of the anonymous author him/herself, I submit that the traditional position of an editor is a masculine, authoritative one. The role of an editor is to regulate and control the content, organization, and on some level the dissemination of a text. Consequently, whether that position is occupied by a man or a woman, the editor serves as a figure of power and patriarchy that validates Unca Eliza's voice as authentic.

and her feminine, uniquely biracial voice clearly emerges. She becomes, for all intents and purposes, one of Vizenor's "postindian warriors of survivance," who arises from the existing Westernized interpretations of Indianness, Indian "mixed-bloodedness," and womanhood, and attempts through the engagement of those "simulations"—copies of copies grounded in Western imagination—to liberate tribal reality (again, I would add feminine reality) from the tradition of oppression. These postindian warriors "bear their own simulations and revisions to contend with manifest manners, the 'authentic' summaries of ethnology, and the curse of racialism and modernism in the ruins of representation. The wild incursions of the warriors of survivance undermine the simulations of the unreal in the literature of dominance" (*Manifest* 12).

This survivance over dominance is located by Vizenor in "the silence of heard stories, or the imagination of oral literature in translation" (*Manifest* 12), in "the shimmers of imagination … [and] an aesthetic restoration of trickster hermeneutics" (*Manifest* 14). In essence, the resistance of Vizenor's postindian warriors is found in the liminal spaces between "liberation and survivance without the dominance of closure," not unlike the agency and survivance of Unca Eliza's authorial voice, which asserts itself over the editorial voice of patriarchy and creates a uniquely biracial and feminine authorial identity (*Manifest* 14).

Rupturing Containment: Defying Conversion, Marriage, Acculturation

At the time of *The Female American*'s 1767 publication, America still operated under the principles of the *feme covert*. Simply put, when a woman married, her identity and any property she owned became legally subsumed by her husband. She literally became "covered" by him, possessing no independent relationship to the state. This was why relationships between white women and Indian men, like the marriage of Mary Conant and Hobomok from Lydia Maria Child's 1824 novel, *Hobomok*, which I will discuss in Chapter 4, were so very troubling for Euro-American hegemony; a white woman was becoming legally "covered" by an Indian. Simultaneously, however, the institution of marriage was a very useful tool for subduing rebellious or independent women, or safely bringing Indianness—female Indianness—into Euro-American society. An Indian bride's position would not only follow her husband's but also be mediated by it. She would, at least ostensibly, become "civilized" and "white" through her marriage, and her threat of otherness, if not entirely erased, would be subdued. She would be colonized through marital domestication, and, as a component of that marriage, also made over as a Christian. The acceptance of and conversion to Christianity was an understood part of any Indian woman's marriage to a white man. Just as Pocahontas publicly declared her acceptance of Christianity, was baptized, and given a new Christian name before her union with John Rolfe, other Indian women who intended to marry Euro-American men and live within Euro-American society were expected to become Christian. Not only would the conversion of the Indian bride-to-be insure the acceptance of the marriage by colonial authority, it would also doubly insure the new bride's subservience to her husband. Legally she was already "covered" by her husband through the marriage; now religiously she would accept that coverage as part of God's divine plan that women be subordinate to their husbands.

Within the text of *The Female American*, the author details two such conversions and marriages between European men and Indian or biracial Indian women: the marriage of Unca Eliza's mother and father, and Unca Eliza's own marriage to her cousin, John Winkfield. Both of these marriages are interesting in that they represent overtly the attempts—and failures—of colonial patriarchy to inscribe Unca Eliza's mother, the Indian princess Unca, and Unca Eliza herself in terms of the Euro-American, male-dominated discourse in which as women, they were to be subordinate to their husbands (and all other male figures) through the naturalized notions of families as hierarchical units reflective of the inherent differences between men and women. In colonial discourses, the religious conversions that accompanied and sanctified such marriages worked in tandem with the domestic union to further define woman's subordinate role in terms of Christian ideology; in other words, the conversion to Christianity, which dictated a woman's submission to God's will, nicely reinforced her submission to her husband in her domestic union. By attempting to bring these two female characters, Unca Eliza and her princess mother, both powerful and independent women in terms of their elevated social status, influence, and wealth, under the thrall of Euro-American marriage contracts and Christianity—but then inscribing those transformations as incomplete—the author is exposing cracks in the surety of patriarchal, colonialist dominance. Neither full-blooded nor "mixed-blooded" femininity are ever completely regulated by it. Instead the uncontainable, trickster-like power of the "mixed-blood"—and in the case of Unca Eliza's mother, her culturally mixed identity—ultimately subvert this domination and silencing.

When Unca Eliza's mother first meets her European soon-to-be husband, William Winkfield, it is in a situation where the Indians, especially Princess Unca, hold all the power. William had come to Virginia with his father, who had begun a successful plantation that was ultimately inherited by William. After an attack on the colony by the neighboring Indians, Unca Eliza's father, William, was taken captive along with several other men. Marched for miles through the wilderness to a remote cabin, William and his fellow captives are stripped naked and encircled by Indians of both sexes. The captives are then bound and, one by one, they are beheaded; however, just as William is about to meet the same fate as the others,

> a maiden, who stood by the king, and whose neck, breast, and arms, were curiously adorned with jewels, diamonds, and solid pieces of gold and silver, and who was one of the king's daughters, stroked [Unca Eliza's] father with a wand. This was the signal for deliverance; he was immediately unbound and a covering, like that the Indians wore was put around his body. (*Female* 49)

William is then led with a woven grass chain placed around his neck to a shady bower by the princess where she "examined him from head to foot, felt his face and hands, but with the greatest modesty" (*Female* 49). Clearly reminiscent of John

Smith's "rescue" by Pocahontas, this scene works to establish Princess Unca's ready recognition of William's superiority over the other captives, and by proxy the superiority of English manhood and culture.[17] Just as Pocahontas presumably felt instant attraction for Smith (and perhaps even romantic desire as Smith hints), consequently enacting his timely and touching rescue, so, too, does Princess Unca feel attraction for William. Only now in the fictionalized world of *The Female American*, the Indian princess and her English paramour will be united in love.

Obviously pleased with her new possession, the princess offers William food and drink, and once he awakens from his post-luncheon nap, she leads him by the chain back to a cabin in which her father, the chief, is waiting. After she passes the lead to her father and he graciously returns it to the hands of his daughter, the princess immediately "break[s] the chain from around his neck, thr[ows] it at his feet, [and] make[s] a motion that he should put his foot upon it" (*Female* 50). Understanding that the princess has given him his liberty, William prostrates himself at her feet and they retire to another lodging together. Unca Eliza's father has clearly been saved from certain death in these passages, she tells her reader, due to his youth, vigor and "remarkable fair complexion for a man, with brown hair, black eyes and [being] well shaped"; however, he has not been fully redeemed to his former status of dominant white manhood (*Female* 47). Still subject to the Indian people around him, especially his princess, William is not in a position of power at this point in the narrative. Although Scarlet Bowen has argued that William, does, indeed, maintain the upper hand in this incident "through his knowledge that various forms of communication or media exist around the world" as compared to his Indian counterparts who are depicted as lacking knowledge of other languages and being in "a kind of pre-Babel state," I would disagree (198). Even though William has been given his freedom and two slaves by Unca, he still must acquiesce to her will and dress, behave, and live in the manner of his captors. While Unca Eliza implies it was physical attraction, perhaps even love at first sight, that draws the princess to William and causes her to save him—investing William with some power of sexuality or exoticism—William clearly does not retain the upper hand in this Pocahontas-John Smith type relationship.

---

[17]   Smith's rescue by Pocahontas does not appear in his earlier accounts of the Virginia colony; it is first recorded by Smith in his *The Generall Historie* of 1624. Of the rescue, Smith notes that while being held prisoner by Powhatan,

> two great stones were brought before Powhatan: then as many as could layd hands on him [Smith himself], dragged him to them, and thereon laid his head, and being ready with their clubs, to beate out his braines, Pocahontas the Kings dearest daughter, when no intreaty could prevaile, got his head in her armes, and laid her own upon his to save him from death; whereat the Empoerour was contented he should live to make him hatchets. (*Generall* 2:259)

There is, of course, much dispute concerning the episode from Smith's *The Generall Historie* in which Pocahontas saves his life. See Norton (*Alternative Americas*), Mossiker (*Pocahontas*), Woodward (*Pocahontas*), Lemay (*Did Pocahontas Save Captain John Smith?*), Barbour (*Pocahontas and Her World*), Rountree (*Pocahontas's People*), and many others for deeper analysis of this event.

However, just as John Smith represents himself as reasserting his authority over both the Powhatans and his savior, Pocahontas, through his European civility and intellect—and John Rolfe is able to further "civilize" Pocahontas through love, conversion, and marriage—so, too, does William reclaim his sovereignty over his Indian princess. Through daily contact with Princess Unca, William "at last … began to understand her language, which redoubled all her past pleasures, when, according to the simplicity of the uncorrupted Indians, she declared that love for him, which he had long before understood by her actions" (*Female* 50). William, by securing the love and devotion of his Indian princess, has now gained the authority in their romantic relationship; he has the power to either accept or refuse the princess' advances and to do so on his own terms. Anglo-European patriarchy is now regaining its role as authoritarian leader. Unca Eliza makes it clear, however, that her father used his masculine control over her mother kindly and prudently. She notes:

> Though a complexion so different, as that of the princess from an European, cannot but at first disgust, yet by degrees my father grew insensible to the difference, and in other respects her person was not inferior to that of the greatest European beauty; but what was more, her understanding was uncommonly great, pleasantly lively, and wonderfully comprehensive, even of subjects unknown to her, till informed of them by my father, who took extraordinary pains to instruct her; for now he loved in his turn. (*Female* 50–51)

William, through learning the tribe's language and taking pains to educate the princess in discourses of European knowledge, has begun the process of subduing the power of the feminine other. However, that feminine other is not yet fully contained. William has not completely reasserted his European dominance. The threat of the sexualized, seductive female other as anxiously expressed in the earliest seals of the Massachusetts Bay colony again resurfaces. Unca Eliza relates that in the flush of love and companionship, her father

> almost forgot his former situation, and begun to look upon the country he was in as his own, nor indeed did he ever expect to see any other again; he now loved Unca as much as she did him, and was therefore willing to make her and her country his forever. (*Female* 51)

William is in danger of succumbing to the degenerative powers of the New World environment and Indianness and "going Native." The discourses of colonialism and patriarchy are complicated and strained through this retelling of the Pocahontas narrative.

The author further complicates these discourses by introducing yet another powerful, female Indian character: Princess Unca's sister Alluca. Just as the seductive, natural Indian womanhood of Princess Unca can enthrall and delight, so, too, the author seems to be suggesting, can that womanhood turn "savage" and threatening, as in the case of Alluca. Alluca is another of the king's daughters who falls under the romantic spell of William. Approaching him one day while he is alone, Alluca tells William, "[K]now, Winca, then, that I have seen you, and that the oftener I have seen you the more I love you; I know my sister loves you, but I am my father's eldest daughter, and as he has no son, whoever married me will be king after his death" (*Female* 52). Of course, the noble William rebuffs this advance, but that only sends the vengeful, passionate Alluca into a rage. She threatens William with death and has him seized by six male Indians who force him to drink a poisonous potion prepared by Alluca. He swallows the potion declaring, "I cannot do too much for Unca; she gave me life, and for her sake I will lose it—I drink Unca's health; her love shall make it sweet" (*Female* 53). Alluca and her henchmen then leave William to die alone in the forest. Fortunately, however, Princess Unca finds him and is able to administer an antidote to the poison her sister gave him and, as a result, manages to "giv[e] [William] life for a second time" (*Female* 53).

This juxtaposition between the literal "good Indian" and "bad Indian" stereotypes is significant, especially in terms of how it presents complex variations of Indian womanhood. Princess Unca, although undeniably the "good Indian" in this binary, is as of yet untamed by the domesticating institutions of marriage, Christianity, and English culture; she could clearly devolve into the "bad Indian" as represented by her sister Alluca, who behaves in an aggressive, threatening manner toward Euro-American manhood. While Princess Unca has begun the process of civilization, that process is not yet complete and the looming figure of Alluca serves to demonstrate what can happen to Indian womanhood when it remains in an "uncivilized," unlearned state of "savagery" or when the process of colonization fails. Although a willing disciple of William's colonialism, the docile Princess Unca always necessarily embodies the potential threat of becoming the uncolonized and destructive Alluca, her alter ego. Consequently, to rein in this threat, Unca must be removed from the wilderness marriage, a move even Princess Unca's father recognizes. The king tells the couple that

> to prevent all future danger, [William] and the princess should be immediately married; and that they should both set out instantly for the place of [William's] abode, and that on his account, he [the king] would enter into a treaty of friendship with his countrymen; and added, that he would give [William] a portion worthy of a princess. (*Female* 54)

William consents to the Indian marriage, as he "considered marriage as a civil, as well as a religious ceremony, and found … that their matrimonial ceremonies had nothing in them contrary to his own religion" (*Female* 54). A few days later, the couple moves permanently to William's planation in the English settlement, bringing a considerable fortune in gold and gems with them, and are married in the English Church. William now begins the final stages of domesticating Princess Unca and containing her power. He "persuade[s] his wife to conform to the European dress … He [takes] every opportunity that offered to send part of his riches over to England … [and] buil[ds] him a more elegant house, which was suitably furnished, and his plantation by far was the best and largest of any about him" (*Female* 55). Princess Unca appears to be fully domesticated and

Anglicized—a success story of colonization not unlike the image of Pocahontas presented in Van de Passe's engraving—by the time Unca Eliza, her daughter and the narrator of the text, is born.

It becomes clear to the reader, however, that acculturation and colonization is not such a linear and uncontested process. Princess Unca begins to demonstrate that she is not entirely acculturated into English society, and in fact violently refuses some aspects of colonization. The destabilizing threat of her Indianness still remains. She does not eschew all of her Indian ways and beliefs for European ones. For example, she refuses to leave the New World and return to England with William. Unca relates that although her father had "no inclination to leave his habitation ... the thoughts of it were highly disgusting to the princess" (*Female* 55). The princess also maintains close contact with her Indian family; her father, the king, often "sent a messenger to inquire after his children, who always attended with some present of fruit, flowers or something more valuable" (*Female* 55). She also dresses her daughter in a uniquely Anglo-Indian fashion that calls attention not only to her own Indian heritage, but also to her daughter's biracial, bicultural identity. Unca Eliza notes:

> My tawny complexion, and the oddity of my dress, attracted every one's attention, for my mother used to dress me in a kind of mixed habit, neither perfectly Indian, nor yet in the European taste, either of fine white linen, or a rich silk. I never wore a cap; but my lank black hair was adorned with diamonds and flowers ... My uncommon complexion, singular dress, and the grand manner in which I appeared, always attended by two female and two male slaves, could not fail of making me much taken notice of. (*Female* 58)

The incomplete conversion of Princess Unca clearly establishes the uniquely bicultural identity of her daughter, Unca Eliza, and sets the scene for Unca Eliza's later adventures based on her biracial status. It establishes Unca Eliza as an amalgamation of cultures and social systems; she is a cultural "mixed-blood" by her own agency, in which

> the trace of what is disavowed is not repressed but repeated as something different—a mutation, a hybrid. It is such a partial and double force that is more than the mimetic but less than the symbolic, that disturbs the visibility of the colonial presence and makes the recognition of its authority problematic. (Bhabha, "Signs" 159)

Princess Unca, through her steadfast refusal to leave the New World for England or ornament her daughter in proper English raiment, is revaluing the assumption of colonial identity through the "deformation and displacement of all sites of discrimination and domination" (Bhabha, "Signs" 159); she is unsettling the mimetic demands of colonial power, performing Bhabha's "almost but not quite." Although Princess Unca is established as functioning in the capacity of the "good Indian" and "good wife"—she has, after all, given up her tribal status and lifestyle and has forfeited her immense wealth to her husband who is stockpiling it in England—she is also functioning as the incomplete Indian convert, the mimic woman who signals the failure of the colonizing process. She becomes a "transitive contradancer," to use Vizenor's term (or "the sign that *remains*," to use Rey Chow's), which has slipped beyond authorial control. In this way, she is just as threatening and disconcerting to colonial identity as her "bad Indian" sister, Alluca, because both highlight the inherent weaknesses in the colonizing process: the possibility of mockery inherent in the mimicry of colonial subjects and the inscrutable, uncontrollable "savagery" of the uncolonized. These sisters work together to illustrate the ultimate realization reached by colonial discourse— "faced with the hybridity of its objects, the presence of power is revealed as something other than what its rules of recognition assert" (Bhabha, "Signs" 160). And what is even more interesting about these Indian sisters is that once their problematic presences are "removed" from the text, they do not stay removed. Instead, both reemerge, in true trickster form, as elements of the agency held by the "mixed-blooded" Unca Eliza.

Meanwhile, back in the Indian village, Alluca is still unable to overcome the romantic slight she received from William. Eventually, she ascends to her father's throne and sends assassins to the couple's home to enact her revenge. Ordered to kill both William and her sister, her henchmen only succeed in attacking Princess Unca. She is stabbed to death, dying in her beloved William's arms. Interestingly, Alluca, because of her power as queen and reputation for unstable behavior, does not suffer retribution, at least from the earthly hands of the English. Her power and reputation are such that the colonists, "considering the infant state of the colony and the temper of the reigning princess ... thought it prudent to avoid every thing that might occasion a quarrel with the Indians," so her act goes unpunished and her rule unquestioned (*Female* 57). Shortly thereafter, however, Unca Eliza reveals that "the queen died of grief" but not before making preparations to have her heart sent to William with a plea for forgiveness and "a very great present of gold dust, and her bow and arrows, of exquisite workmanship for [Unca Eliza]" (*Female* 57). This violent and politically powerful woman seems to have been succinctly contained by the author—first, through her complete infatuation with and willingness to serve an Englishman, and then, through her death by a broken heart. Alluca is "tamed" before her death, indicating her susceptibility as both a woman and an Indian to the superior colonizing forces of the English; even though she does not go down without a savage fight, Alluca's actions were motivated out of admiration and desire for the colonizer.

However, both of these Indian characters—the willing-if-incomplete convert and the destructive-yet-desiring "savage," two points on the imagined spectrum of Indianness—although presumably contained by colonialism and written out of the narrative, vividly reemerge in the figure of Unca Eliza. Without her mother's romantic involvement with her English husband and commitment to his cultural, social, and religious discourses, Unca Eliza could not have existed as an acceptable and rightful "English" heroine. Simultaneously, however, Unca Eliza's character is given American indigenity and made exceptional through her strong ties to her Indian heritage and strength, both in blood and in culture, as granted by her mother but more specifically by her Aunt Alluca, who leaves not only her wealth and the possibility of becoming queen of the Indian nation to Unca Eliza, but also her prized bow and arrows "of exquisite workmanship" (*Female* 57). Yet both Princess Unca and her sister Alluca, after they have done their work of infusing Unca Eliza with authentic "Indianness," are purged from the text. If either Princess Unca or her sister, Queen Alluca, survived, even distantly, in the pages of the narrative, Unca Eliza could always potentially "go Native" again. Unca Eliza's familial ties to Indianness are literally "killed off"—her grandfather the chief, her mother, and her Aunt all die—in order to fulfill the narrative trajectory of colonization, the full acculturation of Unca Eliza into Englishness.

However, Unca Eliza still does "go Native"; she literally lives among the Indians during her time as a castaway, essentially becoming one of them. Unca Eliza adopts their language and lives a fully Indian lifestyle among the tribe, but not exactly as an equal with them. Unca Eliza takes pains to install herself among the tribe as a sort of holy woman or queen—a woman who has complete and utter control over the people; she essentially becomes her Aunt Alluca—a ruler of an Indian nation. Once Unca Eliza decides to go with the tribe to their island to further her Christian mission among them, she tells the tribal elders from inside the oracle statue:

> A person shall come to you ... that person shall be a woman ... You must be sure to show the greatest respect to her, do every thing that she shall command you, never ask who she is, from whence she comes, or when, whether she will leave you. Never hinder her from coming to this island ... You must all believe, and do as she shall instruct you. (*Female* 119)

The commanding, feminine specter of Alluca has reemerged in the text in the figure of Unca Eliza, although in a more subdued, peaceful—and Anglo-acceptable—form. After all, Unca Eliza's purpose for going among the tribe is to bring Christianity to them and her various demands for full and complete obedience are made only to establish her "credentials ... [and] to support the novel [Christian] doctrines [she] was to introduce" (*Female* 118). In this respect, Unca Eliza is channeling the figure of her mother, Princess Unca, the "civilized" and Christianized "good Indian." Neither Unca Eliza's mother nor her aunt has been contained or even erased from the narrative. Instead these powerful figures of Indian womanhood have simply been refigured and revised to become aspects of Unca Eliza's character. Their reemergence in the actions and behaviors of Unca Eliza serve to complicate her character and the trajectory of the text itself. Is Unca Eliza moving toward containment within colonialist discourses as the dominant raced and gendered paradigms insist Indians and women must? Or is she moving further away from the certainty of containment, in fact becoming more "Indian" and more masculine as the text progresses? Unca Eliza's character transgresses and defies both of these extremes, opening a space for the possibility of ambivalence and multiplicity in identity instead of static binaries.

Unca Eliza's Marriage: Irreconcilable Differences

The juggling act of balancing Unca Eliza's uncontainable, "mixed-blood" identity and the fantastic nature of her experiences against the paradigm of colonialism becomes increasingly more complex as the novel progresses. *The Female American* comes to be more at odds with itself, especially when Unca Eliza's ambivalent character is faced with the ultimate act of colonial indoctrination for Indian/"mixed-blooded" woman: marriage to an Englishman. Early in the text, the author introduces Unca Eliza into specifically "English" ways of thinking, living, and believing from a very young age. After her mother's death, she lives in England with her uncle, a clergyman in Surrey, who educates and dotes upon Unca Eliza as one of his own children. She learns classical languages, "polite literature," and is generally accepted by the community, even attracting the attention of several suitors (*Female* 59).

However, the author clearly denotes that Unca Eliza still retains much of her Indianness, despite this "English" upbringing. Unca Eliza is not entirely Anglicized; she can "speak the Indian language as well as English, or rather with more fluency" and still, despite her happy life in England, wants to return to America (*Female* 58). Further, Unca Eliza remains fully aware of her Indian identity and agency as an Indian "princess"; she routinely dresses in Indian clothing and adorns herself with strings of diamonds and other symbols of her wealthy, royal New World lineage, and often carries her Aunt Alluca's bow and arrow with her. In fact, she is so accomplished with these Indian weapons that she brags to the reader that she could "when very young, ... shoot a bird on the wing" (*Female* 58). Unca Eliza might have even been a queen, she confides to her reader, "if my father had pleased, for on the death of my aunt, the Indians made me a formal tender of the crown to me; but I declined it" (*Female* 58). This is a particularly interesting quote because of the dueling sense of subjective agency. On the one hand, it seems Unca's white, European father is the decision maker when it comes to Unca's acceptance or refusal of the Indian crown and her heritage—the offer would have been considered if her father "had pleased." However, the definitive act of subjectivity comes from the narrator, Unca Eliza, when she herself finally declines the offer, clearly subverting patriarchal and Anglo-European authority. When read in this way, the consideration she gives to "pleasing" her father signifies more her deference to his literal pleasure or enjoyment rather than signifying her submission to his controlling, discretionary whims. Clearly, through this carefully described bicultural, and somewhat masculine, identity, the author is stressing Unca Eliza's unique and privileged status as both a highly educated and attractive, wealthy, young English woman, and as a noble descendant of the exotic, autochthonous Indians of the New World.

The author is establishing Unca Eliza's liminal yet integral position as a member of both races and cultures—a hybrid identity—that allows her greater flexibility to move not only between the two cultures of her birth, picking and choosing the elements she wishes to adapt or discard, but also beyond the restrictive gender roles assigned to her as a Euro-American woman; as a Native woman, she is able to participate in activities and to fashion an identity that would be inaccessible to an ordinary Euro-American woman. Further, because of her "mixed-blood" identity Unca Eliza can pursue ventures in Anglo culture that are traditionally reserved for men: education, hunting, travel, and even a distinctly "bachelor's lifestyle" in which she can refuse suitors and remain unencumbered by a spouse or children. She is a uniquely "mixed-blooded" and mixed-gendered figure. However, such an identity has the capacity to slip away from the dominant discourses governing colonization and gender, becoming disruptive to those paradigms, as did the textual identities of Princess Unca and her sister, Alluca; consequently, those raced and patriarchal hegemonies structuring Anglo society demand containment of Unca Eliza's character. Therefore, the reader is introduced to Unca Eliza's future husband, her cousin John Winkfield.

Once she turns 18, Unca Eliza begins to meditate on her bicultural and American roots. During this time of renewed interest in her origins, Unca Eliza's father requests her return to the family home in Virginia and she agrees to go. Accompanied by her cousin John at the insistence of her uncle, Unca Eliza begins her voyage to America. Not long into the journey, she notes with some dismay, that her cousin "neglected no opportunity to renew his address to me, which he had before begun in England" (*Female* 60). Unca Eliza "gravely" tells her cousin "I would never marry any man who could not use a bow and arrow as well as I could" (*Female* 60). Although her cousin persists in his proposals, Unca Eliza merely laughs at him or answers in "the Indian language, of which he was entirely ignorant," until at long last, she "wear[ied] him into silence" (*Female* 60). This is a noteworthy moment in terms of Unca Eliza's agency not only because of her refusal to accept the yoke of marriage, but also because of her mockery of it. Her cousin's proposals are met with bold refusals that are undergirded by her mixed race. She has declared her standards for an appropriate marriage match and they are based in her Indian heritage. Her Indianness grants her, in this case, the authority to refuse to enter into the restrictive covenant of marriage; her biracial identity is what enables her to assert feminine agency.

Although Unca Eliza's voice clearly declares her freedom from the bonds of marriage, at least for now, the author still casts the thrall of marriage as an inevitability for Unca Eliza. The author describes the cousin in such persistent terms and clearly indicates that the latest volley of proposals from him on the transatlantic voyage were not the first, and undoubtedly, will not be the last because, as Unca notes, she only "wearied him into silence" not acquiescence on that front. Consequently, the reader is made aware that Unca Eliza's future may not only contain a marriage, but also a marriage to this young man; for now, her independence is intact, enabling her to end up unaccompanied and at the mercy of the vengeful sea captain who abandons her on the island—interestingly over her refusal of another marriage proposal. Unca Eliza's laughing refusal of marriage, while transgressive, at this point in the text, is not too disruptive of a threat to the raced and gendered discourses of colonialism.

The threat and containment of marriage returns to Unca Eliza more forcibly after her cousin has been left in her care on the island. John begins, once again, to aggressively court her; Unca Eliza firmly tells him, "Hold, this is the language of a lover, ill-suited to the present time and circumstances … Let us consider how you are to be disposed of," shifting the focus of the conversation to the matters at hand (*Female* 140). Just as she has previously done, Unca Eliza shuts down her cousin's attempts at courtship by redirecting John's focus. Later, John reveals to Unca Eliza that he has begun the process of taking holy orders and desires to stay with her, as a missionary, among the Natives, and consequently, has "but one thing more to ask, and that is, Unca Eliza's hand for ever, in return for [his] heart, which she has long had" (*Female* 143). John ends his appeal with the query, "What says my dear cousin?" (*Female* 143). Unca Eliza's response is, once again, one of diversion: "That we must land … for we are upon the shore, and the Indians waiting for us" (*Female* 143). Even her ultimate acceptance of John's numerous and worrisome proposals comes not with an emphatic "Yes!" or even a begrudging, "Okay." Unca Eliza instead, after much haranguing from John, finds that his words "had some weight with [her]" (*Female* 146). Although she admits that she "loved him as a friend and relation, [she] had never considered him as a lover; nor any other person," Unca Eliza's ultimate reason for marrying John is that she realizes she could not be alone with a man "as it hurt [her] modesty" (*Female* 146–7). She has accepted the proposal out of a need to fulfill the Anglo-American, patriarchal expectations of propriety and morality now that a representative of that hegemonic center, her cousin John, has been reintroduced into the text.

This decision puts the narrative directly at odds with itself because previously, Unca Eliza held no thoughts about marriage or any sort of return to an Anglo-American way of life before her cousin's arrival. Her life among the Indians was fulfilling and quite rewarding for her. In fact, once she had found her place among the Indians, Unca Eliza notes:

> How greatly was my situation changed! From a solitary being, obliged to seek my own food from day to day, I was attended by a whole nation, all ready to serve me; and no care upon me but how to discharge the important business of an apostle, which I had now taken upon me. To this purpose, besides my daily instructing the priests in the knowledge of Christianity, I once a week taught the people in public. (*Female* 126)

No doubt, much of Unca Eliza's happiness stems from the fact that she has positioned herself as the ideal missionary to these Indians. She is at once their respected and beloved educator, bringing her proselytes willingly and gently to Christianity, yet she is simultaneously their superior, a holy woman sent by the gods who is "attended by a whole nation." Unca Eliza is able to achieve this "perfect" situation precisely because of her unique position as a biracial woman and her ability to merge two systems of thought: Anglo and Indian. It is her identity/appearance as biracial that wins her acceptance among the Indians, yet it is her gendered identity as a woman that allows her to remain there because, as Roxann Wheeler aptly observes, she "is female and therefore assimilable to the culture of the men with whom she associates" (*Complexion* 171–2). Unca Eliza has achieved an alternative model of colonization that allows for cross-cultural exchanges and the emergence of a dual, mixed culture that melds two systems of thought, unlike the colonial project, which demands full acculturation of the colonized. She is able to adopt some of the Indians' habits and customs, while they adopt some of her Christian habits and customs in a uniquely reciprocal fashion. She also, as Scarlet Bowen has noted, "challenge[s] the privileging of Anglo-British men to be the sole disseminators or mediaries of Anglican teaching" (199). Because of these successes and Unca Eliza's ability to revise and successfully perpetuate a counter-paradigm to patriarchal colonization, she, as a character, has become too transgressive and must necessarily be contained—and silenced—by colonization through the reintroduction of her cousin John.

When Unca Eliza does marry John, her position and authority among the Indians become truncated. Where she was once the sole teacher, minister, and religious authority on the island, John has now taken on those roles. John now gives the religious sermons while Unca Eliza translates for him until he can learn the Indian language. John also takes over the religious education of the male children, leaving Unca Eliza to work with the girls. Unca Eliza even acknowledges, "From the time of my cousin's settling here, or rather my husband, as I now for the future call him, the Indians were properly baptized, married, and many of them, at their earnest desire, admitted to the Lord's supper" (*Female* 149). The wording of this passage seems to indicate that John's masculine presence brings a propriety, a legitimacy, to the work Unca Eliza had previously been doing on her own with the Indians. Now the baptisms and marriages are "proper" because they are officially presided over by a sanctioned colonial and masculine authority: a white male. However, the reader recognizes that with the reintroduction of this sanctioned authority, the text has become a dull report of Christian conversion and moral lessons. It is no longer the exciting adventure dominated by Unca Eliza's intelligent and free-spirited, feminine voice and tales of the glorious adventures she once had as the sole resident of the island. Although patriarchal and colonial hegemony have reined in Unca Eliza's heretofore independent and liminal position as not only a "mixed-blood" woman, but also a female castaway and missionary, this reining in can be seen as the ultimate critique of these discourses. Unca Eliza's increasingly silent and chastened status—much like Maria Kittle's after the reintroduction of her husband—serves only to underscore her previous freedoms and multiple identities that so enthralled the reader; now she is only an Anglo-American wife and helpmeet. This final confinement and calcification of Unca Eliza's identity becomes the text's most pointed depiction of the ideological enclosure patriarchy enacts against female agency and authorship.

After the marriage, the text descends into a cacophony of male voices, beginning with John's, who all seek to "fill in the blanks" about what has been going on in the masculine, colonial world (i.e., the "real" world) while Unca Eliza's personal adventures have been unfolding for the reader. John's voice is accompanied by those of a Merchant Captain and Captain Shore, all of whom relate the fantastic details of how Unca Eliza came to be found through a "wonderful series of providences" that even involved repentant pirates (*Female* 160). Unca Eliza's feminine, "mixed-blooded" voice, which heretofore has controlled the text, is now mediated by the introduction of the format of the dramatic dialogue. Once her cousin arrives on the island, the structuring "voice" of the narrative, that for so long has been Unca Eliza's and Unca Eliza's alone, shifts into an omniscient reporter-like mode, in which each speaker is identified by his/her name or title, and then his/her spoken words are noted directly after. Such a move, while certainly an attempt to clarify and simplify the cacophony of voices speaking at this point in the text, is also a method of reintroducing editorial control—in short, a way to ostensibly re-order the colonial and patriarchal hegemonies Unca Eliza has been evading. Rather than following along with the point of view of Unca Eliza, directly participating in her thoughts and feelings as she/he has before, the reader is now jolted back into a more distant, pared-down relation of this climactic meeting between cousins in which Unca Eliza, the female "mixed-blooded" character, had exerted narrative control.

This dramatic dialogue, after a few brief shifts back into Unca Eliza's own voice, becomes the dominant narrative method for the remaining five chapters of the text, and undercuts the agency Unca Eliza once exercised in the earlier chapters, eventually erasing it altogether. Although Unca Eliza's voice reemerges on occasion, more and more male voices or vacant, third-person-governed dialogues structure the narrative, especially once the character of John Winkfield enters the narrative as a permanent presence. After his crew abandons John Winkfield on the island with Unca Eliza, her voice becomes a random and controlled addition to the text, rather than its controlling feature. Her aggressive agency and pluck are still readily evident, even through this editorial mediation, but on a gradually diminishing scale. Unca Eliza's first-person voice is only heard twice more after this point, once when John finishes his relation and she informs her readers of the return of Captain Shore, and once in the very final sentence of the narrative, when Unca Eliza reveals that she returned her written "adventures" to Europe through the aid of Captain Shore, nicely bringing the idea of the musty recovered manuscript from the editorial introduction full circle (*Female* 162).[18] Although Unca Eliza is still a very visible presence in these passages—the whole object of the men's narratives, after all, is to reveal how they were able to "rescue" her, much like the final passages of Bleecker's *The History of Maria Kittle* are reserved for Mr. Bleecker's narration of how he spent his time prior to reuniting with Maria—the focus on her authority as a woman author and adventurer has been mitigated. Her role becomes that of feminized object in these final pages. She is the focus of the frantic recovery project spearheaded by John, not the subject and author of her own island adventure as she had previously been; she is the wife of an authorized missionary, not the leader of her own revolutionary missionary

---

[18]   In the interim between the end of John's story and the end of the narrative, the two points at which Unca Eliza's first-person voice is briefly reintroduced, the narrative shifts into the usage of the plural first person pronoun "we." The "we" spoken of is obviously Unca Eliza and her husband John, but the abrupt change to a shared identity rather than the previously used individual is interesting to note.

project; she is the lesser half of a married pair, not the independent author of her own life's story. The racist, patriarchal hegemony of Anglo-America has resumed its position as center but, as it is painfully clear to the reader, it is at the expense of Unca Eliza's exciting and radically transgressive identity.

Although she seems to be contained and silenced by the narrative's end through the marriage, the reintroduction of Anglo-American patriarchy, and the moderation of her authorial voice, the figure of Unca Eliza still overpowers and revises any sense of enclosure these systems attempt to enforce. The binaristic concepts of center and periphery, inside and outside, self and other, male and female break down when confronted with her female "mixed-bloodedness" in ways that male "mixed-bloodedness" cannot accomplish. After all, Unca Eliza, in her position on the periphery of the island, had to be regulated in place; the center had to come to her in order for the editorial voice of patriarchal, colonial domination to reassume control of the text. However, in moving the center to the periphery, the author is altering the center, exposing the cracks in its certainty of dominance. How can the center be the center if it is so easily displaced by the periphery? How can the periphery remain the periphery when it, in fact, controls the locus of the center? Unca Eliza Winkfield, even in her acquiescence to Anglo patriarchy in the final pages of *The Female American*, still ruptures the discourses dominating both race and gender and exposes their inherent flaws. Just as Pocahontas's Indian identity disrupts and revises the graven image of "Lady Rebecca" in her European finery, so, too, does Unca Eliza Winkfield disrupt and revise raced and gendered discourses of colonialism when they reenter the narrative.

Unca Eliza slips beyond the boundaries of authorial, racial, and gendered control in trickster-like fashion precisely because she is her own author. Because of the "worn out manuscript" convention introduced by the "editor" at the beginning of the text and the anonymous nature of its production, Unca Eliza's feminine, "mixed-blood" voice is always already dominating the narrative. Even when first-person masculine accounts fill the final pages of the text, the reader recognizes that Unca Eliza cannot be written back into Anglo-American patriarchal hegemony or be "removed" from the text because she circulates beyond its grasp as its author. Her voice, even when evacuated from the final pages of the text, exists *a priori* to any of the masculine ones that invade and scatter the text. Even their stories are contained within her voice, her authorial realm, making her, in the ultimate trickster circumvention, the author of the very discourses that attempt to contain her. She has written herself into existence outside of the raced and gendered discourses of colonial patriarchy, and in doing so, establishes the possibility for the existence of an Anglo female authorial identity that defies containment as well.

Chapter 4
"Mixed-Blooded" Masculinity:
Thomas Rolfe and Charles Hobomok Conant

Part 1
Iconography: The *Sedgeford Hall Portrait*

Transgressive iterations of Indianness, such as Praying Indians, Anglo-acculturated Indians, and even gender-bending "mixed-bloods" like Unca Eliza Winkfield, were, as I have argued in previous chapters, incredibly threatening to Anglo-European discourse and, therefore, very appealing to Anglo women writers seeking to establish their own authorial identities. Such figures with their binary-defying identities could be successfully deployed by female authors to rupture and destabilize colonial discourse, while simultaneously opening a space within the white, masculine New World hegemony where white womanhood and female authorship could emerge. When undergirded by the authenticating power of Indianness, Anglo women authors could rewrite the master narratives governing race, nationalism, and American identity through the appropriation and domestication of that same Indianness. They could posit the possibility of not only a differently raced nation, but also a differently gendered one where they now had a voice—even if their voice came through the appropriation of Indian identity and perpetuation of colonialist Indian fantasy.

Male Indianness, however, was slightly more problematic for these women writers. Although the male Indian was a concept utilized by writers like Mary Rowlandson and Ann Eliza Bleecker to disturb and disorient the certainty of white, patriarchal dominance, the "inappropriateness" of the "real" male Native American who undergirded those textual representations often proved to be too potent for these women and he was ultimately "written out" of textual existence.[1] After all, a male Indian who successfully penetrates and replicates white patriarchy, whether a real historic figure or a fictitious one, is still reproducing patriarchy, even though his presence is destabilizing within that same discourse. This mimicry, Bhabha's *"almost the same, but not quite,"* does, indeed, threaten the "civilizing mission ... [through] the displacing gaze of its disciplinary double," yet the gendered mission, the patriarchal discourses regulating the role of women that many of these female authors sought to interrogate, remains unchallenged ("Of Mimicry," italics in original, 122, 123). Male Indianness, although a threat to the normality of the racist hegemony of Anglo-America, does not necessarily fracture the sexist one. Consequently, even when invoked intentionally by American women writers

---

[1] See the "Narrative" portions of chapters 1 and 2, respectively, for my analysis of Rowlandson's and Bleecker's male Indians.

because of its disruptive potential, male Indianness had to be carefully disarmed and contained.

This also proves to be true for historical—and even fictional, as I will demonstrate in the "Narrative" portion of this chapter—male Native Americans of mixed-raced ancestry. While a mixed-blooded woman, like Unca Eliza Winkfield, could subvert the raced and gendered discourses of colonialism but still "appear" to be contained by both, thereby escaping detection, mixed-blooded men were too disruptive and threatening to remain as unregulated presences in Anglo-American hegemony. Because their biracial-ness prohibits their containment by race, the most significant paradigm governing masculinity, historic mixed-blooded men have to be evacuated from Anglo-American consciousness. Ultimately forced to become "either/or" at the hands of Anglo-American society, and then either "disappeared" into whiteness or literally removed from American consciousness, male "mixed-blood" Indians, because of their privileged gender, have to be voided from white imagination, history, and texts.

A prime example of such historical erasure and obscurity is Thomas Rolfe, the son of John Rolfe and Pocahontas, a figure about whom little is known and of whom only one disputed image exists. Born out of the extended contact between the Indians and colonists at England's first permanent colony in the New World at Jamestown, Virginia, Thomas Rolfe is the embodiment of the complexities and anxieties that characterized New World Anglo-American identity. He is, indeed, the first descendant in a long line of proud Virginians who claim ancestry to "Princess Pocahontas," but yet he is unilaterally de-emphasized in these family trees. It was Thomas Rolfe's marriage and the birth of his daughter, who later married and had a son, that first established the lineage and then enabled it to continue, beginning a New World dynasty which disseminated Thomas's privileged, bicultural lineage to future generations of Americans, many of whom still today proudly claim his ancestry, or rather his mother's.[2] It is not Thomas and his uniquely American, biracial identity that these many descendants embrace; rather they embrace the ancestral links to his mother, Pocahontas, omitting the critical player whose very existence paved the way for their own membership in the "Imperial Family of Virginia" (William Stith as qtd. in Mossiker 319). The biracial, masculine Thomas complicates these lines of descent.

His near erasure from the family legends, lore, and histories surrounding the Jamestown colony and its legacy reveal just how threatening Thomas's biracial identity and, more specifically, his male gender was to the formation of a cohesive New World identity. Not only of biracial ancestry, but also a privileged

---

[2]   Thomas and his wife, Jane Poythress, had one daughter, Jane, who married Colonel Robert Bolling in 1675. The Bollings had one son, John, with whom Jane died in childbirth. Robert Bolling then remarried a white woman, Anne Stith, with whom he had other children, giving rise to two Bolling bloodlines, the "White Bollings" and the "Red Bollings." John, the grandson of Pocahontas and John Rolfe, progenitor of the "Red Bolling" bloodline, had numerous children, beginning the extensive line of descendants who claim ancestry with Pocahontas.

male of high social status in both of his ancestral cultures, Thomas jeopardized the legitimacy of racist, patriarchal discourses that structured the colonial project. While the invocation of his mother, Pocahontas, was a crucial tool for domesticating and claiming dominion over the New World (as I have argued previously in Chapter 3), the invocation and even the idea of her male heir were too destabilizing to the colonial cause and the colonists' understanding of their own identity. Consequently, Thomas's narrative is all but erased from Virginia's (and more broadly, America's) official and mythic history. While Thomas's life has been revived and revised, at least spectrally, in fictional texts, dramas, poetry, and art of the eighteenth and nineteenth centuries which commemorated the life of his mother and claimed her story and noble lineage for white America, he was not a major component in these Pocahontas-revival narratives.[3] Despite the fact that the very nature of the creation of these texts—which was to celebrate and reinforce an indigenous connection of white Americans to the native/Native land and to Pocahontas's originary role in the foundation of America—established the *a priori* existence of Thomas, he remains the unacknowledged "mixed-blood" bridge that allowed Americans to posit these "authentic" (i.e., "blood") claims to Indianness. However, by not overtly addressing Thomas's disruptive and destabilizing identity in these celebratory texts, the fantasy and appearance of colonial dominance is maintained. As a consequence, Thomas's image and identity, although absolutely crucial to the transmission of Pocahontas's lineage, is one that is excised from all types of historic chronicles, even the more creative, aesthetic forms, such as portraiture.

The Sedgeford Hall Portrait*: Earrings and Authenticity*

The *Sedgeford Hall Portrait*, so-called because of its one-time residency in Sedgeford Hall, a Rolfe family property in Norfolk, England, is purportedly a portrait of Pocahontas and her son with John Rolfe, Thomas, as a child; it is the only image of mother and son together, and the only image of Thomas known to exist (see Figure 4.1). It is also perhaps the most disputed of all the Pocahontas engravings, paintings, and portraits in terms of its authenticity, stemming mainly, I would argue, from its visual record of Thomas's mixed-blood existence.

According to lore surrounding the painting, Pocahontas and Thomas reportedly sat for the *Sedgeford Hall Portrait*, or at least for preliminary sketches that would later become the portrait, during the Rolfe family's stay in England in 1616–1617, at the same time as the Van de Passe engraving was made. However, despite their

---

[3] See Rasmussen and Tilton, Abrams, and Tilton for more on the eighteenth- and nineteenth-century proliferations of the Pocahontas narrative. In sum, though, most of these narratives celebrate Pocahontas's contributions to Anglo culture and Jamestown's survival, including her friendship with John Smith and ultimate marriage to John Rolfe. Thomas, if mentioned at all, occurs as kind of a footnote to his mother's narrative, serving to prove the depth of her commitment to Anglo-European society, rather than as an individual in his own right.

Figure 4.1   The *Sedgeford Hall Portrait*, circa 1800. Courtesy of the Borough
Council of King's Lynn and West Norfolk, United Kingdom.

supposedly concomitant creation, there are many more challenges to the authenticity
and validity of the *Sedgeford Hall Portrait* than to Van de Passe's image. The Van
de Passe engraving of Pocahontas is universally accepted as authentic, because as
Philip Barbour notes, it "is signed by the artist, … [and] the date when prints of it
were available is attested to by John Chamberlain" (232).[4] On February 22, 1617,

---

[4]   John Chamberlain, a London gossip and letter writer extraordinaire, authored a
series of letters between 1553 and 1628, chiefly to Sir Dudley Carleton, concerning life in
England which are so reliable and knowledgeable, it is, as Maurice Lee notes, "just about

in a letter to Sir Dudley Carleton containing a copy of Van de Passe's engraving of Pocahontas, Chamberlain scathingly remarks, "Here is a fine picture of no fayre Lady ... with her tricking up and high stile and titles you might thincke her and her worshipfull husband to be somebody" (2:56–7).[5] Barbour, as well as other scholars, cites this reference from the reliable Chamberlain, along with the fact that the engraving is signed and dated by the artist, as evidence of the image's authenticity. As a result, the Van de Passe engraving is an image authenticated through historical record and white patriarchy. It enjoys a validation, a credibility, that other depictions of Pocahontas do not; it is an image that is widely accepted as "true," as a snapshot of Pocahontas's real-life physical appearance and a testament to her successful transition from "savage Indian" into a "a great lady of the Jacobean court" (Townsend 151). The Van de Passe engraving, despite its evident tensions between the Anglo self and Indian other, which I discuss in Chapter 3, preserves the colonialist, patriarchal fantasy of Anglo male jurisdiction and authority over Indianness and womanhood.

However, the *Sedgeford Hall Portrait*, with its depiction of both Pocahontas and her son, Thomas, represents a more problematic and destabilizing relationship of Anglo-Europeanness to Indianness. This portrait represents the physical reality of miscegenation with the Indian other and a resultant hybrid identity in the figure of Thomas that was neither purely Indian nor Anglo-European. It depicts the melding of Anglo-European and Indian identities rather than their separation and, perhaps more disconcertingly for Anglo-European patriarchy, represents a challenge to the "superiority" of white masculinity through the figure of Thomas. Although the provenance and legitimacy of the *Sedgeford Hall Portrait* are, indeed, historically unfounded and rather sketchy, as I will fully discuss, which make the image's authenticity understandably open to debate and dismissal, there are aspects of the portrait, like the earrings the young woman wears in it, that somehow retain a historic legitimacy and are accepted as "real." The earrings are embraced as documented proof of the "Indian Princess" Pocahontas's legacy while the painting itself is dismissed out of hand as apocryphal. This is at least partially due, as I will argue here, to the biracial, unsettling presence of Thomas Rolfe.

A strikingly beautiful and complex image of post-colonial American identity about which the artist and date are unknown, the *Sedgeford Hall Portrait* is similar in many ways to the *casta* portrait tradition of eighteenth-century Mexico. These portraits of racially mixed families which typically depicted both parents and at least one child were produced, as Ilona Katzew has observed in *Casta Painting: Images of Race in Eighteenth-Century Mexico*, to provide visual stability in a colonial social system undergoing rapid growth and changing ideologies of race and power. Katzew illustrates how these paintings, hundreds of sets of them,

---

impossible to write about any aspect of the Jacobean period without quoting Chamberlain at least once" (3).

[5]   See Robertson, Townsend, and Mossiker for extended readings of Chamberlain's comments about the engraving which are clearly fraught with racist, sexist, and elitist overtones, to say the least.

were made for the consumption of Spanish elites who harbored anxiety over the blending of races—African, Spanish, and Indian—in the New World. She writes, "[W]hile *casta* paintings fit within European concepts of the exotic and follow the trend to classify in the eighteenth century, the works also reveal a special concern with the construction of a particular self-image" and work to underscore "the legitimacy of racial hierarchy" (Kastew 1, 4). These paintings contributed to the construction of a Spanish colonial subjectivity rooted in race and social status in many of the same ways the Massachusetts Bay Colony seal, Van de Passe's engraving, and, as I will argue, the *Sedgeford Hall Portrait*, worked to establish a stable and superior Anglo-American colonial subjectivity at the exclusion of other identities. While the *Sedgeford Hall Portrait* is not exactly within the *casta* tradition because only one parent of the biracial union is pictured and the identities of the subjects are, indeed, unverified as being bi- or multi-racial, it still is an image that struggles to reconcile miscegenation, masculinity, and Anglo-European identity, especially when its fabled connection to Pocahontas and Thomas is factored in.

The *Sedgeford Hall Portrait* depicts a young, seated Indian woman, presumably Pocahontas, with her right arm loosely draped behind the shoulders of a young Indian boy, presumably Thomas, at about three or four years of age. Both the woman and the child are looking straight ahead, directly into the eyes of the viewer, although the child's body is positioned perpendicular to that of the forward-facing woman, so that his chest and stomach rest lightly against her thigh. Neither the woman or child is smiling, but they aren't gazing unhappily out of their woodland background, either. Rather, they are regarding the artist, the viewer, with a composed, relaxed confidence. The duo is beautiful, peaceful, and intimate with each other; they are also clearly raced as Indians.

The mother wears her sleek, black hair parted in the center and hanging loosely down her back—no elegant or complicated up-dos. Her black eyes, prominent cheekbones and nose, and olive skin clearly indicate her non-western European ancestry. The child is equally as "dark" with a fringe of glossy, black bangs that hang across his forehead and almost over one eye. Further enhancing the Indianness of the duo is the natural landscape in the background. Posed as if in front of an arched window, a broad expanse of cloud-filled sky and leafy boughs hang down behind the pair. The portrait depicts a little bit of nature—both the landscape behind and the Indians at center—brought in and contained by European sensibility in not only the calcifying moment of the portrait but also in the display of the culturally stabilizing accoutrements within it. The portrait is not unlike the seal of the Massachusetts Bay Colony or the Van de Passe engraving of Pocahontas when considered in these terms; Indianness is "captured" and "domesticated" so that non-Indian viewers can gaze at and ingest the authenticity of "otherness" in order to form their own senses of self.

This portrait is strikingly like these images in another way; the Indians at the center, while clearly raced as "other," are also clearly cultured as European. Their clothing, environment, and even the physical artifact of the portrait itself are entirely European. The mother is dressed in a red embroidered bodice with three-quarter length poufed sleeves and an olive skirt, both decorated with ornate silver embellishments. She is also wearing what appears to be a string of graduated pearls around her neck and unusual shell earrings in each ear. The child is wearing the same colors and European-style clothes as his mother. This portrait with its mixing of Indian and English markers is clearly attempting to work out the same anxieties present in the Bay Colony seal and the Van de Passe engraving over the melding of New World identity. The woman and her child are displayed in this portrait as having convincingly adopted Englishness in their poses and dress; they have become the model, Anglicized Indians the colonists sought to produce. At the same time, though, these figures have also clearly remained the Indian "others" with their dark skin, eyes, and hair, signifying the immutable and stable nature of racial identity, an uncertain conviction that continually needed validation in colonial imagination. In short, this woman and her child are the ideal "mimic men" of Bhabha—they are "almost but not quite" European in an aesthetically pleasing form. They underscore the ambivalence of colonial dominance through their imperfect replication of the colonizer's identity. However, when inscribed with the identities of Pocahontas and Thomas Rolfe, the pair from the portrait become more than just mimics of the colonizer—the young boy becomes the colonizer and his mother becomes his indelible ties to Indianness. The child in the portrait, Thomas, visually defies the binaries that regulate race and identity, straddling the divide between Anglo-American/Indian, "civilized"/"savage," and embodying both; he is Rey Chow's "sign that remains," the literal "being-there, an externalization and an exhibition—in the aftermath of a process of sacrifice" (90). As a consequence of this ambivalent figure of Thomas, the authenticity of the *Sedgeford Hall Portrait* as a true-to-life depiction of Pocahontas and her son is hotly debated.

Also known as the *Heacham Hall Pocahontas* after the residence where it originated, the portrait has many critics of its authenticity. The history surrounding the painting indicates that it was supposedly painted during the time of Pocahontas's visit to her husband's family in Heacham near the end of her seven month stay in England sometime in 1616 or 1617, or possibly may have been made at a later date from sketches obtained during this visit. After the death of Pocahontas and John Rolfe's subsequent return to Virginia without his son, whom he left in the custody of family in England, Rolfe reportedly had the painting sent to him in America. The timeline of the portrait becomes sketchy after this initial transport to the New World; it is unclear how long the painting remained in America or how it found its way out of the Rolfe family. It is only acknowledged that some time later, according to the *Rolfe Family Records*, the portrait was finally returned to the possession of the Rolfe family when it was purchased sometime in the late nineteenth century by Eustace Neville Rolfe of Heacham Hall from a "Mrs. Charlton, who stated that 'her husband had bought it in America years ago'" (as qtd. in Barbour 235). It then hung in the home of Mrs. Alexander J. Stevenson of West Calder, Midlothian, a grand-niece of Eustace Neville Rolfe, for many years as a family relic and portrait of the "Indian princess." Presently, the portrait resides in the custody of the Borough Council of King's Lynn and West Norfolk, King's Lynn, England, where it hangs in a place of honor, still identified as the *Sedgeford Hall Portrait*, after a Rolfe family property.

According to Philip Barbour in his *Pocahontas and Her World*, however, the portrait "has nothing to do with Pocahontas" (235). Barbour consulted Dr. William C. Sturttevant of the Smithsonian Institute on the matter, noting that Sturttevant seconds Barbour's opinion and reveals to him in a personal letter that the portrait may instead represent "an 18th-century Iroquois woman and child" (235). Additional critics similarly assert that the painting is of eighteenth-century origins based on its style (Tilton 108). Others cite the apocryphal age of the child as evidence of the portrait's spuriousness. They note that Thomas would have been only about two when the portrait would have been painted or sketches made in 1617; the child in the portrait is clearly older than that—perhaps about four years of age—and consequently, could not be a representation of Pocahontas or her son. For this particular group of critics, there are no "maybes" or equivocal statements about the portrait that indicate there are other possibilities to explain these inaccuracies. The portrait and its mythology are simply untrue; the *Sedgeford Hall Portrait* does not and could not possibly depict Pocahontas or her son.[6]

There are, however, legends surrounding the painting and its authenticity which dispute these criticisms. For example, it has been suggested that the painting in

---

[6]   Certainly, nearly all images of Pocahontas have been scrutinized and criticized for their various "artistic liberties" and authenticity. For example, the nineteenth-century paintings of Pocahontas by Edward Corbould, Alonzo Chappell, and the series of portraits of her by both Thomas Sully and Robert Matthew Sully have been critiqued for their romantic, Anglicized portrayals of Pocahontas. However, these portraits, which were based upon pre-existing images or even produced from pure imagination, are never doubted as being representations of Pocahontas. I will suggest that while the *Sedgeford Hall Portrait* is, in some ways, more historically connected to Pocahontas and her son, Thomas, it is summarily rejected as an authentic depiction of them because of the "mixed-blood" presence of Thomas. See Tilton and Abrams for excellent analysis of the many and varied Pocahontas-related images, although neither deals with the *Sedgeford Hall Portrait* in any depth.

Tim Thorpe, the curator of the King's Lynn Museum, where the *Sedgeford Hall Portrait* resides, reports that in 2010, a drawn version of the portrait was discovered by a researcher in the January 29, 1848, edition of *Illustrated London News*, a popular Victorian magazine. This published version of the image, which is undeniably based on the *Sedgeford Hall* portrait, is entitled *The Wife and Child of Osceola, the Last of the Seminole Indian Chiefs*. This discovery has led to the reidentification of the woman in the portrait as Pe-o-ka, the wife of Osceola, rather than as Pocahontas. While this new information certainly adds a layer of historical interest and context to this portrait (and definitely invites further analysis), it does not alter my ultimate point in this chapter as my focus is on the Pocahontas lore (not fact) surrounding the image and the way race and identity are constructed based on that lore. My gratitude goes to Mark Fuller of the King's Lynn Borough Council for pointing this out to me.

existence today is an eighteenth-century copy of the now lost original, hence the anachronistic style and wardrobe of the subjects. The jump in the child's age, it has also been argued, stems perhaps from the same copyist in the eighteenth century who, in an overly imaginative way, took artistic liberties with the content of the original painting and altered the child's aged appearance for whatever reason—not unlike the ways in which Simon Van de Passe's engraving of Pocahontas has been artistically reimagined through the years. Additionally, believers in the veracity of the portrait finally note quite simply that the careful preservation of the picture and its lore proves that its value was appreciated and that its regal identity was known. However, perhaps the most potent and tangible element cited by believers that validates the authenticity of this painting for them is the unusual pair of earrings worn by Pocahontas in the portrait that are still in existence today (see Figure 4.2).

These earrings, "of a peculiar white shell, set in silver," are, interestingly, much less contested artifacts than the painting in which they appear (as qtd. in Barbour 236). They are described in the *Rolfe Family Records* as, at their earliest documentation in the mid-nineteenth century, belonging to John Girdlestone Rolfe and as being "identical with the earrings represented in the Sedgeford portrait" (as qtd. in Barbour 236). Each earring is formed of a rare, white, double mussel-shell of a kind "found only on the eastern shore of the Berings [sic] Strait" that were reserved "exclusively for the adornment of priests and princes" (Palmer). The setting of the earrings, which is sterling silver inlaid with small steel points, indicates that they most likely were set in England and perhaps even given to Pocahontas by her husband's family during her visit with them in 1616.[7] When Pocahontas died shortly thereafter at the outset of her return journey to Virginia in 1617, the earrings apparently passed into the family of John Rolfe's brother, Henry Rolfe, along with the young child, Thomas, who would live with his uncle in England until maturity. The earrings were then passed down through the Rolfe family with occasional references being made to them, as in 1866 when a new bride in the family was presented with the earrings and was told they were Pocahontas's (Prudames). Now touted more consistently as "Pocahontas's earrings," they were put "on exhibition at the World's Fair in Chicago in 1893, and were shown again at the Jamestown Exposition in 1907" (Palmer). In 1923, however, a second wife of one of the Rolfe men bequeathed the earrings to her sister, Mrs. Jessie Hodgson Meggy, rather than another Rolfe family member, thus ending their possession by the Rolfes (Palmer).

---

[7]   Interestingly, there are additional legends circulating that these double shell earrings were reset for Pocahontas in the silver mounting by the Earl of Northumberland while he was imprisoned in the Tower of London. See Palmer ("Pocahontas's Earrings"), Woodward (*Pocahontas*), Quarles (*Pocahontas: Bright Stream Between Two Hills*), and Museum of London Group ("Pocahontas Jewelry Returns to London"). That the earrings from the portrait have such a specifically grounded (and infamous) lineage certainly adds not only to the mystique and power of the portrait, but also complicates the disavowal of the portrait by critics.

Figure 4.2   Pocahontas's earrings. Photograph by Katherine Wetzel. Courtesy
of Preservation Virginia.

In 1935, the officers of the Association for the Preservation of Virginia
Antiquities (APVA) even secured them temporarily to be put "on private view
at the John Marshall House" (Palmer). Although the APVA actively pursued the
purchase of the earrings from the Meggys to make them a permanent part of
their collection, their exorbitant price in 1935 of $5,000 was prohibitive for the
Association (Palmer). Finally, however, the Association was able to acquire the
earrings in 1941, and ever since, they have been a key part of their collection, being
displayed most often at Historic Jamestowne, but also being shown in England in
2005 along with other relics from the Jamestown excavation site in commemoration
of the 400-year anniversary of the founding of England's first permanent settlement
in the New World. Shown alongside a natty silver ear picker, quartz arrowhead
points, Native-made pottery, and other relics that were actually unearthed from
Jamestown soil, these earrings, simply by their proximity to genuine Jamestown
artifacts, received validation as authentic, historically grounded, tangible
possessions that once belonged to the legendary Pocahontas. With just as little
or less factual information existing about them than the *Sedgeford Hall Portrait*
(the portrait is the only physical evidence that corroborates a connection between
the earrings and Pocahontas; all other connections are based on family lore), they
are still referred to by the Historic Jamestowne curators in their current museum
exhibit as "White mussel shell earrings" that "tradition claims … belonged to

Pocahontas" (*Historic Jamestowne*).[8] And this is despite the fact that tests run on the earrings in 2006 by the London Assay office at the request of the APVA have shown the earrings were most likely produced sometime between 1830 and 1900—some 200 years after Pocahontas's death.[9] Yet the earrings are still described, quite sincerely and assuredly, as having some kind of tie to the most famous of Indian converts. For example, Catherine Dean, the Curator of the Collections of the APVA, notes in her 2012 work, *Jamestown*, that although the earrings have been dated as having been created after Pocahontas's lifetime, "it is possible that the shell ovals belonged to her and had been reset" (96). Several museum gift shops run by the APVA, including the one at Jamestown, even sell replicas of the earrings, and although the fine print in the ad describing the baubles at the APVA's online Museum Store and on the romance card accompanying the earrings guardedly notes that they "have a tradition of ownership by Pocahontas," they are still boldly and clearly marketed as replicas of "Pocahontas's Earrings" (*APVA Museum Store*). Why would these earrings, although no less tangible or surrounded by uncorroborated legend than the *Sedgeford Hall Portrait*, be so much easier to accept as authentic, as a legitimate and "true" representation of and connection to the figure of Pocahontas?

Clearly, both the earrings and the portrait are potent markers of the originary connection between Indianness and Europeanness. They both showcase the positive, transformative effects of European civilization on the "savage" Native other. However, the earrings, which represent a direct lineage to Pocahontas and all of her laudable and legendary experiences as well as her regal status, maintain a clear distinction between the colonizer and the colonized that the painting does not. With the earrings, both believers and non-believers in the legend can unproblematically accept or reject a connection with the Indianness that undergirds Anglo-American identity. In other words, by accepting the earrings as actual relics of the "Princess Pocahontas," believers can embrace an Anglicized link with Indianness that only flows in one direction; they can appreciate the elegant, "civilized" baubles that Pocahontas accepted and wore, much as she accepted Anglo-American culture, yet they can do so without having to accept any element of Indian culture or identity in return. They can remain separate from the "taint" of Indianness while still enjoying a proprietary connection to it. The earrings represent the positive transformation of "savage" Indianness by Anglo-American-ness without the anxiety of reciprocation or Indianness transforming Anglo-American identity. The portrait, however, with its depiction of both Pocahontas and her son, Thomas, confronts its viewers with

---

[8]   Additionally, in 2005 during the showing of the Jamestown materials in England, Bly Straube, then the curator of the Jamestown Rediscovery Project, noted in an interview that while it was not known for sure if the earrings were actually Pocahontas's, "the circumstantial evidence provides a decent case" (Prudames). Such statements, staged showings of the earrings, and their "Pocahontas" title all clearly validate and confirm the authenticity of the earrings in a way that the *Sedgeford Hall Portrait* is not authenticated.

[9]   My thanks go to Catherine Dean for bringing these test results on the earrings to my attention. The report from the London Assay office reveals with a 99 percent probability that the earrings were manufactured during the nineteenth century (APVA "Results").

the hybrid "mixed-blood" that, in order to maintain colonial identity, mastery, and utter difference from Indianness, must be rejected and overwritten, and so must the biracial reality of one of the subjects of the painting: Thomas Rolfe.

Destablizing "Mixed-Bloodedness": Thomas Rolfe

Born in 1615, Thomas Rolfe, almost certainly named after the governor of Jamestown colony, Sir Thomas Dale—the "patron" of John and Pocahontas who granted their request to marry—was literally a hybrid of American identity. His mother, the favorite daughter of Chief Powhatan, came to historical attention through her "salvation" of Captain John Smith during his captivity among the Powhatans in 1607. After experiencing a captivity of her own among the English at Jamestown, she eventually became a converted, transculturated Indian who not only took up the cultural values and accoutrements of the English colonists, but also changed her name and religion in order to marry one of them.[10]

Thomas's father, John Rolfe, was a newly married man of 24 when he first came to Jamestown in 1609 seeking his fortune as a merchant, later finding it as a tobacco farmer. After his English wife's death and subsequent extended contact with Pocahontas during her captivity in the Jamestown area, perhaps in the capacity of an English tutor, Rolfe realized his love for Pocahontas. In a 1614 letter to Sir Thomas Dale that covered both sides of four pieces of paper, Rolfe poured out his heart and asked the governor's permission to marry Pocahontas, noting that she was "to whom my hart and best thoughts are and have byn a longe tyme so intangled & inthralled in so intricate a Laborinth, that I was even awearied to unwynde my selfe thereout" (qtd. in Barbour 248).[11] Dale granted Rolfe's request and the couple were married that same year, but only after Pocahontas publicly declared herself a Christian, accepted Baptism, and received her new name of Rebecca.[12] The couple's marriage began the so-called "Peace of Pocahontas" that calmed the "war that had sporadically broken out between them [the Powhatans and the English], caused as much by English violations of custom, persons, or property as by Native fear, suspicion, and anger at the foreigners' incursions" (Allen 207). The peace lasted until about 1622, five years after Pocahontas's death, when Opechancanough, her more hostile uncle, launched open war against the English; this was perhaps "the first time that open warfare rather than sporadic armed conflict raged" in the colonies (Allen 207).

After their marriage, Rolfe and Pocahontas, now officially Mistress Rebecca Rolfe, lived on Rolfe's property across the river from Jamestown and began

---

[10]   In 1613 when she would have been about 16 or 18, Pocahontas was taken captive by Samuel Argall in order to gain leverage against Powhatan. See Samuel Purchas and Ralph Hamor.

[11]   For further discussion of Rolfe's "love letter," see Townsend, Faery, and Price.

[12]   The order of these events—Rolfe's official declaration of intent to marry Pocahontas, then Pocahontas's conversion and name reassignment, and finally, the marriage—has been analyzed as a significant indicator of Pocahontas's/the Powhatans' agency in dealing with the English. See Allen and Townsend for further discussion of these events.

conducting agricultural experiments with tobacco seeds from a species of the plant grown in the Spanish Caribbean. Before long, Rolfe was sending his first shipment of the milder tobacco to England for a hefty profit, not only turning the colony's bedraggled fortune around, but also breaking the Spanish monopoly on the exportation of tobacco. Rolfe's success with the tobacco may have been directly related to his Indian wife, who perhaps acquainted him with the much more effective method of carefully hanging each leaf to dry as the Indians did, or showed him how burned woodland and a southern exposure would aid in the crop's growth.[13]

Within a few months of his marriage to Pocahontas, Rolfe was appointed to the position of secretary of the colony, a position that brought with it a salary and increased rank. Rolfe consequently hired help to do the more menial chores around the farm that he and he wife would no longer be able, much less be expected, to do. Undoubtedly, many of the people who worked for the Rolfes were Natives, because as Camilla Townsend has noted, "Eight years later, when there were far more immigrants available and John was financially better off, he had only three white indentured servants laboring with him in the fields, and they were recent acquisitions" (131).

As a result, Rolfe's young wife, aged about 17, would have been surrounded by Indian companions who could converse in her own language and help her maintain a close link to her Native roots. It was also most likely these Native attendant-companions who aided Pocahontas with the birth of her son Thomas about a year after her marriage. The mother and her baby boy thrived due, no doubt, to the more sanitary and comforting birthing methods used by Pocahontas's Native American companions. This must have been a relief to Rolfe; he had already lost one child shortly after its birth, a daughter born in Virginia in 1610 of his first wife, who also died shortly thereafter due to complications from the birth. Thomas, unlike Rolfe's first born, however, would survive into adulthood.

In his childhood, Thomas would have lived a singularly bicultural lifestyle. Although born as the product of a mixed-race union between the "superior" English and the "inferior" Indian other, he would have publicly and officially lived an Anglicized existence. However, behind closed doors or out in the fields Thomas was probably as well acquainted with his Native roots as he was with his English, at least in his early years. Considering the close proximity of Pocahontas's family, neighboring tribes, and the presence of Native attendant-companions on the Rolfe farm, Thomas would have undoubtedly had intimate and extended contact with tribal peoples besides his mother. Helen Rountree notes that during the peaceful time after Pocahontas's and Rolfe's marriage and the birth of Thomas, the Rolfe family would have frequently visited the Powhatan settlement, because "keeping up with relatives was highly valued in both [English and Native] cultures" and that John Rolfe even met and became friends with Pocahontas's uncle, Opechancanough (*Pocahontas, Powhatan, Opechancanough* 167). Additionally, because of

---

[13]   Among the scholars who suggest Pocahontas's essential role in Rolfe's agricultural success are Mossiker, Allen, and Townsend.

Pocahontas's own proximity to Indianness, she would have been an active source of Indian culture herself for young Thomas, as well. Thomas would have lived his young years as more than just a person of biologically mixed ancestry who was culturally, linguistically, and socially identified as English; he would have lived a Native existence as well. He would have been conversant and knowledgeable in both cultures, both worlds, and although young, could have functioned comfortably in both, much as the adult James Printer would have in New England. However, Thomas might have been even more threatening and destabilizing to the colonists around him than a James Printer figure would have been because Thomas would have actually embodied both worlds; he was not just a cultural/ social crossover. Thomas was a literal, biological crossover, a mixture of identities that had heretofore been awkwardly and anxiously and repetitively demarcated as separate and opposite by the colonizers. He would have represented what the colonists had repeatedly told themselves could not exist, for if it did, it would void not only their own superiority and purity, but also their very existences.

Aside from a few short mentions in colonial historical records and his depiction in the *Sedgeford Hall Portrait*, Thomas Rolfe, after the death of his mother, all but ceases to exist. Very little is known about Thomas after about the age of two, and even less is known about his life as an infant in Jamestown—even "his birthplace is unknown … [and] his birth date is equally a mystery" (Rountree, *Pocahontas, Powhatan, Opechancanough* 167). What is factually known is that after living his entire life beyond the age of two in England, Thomas returned "to Virginia upon reaching manhood, arriving in the colony sometime in the mid-1630s, possibly as early as 1635 (at age twenty), not later than 1640 (at age twenty-five)" (Mossiker 311). A large inheritance of land, including a 400-acre plantation across the river from Jamestown that was left to him by his father, and an adjoining tract "three times as large" from his mother's uncle, Opechancanough, awaited him upon his arrival (Mossiker 312). Some scholars indicate Thomas's entire land holdings may have been as large as "two thousand acres" and that he "became a successful Virginia planter in his own right" (Price 271). Virginia records indicate that Thomas petitioned the governor in 1641 to go and visit his great-uncle, although it is unclear whether or not the visit actually occurred, and that in 1646, he was "commissioned a lieutenant in the colonial militia, assigned guard duty at Fort James in defense of the colonists against the Indians" (Mossiker 313). It is known he married Jane Poythress and had a single daughter with her, also Jane, but the dates and pertinent information about these events are not recorded. Thomas's name is finally mentioned in a land patent from 1658—the last time, one of the few, his name appears in historical record.

There is also a conspicuous absence in the mountains of Pocahontas scholarship where Thomas is concerned, perhaps stemming from (or continuing) his historic omission.[14] He becomes the prototype for the vanishing Indian or the tragic

---

[14]   Among the scholars who devote any discussion to Thomas at all—besides simply acknowledging his existence—include Helen Rountree, Frances Mossiker, Rebecca Blevins Faery, David Price (*Love and Hate in Jamestown*), and Camilla Townsend.

"mixed-blood" by virtue of his erasure from colonial memory. He left Jamestown at about the age of two in 1616 with his mother, father, and retinue of Indian "specimens" and attendant-companions bound for London so that his mother "might serve as a living advertisement for the Virginia Company's enterprise" and garner additional funds to keep the tobacco-growing endeavor afloat a bit longer (Faery 127). She, along with 20,000 pounds of the colony's finest tobacco, was, no doubt, intended to serve as an exemplar of the colonial enterprise, an "Indian paragon of missionary zeal and [a] cash crop, indicator[s] of solid investment opportunities" (Allen 271). Setting sail on the *Treasurer*, captained by Samuel Argall,[15] the Indian "princess" and her retinue arrived in London to an entirely different world. Given a stipend of four pounds a week by the Virginia Company, "Lady Rebecca" was suddenly expected to "dress like a Jacobean grande dame and feed her attendants decently" (Townsend 139). She would have to perform not only her exceptionality as an Indian princess, but also her fluency and ability as an English lady.

For all of the effort and bewilderment such accoutering may have caused Pocahontas, her efforts were rewarded. Mentions of "Pokahuntas" began appearing in diaries and letters such as those by John Chamberlain, and invitations began to arrive. Pocahontas was entertained, visited by, and remarked upon by the important and elite of London society; she was even invited to the annual Twelfth Night masque at the Court of King James, where she would have had a formal audience with the king. However, in all of these mentions in missives and diaries and public appearances, Thomas, Pocahontas's young son, who would have now been walking and talking, perhaps even uttering a pidgin-like amalgamation of Powhatan and English words, is conspicuously absent.

Although he would have only been around two years of age and certainly not a consideration when party invitations were issued or gossipy letters penned, Thomas's existence is not even registered as a passing remark by those who met with Pocahontas, both publicly and privately. Even John Smith, who visited her at her lodgings in England in late 1616, and takes pains to record her impassioned response to his refusal to accept the address "father," makes no mention of meeting Pocahontas's son and barely even acknowledges his existence.[16] Surely, Pocahontas would have been eager to show off her young son, especially to Smith, one of her oldest English acquaintances and someone whom she regarded with enough familiarity to address as "father"—whether for political reasons or

---

[15]   This, ironically enough, is the same boat sailing under the same captain that took Pocahontas downstream as a captive from her family and village to James Fort in 1613.

[16]   In the Fourth Book of the *The Generall Historie*, Smith mentions Thomas a mere handful of times and only in passing. For example, Smith notes that Pocahontas was "the first Christian ever of that [Powhatan] Nation, the first Virginian ever spake English or had a childe in marriage by an Englishman" (*Generall* 2:259–60). He also notes that upon Pocahontas's death, "Her little childe Thomas Rolfe ... was left at Plimoth with Sir Lewis Stukly" (*Generall* 2:262).

genuine affection.[17] And Smith, given his seeming fondness for Pocahontas as evidenced through his journey to visit her and the letter he wrote on her behalf to Queen Anne—again, whether motivated by his desires for self-promotion or by true attachment—surely would have been anxious to see and meet the child if only to use the moment as more grist for his own publicity mill.[18] The existence of this child would have undoubtedly been common knowledge to Smith and to others in England and might have been an exotic object of curiosity from the strange New World, just as his mother and her retinue were. Thomas would have ostensibly symbolized the reality of the commitment between Pocahontas and her English husband; Thomas would have been a physical realization of the "civilizing" effects of colonization and the rehabilitation of non-European others. However, there is no record, no preservation, no analysis of Thomas's existence among the dozens of portraits, stories, letters, histories, and plays that memorialize his mother's.

Thomas was the embodiment, the result, of the successful colonial project; he represented both the appropriation of the useful traces of Indian identity—its indigenity and nobility—and the domestication and colonization of its "savage" underbelly—he was, after all, an "English" man. He is what makes the many descendants of Pocahontas who and what they are. Without Thomas Rolfe, "the only aristocracy in America" would not, could not, exist; yet that existence is continually obscured from American cultural consciousness in favor of his mother's iconic "Indian princess" status (Edith Wilson as qtd. in Abrams 12). Despite his more securely Anglo-American identity and his patrilineal connections to elite families of both Native and English societies, Thomas's life is consistently overwritten by the narrative of his mother's.

Within Anglo-American society "mixed-bloodedness" was a transgressive and threatening construct not easily accepted or even understood. Cherokee scholar Jace Weaver observes that in Anglo-American imagination, in between the stereotypes of the "good Indian"—those Indians who live in harmony with nature in a state of simple, loyal liberty—and the "bad Indian"—the bloodthirsty, destructive "savage"—developed the even more derogatory stereotype of the "half-breed." Weaver writes, "An extension of the 'bad Indian' image, half-breeds have no redeeming virtues. They are neither White nor Indian. As such, they are the degenerate products of miscegenation, distrusted by both cultures and fitting in nowhere" (104). Clearly reflective of the dis-ease and anxiety caused by their hybrid identity, the marking of "mixed-blooded" people as without value in terms Anglo-American discourse and society was the colonizers' attempt to reassert the binary, to contain and regulate these disruptive hybrid bodies. The "almost but not quite" status of Indian "mixed-bloods" was simply too unsettling for Anglo-American subjectivity. Whereas a female and fictional mixed-blood like Unca

---

[17]   John Smith came to visit Pocahontas sometime in the fall of 1616 in her lodgings in Brentford, England. See Daniel Richter (*Facing East from Indian Country*), Paula Gunn Allen (*Pocahontas: Medicine Woman, Spy, Entrepreneur, Diplomat*), Camilla Townsend, and Philip Barbour for analysis of the meaning of this exchange.

[18]   John Smith wrote to Queen Anne in 1616 at the behest of the gentlemen of the Popular Party to interest her in receiving Pocahontas (Smith, *Generall* 2:258–60).

Eliza Winkfield could appear to be contained, at least on the surface, by discourses governing her gender, a male mixed-blood like Thomas Rolfe caused too much dis-ease and uncertainty in the minds of his contemporaries and descendants. Rather than being as marked "without value" as Jace Weaver asserts, a biracial Indian with "royal" heritage like Thomas were simply downplayed and forgotten by Anglo-Americans.[19] The earrings in the *Sedgeford Hall Portrait* can stay, but the historic reality of the biracial little boy has got to go.

Beyond his "mixed-bloodedness," however, Thomas is threatening to the project of colonization for another reason: his gender. Because Thomas was a biracial man, he further disrupted the colonial project of constructing a gendered, as well as raced, American identity. As I have previously discussed in Chapter 2, nations are ultimately social constructions that magnify the differences between dominant power groups and the excluded and powerless fringes in order to institutionalize the idea of the inequality among the citizens. Most often and most universally, these exclusions are gendered, leaving the terms of any nation-state to be defined by male desires, male difference, and male power. A figure like Thomas, who embodies markers of both the dominant power group—wealth, significant heritage, education—and the excluded, subaltern group—a "savage" race, culture, and physical appearance—all in a male body, creates conflict in the creation of a cohesive national narrative. His maleness, lineage, and wealth warrant recognition and a place in the construction of the new nation. He validates nation building through the transmission of Native land, power, and identity to the colonizers through blood inheritance, yet his Indianness combined with his maleness undercuts that transmission. Consequently, attempts to consolidate and construct the identity of a white, male American nation that is culturally separate from England becomes thwarted by the existence of a figure like Thomas Rolfe.

Thomas's presence, his masculine, "mixed-blood" status, highlights what Bhabha calls the "partializing process of hybridity" in which "the hybrid object ... retains the actual semblance of the authoritative symbol but revalues its presence by resisting it as the signifier of *Entstellung—after the intervention of difference*" ("Signs" 163–4, italics in original). In other words, Thomas occupies a space in between the colonizer and colonized, not merely blending the two identities, but transforming both, without fully resembling or performing either one. He shatters the binary sensibilities of difference that inflect and simplify colonial understanding. Consequently, such a transformative identity interrupts the hierarchical alignment of subjects in colonial discourse posing a "paranoid threat" to colonial power (Bhabha, "Signs" 165). The threat of the hybrid is "finally uncontainable because it breaks down the symmetry and the duality of self/other, inside/outside. In the productivity of power, the boundaries of authority—its reality effects—are always

---

[19] Although he was never to see his son again, John Rolfe did make reference to his son shortly after his return to Virginia in a letter to Sir Edwin Sandys in June of 1617. After meeting with the Indians to inform them of Pocahontas's death and explain Thomas's absence, Rolfe notes "The Indyans [are] very loving ... My wive's death is much lamented; my childe much desired, when it is of better strength to endure so hard a passage" (*Records* 3:70–71)

besieged by 'the other scene' of fixations and phantoms" (Bhabha, "Signs" 165–6). Thomas, therefore, must be purged from colonial consciousness, "sacrificed" through the "representational politics of the mutuality of loss and gain, and of surrender and redemption" that undergird colonialist hegemony (Chow 90). Yet this cannot ever be completely accomplished because hybrid, "mixed-blood" male figures like Thomas did, indeed, exist and their uncontainable, racially ambiguous identities, which were essential to the formation of a truly "American" lineage, did emerge in historic fact, record, art, and narratives, puncturing and fracturing the racialized boundaries of colonial power. Anglo-American women writers realized this disruptive potential. Just as previous iterations of colonial imagined Indianness—the pleading/threatening supplicant of the Bay Colony seal, the culturally ambivalent Christian Indian of Rowlandson's captivity, the duplicitous friend/foe Indian of Bleecker's narrative, the fluctuating Van de Passe engraving of Pocahontas, the biracial Unca Eliza Winkfield—were appropriated and exploited by Anglo women writers as avenues to provide legitimacy for their own authorial identities, so, too, was the male "mixed-blood."

Part 2
Narrative: Little Hobomok

In many ways, Charles Hobomok Conant, the son of Mary Conant and the noble, English-friendly Indian Hobomok in Lydia Maria Child's 1824 novel, *Hobomok*, is the literary equivalent of Thomas Rolfe. Born into an interracial marriage of notable Indian and English ancestry in one of the earliest English colonies in the New World, "Little Hobomok" as he is called by Child, lives a fictional life parallel to Thomas's historic one. Little Hobomok suffers the loss of his Indian parent at a very young age, just as Thomas did; after the age of about two, he lives a purely Anglicized life among the English side of his family, just as Thomas did; and he eventually ends up in England, leaving all remnants of his Indian heritage behind him in the New World, becoming an "Englishman" for all intents and purposes, just as Thomas did. Little Hobomok and his problematic "mixed-blood" presence, that biologic connection to Indianness, is essentially "erased" from Child's novel by its end, just as Thomas was "erased" from the historic lore surrounding the foundation of Jamestown and his Indian princess mother. The parallels are striking and not without significance.

Charles Hobomok Conant, like Thomas Rolfe before him, exemplifies the problematic existence of biracial children/people—particularly biracial males—in the formation of a distinctive New World Anglo identity. As I have discussed previously, the Indian (the colonialist-created fantasy) was a necessary component for the formation of a unique Anglo-American identity that was distinct from but also not simply a degenerate version of English identity. The Indian served colonialist discourse as an originary link to the American landscape and an "authentic" American identity, but also functioned as a savage anti-self for the English that could anxiously reaffirm their civilized and superior nature.

For Anglo-American women writers, though, the figure of the Indian served an additional purpose: she or he could validate and even excuse the writings of these authors when Indianness was invoked specifically in their texts. As we have seen with Mary Rowlandson and Ann Eliza Bleecker, the Indian could function as both a threatening menace to and surprising validator of white womanhood and the domestic realm, implicitly reiterating the value and importance of this sphere—and the female-authored texts about it. The appropriated figure of the Indian in these texts challenged the racist and sexist discourses that structured the newly forming American nation and identity. However, when the "Indian" being invoked in a text is no longer the unequivocal Other because of a literal "mixed-blood" identity and the added privilege of patriarchy, as in the case of the historic Thomas Rolfe and the fictional Charles Hobomok Conant, the legitimacy of the racial binaries and patriarchal discourses that underpin Anglo-American society can be pointedly critiqued.

Subtitled *A Tale of Early Times* and initially published anonymously and signed only "By an American," Lydia Maria Child's *Hobomok* relates the story of Mary Conant, the privileged daughter of a religiously intolerant Puritan father and an ailing mother, who is struggling to make a life in the rugged New World colony of Salem in the early seventeenth century. Mary's lover, the Episcopalian Charles Brown, is exiled from the colony for "fomenting disturbance" with his religious teachings and is supposedly killed in a shipwreck, leaving Mary on the verge of despair after suffering through the previous deaths of her beloved mother and visiting friend (Child 70). Distraught, Mary elopes with the Indian Hobomok, a friend to the English who had always held Mary in special regard. She lives with Hobomok in his Indian village outside of the English settlement for two years, even having a son with the Indian—the Thomas Rolfe-like Little Hobomok—until Charles Brown unexpectedly returns. True to his "Noble Savage" form, Hobomok symbolically divorces Mary, vanishing from the scene so Mary and their son can build an English life with Mary's original love. The groundbreaking novel, according to Carolyn Karcher, is ultimately based on an insight that would guide the remainder of Child's career as an activist and writer: to explore "interracial marriage [as] symbolizing both the natural alliance between white women and people of color, and the natural resolution of America's racial and sexual contradictions" (Introduction, xx). Most scholars who have examined *Hobomok* agree that Child's ultimate intent was to rupture and revise both the racist and patriarchal paradigms governing Anglo-American society.[20] However, within all

---

[20]   Additional critics who have examined Child's various re-visionary techniques in *Hobomok* include Carolyn Karcher, Shirley Samuels, Renee Bergland, Bruce Mills (*Cultural Reformations*), Mark G. Vasquez ("'Your Sister Cannot Speak to You and Understand You As I Do': Native American Culture and Female Subjectivity in Lydia Maria Child and Catharine Maria Sedgwick"), Carl H. Sederhorn ("Dividing Religion from Theology in Lydia Maria Child's *Hobomok*"), Robert Abzug (*Cosmos Crumbling*), Leland Person ("The American Eve: Miscegenation and a Feminist Frontier Fiction"), Harry Brown (*Injun Joe's Ghost*), and Laura Mielke (*Moving Encounters*), to name just a few.

of the critical discussion of Child's radical revisioning of facets of the racist and patriarchal colonial encounters at Salem (Naumkeak) and Plymouth, the settings of her novel, perhaps the most radical of her revisions—her introduction of a mixed-race child whose mother is white and father is Indian—warrants closer examination. [21]

It is Child's use of Indianness, particularly the presence of the biracial Charles Hobomok Conant, which serves as a ground from which she can not only validate her own identity as a female author but also launch her critique of early American hegemony. Child had to do so carefully, though, because of the masculinity that undergirded her Indian characters. She had to mine the indigenity of Native identity in order to write white womanhood—and white female authorship—into existence, but she must not inadvertently write a version of Indian masculinity into existence in the process, giving it dominance over Anglo-American women and equality with Anglo-American men. Consequently, little Hobomok's "almost but not quite" status as a "mixed-blood" child and his masculinity, while in infancy, serve to support Child's work in validating white feminine agency; in adulthood, though, Child must necessarily write this character into a marginalized existence, relegating him to an entirely acculturated Anglicized existence away from American soil—a de-emphasized fate strikingly similar to that of Pocahontas's only son, Thomas Rolfe. Male "mixed-bloodedness" was simply too uncontainable and too threatening to Anglo-American identity to remain unchecked, and in the case of Child, too threatening to her American feminine authorial identity because of its potential to reify patriarchal hegemony; as a consequence, it had to be carefully regulated and downplayed in her text—to be literally removed from contact with Americanness through an evacuation to England. [22] She has to write Indianness out of textual existence in order to write Anglo women and their agency into it.

Gender Trouble: Flipping the Binary

Child engages in a daring experiment with her characters not only by creating a character of mixed race—Charles Hobomok Conant—but also through the reversal of the races and genders of this child's parents from the accepted "norms" of interracial love and attraction. In the standard narratives of colonization, such

---

[21]   Harry J. Brown, in his *Injun Joe's Ghost*, addresses, although briefly, the implications of Hobomok and Mary Conant's child. Karen Woods Weierman also discusses the implications of Mary and Hobomok's marriage in her *One Nation, One Blood*, as does Nancy Sweet in "Dissent and the Daughter in *A New England Tale* and *Hobomok*."

[22]   Nancy Sweet ("Dissent and the Daughter in *A New England Tale* and *Hobomok*") briefly addresses this "whitening" of Little Hobomok, but reads it as a move by Child to redeem "the disobedient daughter-heroine" of Mary Conant (121). Sabina Matter-Seibel ("Native Americans, Women, and the Culture of Nationalism in Lydia Maria Child and Catharine Maria Sedgwick") also mentions that Child's assimilation of Little Hobomok is evidence of Child's belief that "Native Americans are capable of gradual assimilation into white culture through proper education" as a part of her larger argument about race and nationalism in the works of Sedgwick and Child (435).

as narrative of Pocahontas's and John Rolfe's union, it is the "savage" woman who engages in a relationship with the "civilized" Anglo-American male. Even in the imagined, romanticized versions of Pocahontas's life, popularized in the nineteenth century and later in the 1985 Disney version, *Pocahontas*, and the 2005 Terrence Malick film *The New World*, in which she carries an unrequited love for John Smith instead of Rolfe, the flow of desire and masculine authority remains intact; it is the feminine other cleaving unto the masculine colonizer.[23] This order of coupling was, as Margaret D. Jacobs notes, widely "tolerated within American society. Liaisons between white men and non-white women did not violate the hierarchical order that developed between European Americans, African Americans, and American Indians. Rather, they represented extensions and reinforcements of colonialism, conquest, and domination" (31).

Child deviates from this standardized narrative in *Hobomok*, however, and inscribes Little Hobomok's father as the noble, high-ranking Indian friend of the English, and his mother as the equally high-ranking Puritan woman who commits herself to an Indian marriage. This radical move was especially bold on Child's part, because "there was widespread opposition to marriage between white women and Native American men" in colonial America (Jacobs 32). Additionally, "[w]hen white women and non-white men engaged in sexual relationships or married, they violated the colonial, racial, and patriarchal order. Within this order, white men dominated both their daughters and wives as well as groups of subjugated peoples, including American Indians and African Americans" (Jacobs 31–2).

Such unions gave the colonized, dominated Indian male "a power and a prerogative [over white women] that many white men believed should be theirs alone" (Jacobs 34). Interracial marriage was, in general, frowned upon in the nineteenth century. Karen Woods Weierman notes, "Interracial marriage was a dangerous threat, both in its production of biracial children and in its implication of equality for people of color ... [it] thus formed a powerful narrative of disruption, threatening the very foundation of [American] racialized society" (4). However, interracial marriage between a white woman and a man of color was even more destabilizing. Consequently, Child's choice to reverse the gender and race of her most significant characters rewrites not only the master narratives governing New World interracial relationships, but also the discourses governing Anglo-American masculinity and authority. She has introduced a liaison in which white patriarchy has no governance over the behaviors and actions of either of the two main actors within the relationship, Mary and Hobomok, and a situation in which colonial discourse fails to dominate the two main objects of its control: white women and non-white men. Child has thwarted patriarchal hegemony and created a point of rupture through which white womanhood can textually assert its own agency by making choices and living a lifestyle—at least temporarily, as in Mary's case—that is beyond the regulatory framework of the gendered and raced

---

[23]   Unca Eliza's mother, Princess Unca, in *The Female American*, deviates from this pattern as I demonstrate in Chapter 3. However, her challenges to the paradigm of the female other cleaving unto the male colonizer are, of course, intentionally veiled by the author.

discourses of colonialism. Further, by recording that narrative into textual form, Child has inscribed feminine agency and, more importantly, a feminine authorial voice, onto the standard narrative that she is aggressively rewriting.

Child further builds her specifically feminine and American authorial identity through her narrative structure, which alternates among multiple authorial voices as well as two distinct time periods. The novel begins with a short preface in which the genesis of the text is revealed through an anecdotal story told by the "friend" of the text's author. "Frederic" relates how his friend, a young, unnamed man of "an awkward and unprepossessing appearance" (Child 4) set out in the summer of 1823 to write a "New England novel" (Child 3) with only some encouragement and historical pamphlets, both of which are provided by Frederic. Immediately following this preface is chapter 1 in which the actual "novel" drafted by the awkward young man begins. However, before the plot of *Hobomok* is put into narrative action, there is another short "introduction" at the beginning of chapter 1 in which the awkward young author waxes poetic on his nationalistic pride as a native New Englander and the "mighty effort" of the American forefathers some 200 years ago whose "bold outlines of ... character alone remain to us" (Child 6). The reader is then told that although the day-to-day details of the lives of these colonial leaders are generally lost to contemporary audiences, some of those details "have lately been unfolded in an old, worn-out manuscript, which accidentally came in [his] way" (Child 6). The manuscript, purportedly written by one of the author's ancestors who as a young man fled religious persecution and arrived in Salem (Naumkeak) "about the middle of June 1629," is then recorded almost verbatim by the young author, constituting the body of the narrative and placing the remainder of the action in the narrative squarely in the seventeenth century (Child 7).

This narrative, which thus far moves between multiple narrators—three young men to be exact—and two different time periods—the "present" of Frederic, the awkward young author, and Child herself, and the "ancestral past" of Salem in 1629—employs strategies used by Child to ground her text, and her revisionary ideas within it, in both patriarchy and history so she can then rewrite them. By setting her text in the earliest and most hallowed moments of colonial history and giving it the most revered of voices—a religiously persecuted male ancestor—Child is providing her text with a sense of authenticity and authority that lend her words and her story weight, connecting her words to the ancestral past and genesis of the American nation. She is able, as Carolyn Karcher observes, to "evade sanctions against female authorship by speaking through a series of male narrators" (*First Woman* 22). Molly Vaux has similarly argued that the preface functions as "an elaborate cover story in which Child not only masks her gender but also supports herself with a double" in the form of a young male writer in order to "open a space where she [Child] can safely express her own ambitions and inhibitions" (131, 132).[24] Additionally, by providing her text with a native

---

[24]   Paula Kot ("Engendering Identity: Doubts and Doubles in Lydia Maria Child's *Hobomok*") has also noted that the layers of narrators in the preface allow Child to "challeng[e] what the novel seems to optimistically affirm: the fulfillment of America's

American setting and an Indian protagonist, whose name provides the narrative its title, Child is establishing her narrative as representatively and foundationally American; it is an indigenous text. As author, Child is reaching back from her present day and time of 1823–1824 in order to position her ideas as coeval with the founding of the American colonies and as authentically "American" so that she can begin her revision of history.

With numerous "editorial" interruptions from the author in which he "takes the liberty of substituting [his] expressions for [the] antiquated and almost unintelligible style" (Child 7) and a bold acknowledgment by the author's friend Frederic in the preface that this work of fiction was written through the aid of "many old, historical pamphlets," Child undercuts the austerity and reverence bestowed upon such sources (Child 4). As Carolyn Karcher has noted, such authorial moves allow Child "to appropriate the narrative authority of the Puritan chroniclers while rewriting the hagiography they had bequeathed to posterity" (Introduction, xx). She cloaks herself in patriarchy and history in order to expose and revise the selective memory and exclusions practiced by these institutions. At the same time, however, and more interestingly, there is Child's erasure of any evidence of Indianness in these initial, foundational moments of the formation of America. Hobomok, the titular character of the text, doesn't even appear until the very end of chapter 1, and then, it is as a mysterious figure who springs into the circle of Mary's husband divining ceremony and has to speak to Mary in order to "convince her that he was real flesh and blood" (Child 14).[25] Hobomok is a one-dimensional, stock character, the "lovesick young man," whose Indianness serves only to propel Child's agenda of refiguring the patriarchal and racist systems of Euro-America. He is not grounded in specific cultural and historical moments; rather he is the Indian from the Massachusetts Bay Colony seal, begging for European domination through domestication. He is an updated version of Mary Rowlandson's flattened out Indians and Ann Eliza Bleecker's domestic-destroying Indians; however, instead of being a wild-eyed, blood-thirsty "savage" as Rowlandson's and Bleecker's Indians were, Hobomok is now a laudable "Noble Savage"—more in line with Pocahontas and Unca Eliza Winkfield—seeking all the accoutrements of English civilization through a romantic union, a steam-rolled image of Indianness that is just as problematic as (although less "savage" than) Rowlandson's and Bleecker's versions are.

While Child is obviously banking on the colonial fantasies of Indianness and Hobomok's future marriage to Mary to ground her ideas in a Native authenticity at this early point in chapter 1, she is also removing the historical fact of Hobomok's Indianness from the political, religious, and colonial focus of her text. These first few pages of the text deal overtly with the historicity of the newly arriving colonists, the dire situation of the colony at Salem, and the religious

---

quest for an independent and 'native' American identity, embodied in its masculine narrator and his Puritan forefathers" (81).

[25]   For more in-depth readings of Mary's witch-craft like ceremony for a husband, see for example Karcher, Sederholm, Person, Maddox, Bergland, Samuels, and Brown.

(and patriarchal) intolerance governing not only the central character of Mr. Conant, but male authority in general. Hobomok, however, only enters into the text as an illusory and forbidden love match for Mary, an ahistorical spirit of the forest out to "watch the deer tracks" and to "make the Manitto Asseinah green as the oak tree" (Child 14), not as a political, physical reality in terms of the colony's historical corporeality. He is present, but displaced from the actual historical occurrences (and significances) in the text. "Real" Indianness is removed to where it can't be seen, or at least doesn't really "count"—to the romantic world of love potions and silly lovesick girls. While Hobomok is pivotal to Child's narrative and is a necessity for her ultimate critique, he is also a threatening reminder of the "real live" Indianness underpinning the colony's (and America's) existence that must be textually removed to a place where he can't really matter so that what does matter—Anglo womanhood and female agency—can be explored.

In *The National Uncanny: Indian Ghosts and American Subjects*, Renee Bergland has observed that "Child's work ... uses the metaphors and plots of Indian spectralization and romantic love to assert female subjectivity and to claim the body and the political community for white American women" (63). She argues that "[w]hite women and dark men dwell together in an American netherworld" and that Child's primary purpose in the text is "to bring white women out of spectrality" (Bergland 69, 70). While Hobomok is certainly minimized as a character in the opening chapter of the text—he is essentially a romanticized stereotype—he and Mary are never entirely spectralized by Child. Although each character is, indeed, at times described in apparitional terms, Mary and Hobomok are developed by Child as concrete, embodied entities who actively participate into her re-visioning of colonial history, most especially through their physical union as husband and wife and the birth of their son. It is this union with Hobomok and his Indianness that becomes the footing from which Mary is able to assert her own agency and Child is able to launch her critique of white patriarchy. Rather than being a disembodied specter from which Mary, and Child as a white woman herself, seek to escape, Hobomok's Indian presence in the novel is instead the foundation that authenticates Mary's, and Child's, voice as being "American." Although his Indianness is mediated and redrawn by Child to suit her authorial goals, the character of Hobomok, after his initial encounters with the reader, becomes a substantial—albeit at times a flattened—presence rather than a spectral one. Child's entire premise of disrupting the colonial discourses to posit new possibilities for white womanhood through Mary's marriage to and production of a child by Hobomok requires the fact of Hobomok's very real presence. Simply put, Hobomok has to be "real" in order for his son—and Child's critiques—to be real.

Domesticating Indianness, Revaluing White Womanhood

As the plot of *Hobomok* advances, Hobomok, as a character, figures into the action of the text more significantly. Child develops Hobomok's adversarial relationship with the anti-English Indian Corbitant, which ultimately leads to Hobomok warning the English of an impending Indian attack, and Hobomok's well-known reputation, even among his own tribe, as one "whose loves and hates had become identified with the English" (Child 31). Child also develops the affections of Hobomok, an Indian "cast in nature's noblest mould," for Mary Conant (Child 36). Child describes Hobomok as an Indian who "looked upon [Mary] with reverence, which almost amounted to adoration," even facing taunts from his own tribe because of it (Child 33). Corbitant, for example, while arguing with Hobomok about the threat posed by the English colonists to the area Indian tribes, "sarcastically" sneers at him, "Hobomok saves his tears for the white-faced daughter of Conant, and his blood for the arrow of Corbitant" (Child 31). He is, as Nancy Sweet has pointed out, "such an exemplar of Christian virtue that for Child's characters—and some readers—he no longer plausibly resembles a Native American" (120). Clearly, Hobomok's affection for Mary (and consequently, the English), which is described by Child in stereotypical terms tinged with racist undertones, is the single dominating characteristic of his character. It is what motivates all of his actions within the course of the novel: his informing the English of the Indian attack against the colony; his marriage to a raving Mary after she suffers through the death of her mother, her good friend, Lady Arabella, and her lover, Charles Brown; and finally, his release of Mary and their son from their ties to him at the end of the novel so that she can be reunited with her white lover, Charles.

For Child, Hobomok's recognition of Anglo-American superiority and his desire for white womanhood, while certainly portrayed as pure of motive, do not need to be questioned or even explained. There is no need to justify Hobomok's choice of Anglicized lifestyle and possibly insane white wife; the allure and power of white womanhood and the domestic unions that result from it, Child Anglo-centrically implies, are explanation enough. Child figures Hobomok's English-loving Indianness so that it serves to validate the potency of the feminine domestic through his desire for it and ultimate acceptance of it. Because Hobomok is literally one with nature—he originates from "nature's noblest mould" and exits the novel by "plung[ing] into a thicket and disappear[ing]" (Child 36, 141)—his acceptance of Child's domestic plan validates it in a way that Puritan patriarchy with its worn out, verbose old manuscripts and man-made laws can never be validated. Indianness, in this instance, while relegated to a one-dimensional form that keeps it cartoonishly unreal and distant from the historical moment of the text, authenticates Child's ideas and ties them to an autochthonous New World identity, separate from patriarchal hegemony.

However, at the same time, Child must disavow the validation and agency provided by Hobomok's Indianness. If she places too much stock in the power and authority of a male Indian figure, Child runs the risk of undermining her entire critique. Child must walk the fine line between investing her Native character with too much power, making him and his Indian blood the only authoritative New World identity, and dismantling Hobomok's natural authority as a New World indigene whose acceptance of white domesticity empowers Child's alternative plan for civilizing America, much as Ann Eliza Bleecker did with her critique of nationalism in *The History of Maria Kittle*. Just as Bleecker carefully measured her use of Indianness, mediating between stereotypical but potent images of "bloodthirsty," destructive "savages" and images of Indians who valued white domesticity, in order to successfully critique the masculine discourses of nationalism, so too must Child mediate between versions of Indianness as being authentically, independently "American" and as longing for Anglo-American domestication. Both women artfully rewrite Indian identity—particularly male Indian identity—in order to create their own identities as women writers of history.

To temper Hobomok's authority and maintain her own as a white woman writer, Child enables the attraction between Mary Conant and Hobomok to grow, but under uneven conditions—Hobomok is far more invested in loving Mary than she is in loving him. Child is careful to establish Hobomok's Indianness and the autochthony that goes with it, as subject to Mary's white womanhood. Hobomok's affection for Mary is direct and unwavering throughout the text, but Mary's reactions toward Hobomok are more ambivalent; the flow of desire only moves in one direction—toward the colonizer. When the reader is first introduced to Hobomok as he leaps into Mary's marriage-divining circle in the moonlight her reaction is one of horror and disbelief; she utters an "involuntary shriek of terror" and is on the verge of "retreating from the woods" even after she recognizes her Indian friend (Child 14). Charles Brown then appears, and "Mary eagerly [catches] his arm, and seem[s] glad amid her terror and agitation, to seek the shelter of his offered protection" (14). Later the next day, she tells her friend Sally Oldham that she has done "a wicked thing" that "frightens [her] to think thereof" (Child 20). Hobomok's presence in this circumstance—in the forest alone at midnight with Mary—incites much anxiety and fear for the young white woman. He is the "unthinkable" for Mary in numerous ways.

However, in the safe confines of her home surrounded by her parents and the "civilization" of Naumkeak, Mary finds Hobomok an intriguing and even desirable companion. After her white lover, Charles Brown, has been exiled to England, Mary suffers through a "long and dreary winter," during which there "was nothing to break the monotony of the scene, except the occasional visits of Hobomok" (Child 84). Hobomok becomes even more attentive to Mary at this point in the narrative, bringing her furs and other tokens of his affections, because "love deep and intense, had sunk far into [his] bosom" (Child 84). Mary, suffering through the absence of her beloved Charles, enjoys, albeit guiltily, these overtures. Child notes:

> A woman's heart loves the flattery of devoted attention, let it come from what source it may. Perhaps Mary smiled too complacently on such offerings; perhaps she listened with too much interest, to descriptions of the Indian nations, glowing as they were in the brief figurative language of nature ... [F]emale vanity sinfully indulged [love's] growth. (Child 84–5)

Mary also, in gushing gratitude for the exquisite gray fox furs and shells Hobomok has brought her, tells him, "I am going to make you a wampum belt of the shells you brought, and I want you to tell me how to put them together," not only stoking the fires of his attentions, but also showing her willingness to spend more time with

Hobomok and learn about his culture (Child 86). Additionally, Mary hangs on the words of Hobomok's stories, prompting him to continue and asking questions as the Indian tells the tales of his Native culture; she even accompanies Hobomok and his friends, chaperoned of course, on a nighttime deer hunt during which Hobomok displays his ample skill with a bow. Clearly, Mary is interested in, if not encouraging, the attentions Hobomok is bestowing upon her. She is also just as clearly interested in Hobomok's Indian identity. Through her willingness to learn about and even adopt some of the cultural markings of Indianness as introduced to her by Hobomok, Mary is flirting with Native identity. By having Mary accept the furs and shells, and learn Hobomok's stories and traditions with relish, Child is not only setting the seeds for the future marriage of the young couple, she is also having Mary "absorb" Indian indigenity. Mary is becoming N/native through her relationship with Hobomok. Although the idea of Mary's whiteness being a blank canvas that can imbibe prime bits and pieces of Indianness is certainly reflective of the colonial hegemony Child is writing against, it is also a bold move by Child that invests Mary (and other Anglo women by proxy) with N/native authority and a truly American identity that white patriarchy does not have.

Child is sure to make clear, however, that Hobomok's intentions toward Mary are innocently, and quite naturally motivated. Child writes that

> the untutored chief knew not the strange visitant which had usurped such empire in his heart; if he found himself gazing up her face in silent eagerness, 'twas but adoration for so bright an emanation from the Good Spirit; if something within taught him to copy, with promptitude, all the kind attentions of the white man, 'twas gratitude for the life of his mother which she had preserved. (Child 84)

Hobomok's feelings for Mary stem from both gratitude and a cognizance of her innate goodness, as well as a deep-seated desire to adopt the ways of white man. He is, as Sabina Matter-Seibel has shown, "a domestic character" despite his hunting and fighting prowess (417). He is desirous of winning the recognition and acceptance of the colonizers, particularly those of the blushing, youthful Mary.

Here, Child is developing the attachment between Hobomok and Mary Conant in carefully measured steps. If there were no return of affection on the part of Mary, Hobomok's pursuit of her would become aggressive and threatening to white patriarchy and white readers; he would become the "savage other" who desires and corrupts white womanhood with his dark desires, even vaguely threatening kidnap and capture. However, if Mary is too receptive of Hobomok's overtures, she becomes too rebellious to be given any credence as a character. She becomes the ungovernable, passionate woman whose protection and management the patriarchal paradigms of society were purportedly enacted to protect. Child circumvents such issues by bringing Mary to the brink of infatuation with her Indian suitor, but with the full realization that what she is doing is unacceptable; for example, Mary regards her relationship with Hobomok with "shuddering superstition" (Child 85). Additionally, Child depicts Hobomok as genuinely and innocently infatuated with Mary's English goodness, essentially making him into the colonizer's willing—but chaste—love-slave. As Carolyn Karcher notes, "Child's symbolism hints at the factors that create a natural alliance between white women and people of color" (*First Woman* 28). Such a combination allows Child to pursue her interracial love affair and simultaneous restructuring of patriarchy unopposed. However, when it comes to the actual marriage of Mary and her Indian lover, Child turns many accepted norms on their ends. While she quickly moves to make Mary's decisions and behaviors toward Hobomok excusable/understandable for her readers, she also puts Mary in the driver's seat of that relationship.

Mary's marriage to Hobomok occurs shortly after and in direct response to the deaths of her mother and her dear friend, Lady Arabella, in chapter 15, and that of Charles Brown in a shipwreck immediately after in chapter 16. Initially, after the deaths of the two women, Mary, although devastated, is able to "discharge her daily duties with tolerable cheerfulness" (Child 115). The ideas of "asking her father's permission to return to England" and the "prospect of Brown's arrival in the ensuing spring" keep Mary's spirit alive and her thought processes intact (Child 144). However, when Hobomok appears a short time later, bearing a letter from Plymouth that reveals Charles Brown was a passenger on a shipwrecked East India vessel, Mary's "heart reel[s], and the blow threaten[s] to suspend her faculties" (Child 117). And destroy her faculties it does. Mary becomes a pale and trembling shell of herself, suffering "a partial derangement of [her] faculties" and "[a] bewilderment of despair that almost amounted to insanity" (Child 120). With her brain in a "burning agony" she visits the grave of her mother where Hobomok finds her and tells her he "wish he could make [her] happy" in the stereotypical broken English of Indians (Child 121). With the remembrance of "the idolatry [Hobomok] had always paid her, and in the desolation of the moment, [Mary] felt as if he was the only being in the wide world left to love her" (Child 121); so, in "the midst of this whirlwind of thoughts and passions" she proposes to Hobomok. Mary says, "I will be your wife, Hobomok, if you love me" (Child 121).

This scene of consensual miscegenation has polarized readers and scholars since the publication of *Hobomok* in 1824. Originally described by a reviewer in the *North American Review* as "unnatural … [and] revolting," Mary's proposal to her Indian lover is no less disruptive and disputed among scholars today. For example, Harry Brown notes the scene is one more reminiscent of "an abduction rather than an elopement" that occurs as a "tragic consequence of the collapse of [Mary's] will" (57), while Carolyn Karcher sees it as a moment where Mary seizes "the right to define her own fate, choose her own religion, reclaim her own sexuality, assert her own worth" (Introduction, xxx), and Renee Bergland suggests Mary's proposal was "an attempt to evade death, and to claim her own fate" (75).[26] While these readings do focus on Mary's agency (or lack thereof) in her proposal

---

[26] Additionally, Nina Baym sees the scene as one in which Mary's proposal "is a maddened attempt to escape from a community to which she is so far superior, and in which she is totally isolated" (156), and Karen Weierman as the first step in Child's progression toward depicting interracial marriages as "loving, mutually rewarding relationships between equals" in later texts (95). Laura Mielke sees the marriage as indicative of Child's acknowledgment and support of a "biological structure, the family" (31).

to Hobomok—and Child's revisionary efforts as author—they ultimately do not underscore the complexity of Child's maneuverings in this scene. There is an intricate and bold textual negotiation by Child between Indianness and womanhood, a careful moderation of binaristic extremes that enables the emergence of female authorship, one of many Child makes in the narrative. Mary neither completely collapses and "gives up" nor flagrantly asserts her rights in this scene. Instead, Child has her carefully walk a line between the two extremes, bringing Mary to the brink of full and conscious rebellion and to the edge of being absolutely incapable of reason, and therefore, not responsible for her actions. Mary's "insanity" is, after all, only temporary and rightfully due to the overwhelming grief she suffers from the loss of her mother, her friend, and her lover. Mary's lapse in judgment and subsequent Indian marriage is therefore justified, almost understandable.

Because Mary's actions fly directly in the face of the racist, patriarchal paradigms under which she lived in the seventeenth century and Child still lived in the nineteenth century, Child must carefully temper Mary's aggressive actions of feminine rebellion through the reactions and behaviors of the Indian Hobomok. Child balances Mary's disruption of patriarchal hegemony through her dominant, masculine act of pursuing a husband and marriage by reinforcing colonial hegemony through Hobomok's eager and worshipful acceptance of the proposal. This is made clear when Hobomok confesses the nature of his love to Mary. He says, "Hobomok has loved you many long moons … but he loved like as he loves the Great Spirit" (Child 121). Hobomok's love is not a lustful, carnal one, but rather one of distant adoration undergirded by a sense of his own inadequacy as an Indian and his perception of Mary's superiority as an English woman. He loves and worships Mary almost as one would a deity, a "Great Spirit," making his acceptance of Mary's proposal into a model of what the "acceptable" relationship of the colonized to the colonizer should be: pure subservient veneration. Consequently, Mary's aggressive and threatening act of agency is mediated by the positive result it achieves: a sort of willing "domestic colonization" of the Indians. The marriage also, as Nancy Sweet has suggested, allows Mary to undergo a positive "transformation … that finally reconciles and fits her for life in America" something she has previously railed against (119). Rather than simply working to reinforce or disrupt the colonial system, Child has used Hobomok's Indianness, and its colonial-perceived compliance, as a justification for Mary's radical act. The ends justify the means, or so Child seems to boldly suggest.

Child further mediates these bold assertions by placing Mary into a state of "unreasonableness of mingled grief and anger," and under a "stupefying influence," so that she only delivers "mournful and incoherent soliloqu[ies]" when she speaks at all (122–3). Mary is understandably, legitimately, heartbroken and bereft over the loss of so many people who were close to her, so her breakdown in reason is not a sign of weakness, but rather a sign of her sensitive nature and is excusable. Yet, a woman who is deemed "mad" by her future mother-in-law is clearly not capable of making sound decisions about whom she should marry and for what reasons, whether her "madness" stems from legitimate reasons or not (Child 124). Consequently, Mary's choices and actions are devalued or at least downplayed in the narrative even though the cause of her incoherent state is reasonable. Although Mary has exercised agency in negotiating relations with the Native other, much as Maria Kittle did when she brokered a peace treaty with an Indian party in Bleecker's *The History of Maria Kittle*, the potency of that agency is undercut because of its entanglement with Indianness, and in Mary's case, insanity—albeit a justifiable and temporary insanity. A deal made with an Indian, even if based on progressive ideas of unity rather than disunity (as both Kittle and Mary Conant establish) isn't really a deal at all, at least in Anglo-American terms, because it was made with a non-citizen—an "uncivilized savage." Similarly, such a choice, even a radical one, isn't much of a choice—or a threat to established authority—if you make it while not in possession of your faculties. Bleecker and Child both suggest the power of Indianness for establishing white, feminine identity and authority in instances such as these. These women authors are aware that Indianness, especially male Indianness, is what can legitimize the actions of their female protagonists in ways that white patriarchy cannot and will not; however, it is ultimately a fraught legitimacy, because it has to be so carefully justified and distanced from the Indianness that enables it and because it often must occur at the problematic expense of feminine agency.

Returning to the Fold: The Marriage that Never Was

Further veiling Mary's feminine agency and advancing the notion that Mary's choice to marry Hobomok was a non-choice, a fictional non-reality, is the process through which Hobomok ends his marriage to her. Once Charles Brown has returned from his presumed death and is ready to renew his relationship with Mary, Hobomok, upon encountering Charles in the woods before anyone else, agrees to relinquish his hold on Mary and the couple's two-year-old son, Little Hobomok. Hobomok tells Charles, "Good and kind [Mary] has been; but the heart of Mary is not with the Indian … Hobomok will go far off … and Mary may sing the marriage song in the wigwam of the Englishman" (Child 139). Before Brown can protest, Hobomok is gone, disappearing into the wilderness, leaving Charles free to rekindle his love with Mary. Later on at the home of Mary's good friend, the now-married Sally Oldham Collier, a note is found attached to the carcasses of three foxes and a huge deer. It is from Hobomok and reads:

> This doth certifie that the witche hazel sticks, which were givene to the witnesses
> of my marriage are all burnt by my requeste: therefore by Indian laws, Hobomok
> and Mary Conant are divorced. And this I doe, that Mary may be happie … The
> deere and foxes are for my goode Mary, and my boy. (Child 146)

Although dictated to and signed by Governor Edward Winslow and containing the mark of Hobomok, the note underscores further, at least for English audiences, the "unreal" state of Mary's marriage. Her commitment to Hobomok is severed by the "mere" burning of a few twigs and Hobomok's declaration (the word of an Indian, no less) that the marriage is finished. There are no appeals to either colonial or

Christian religious authorities to dissolve this union; instead, Indians who bore witness to the marriage are the authorities asked to grant the divorce by burning symbolic sticks. This was clearly a union that was only recognized and sanctioned within the Indian community, and is not, Child is suggesting, anything to be held against Mary or prevent her return to the colonial fold because it was not "real" in terms of English law. Additionally, the animal offerings Hobomok leaves behind, particularly the deer, signify an interchangeability between the dead animal and Hobomok's own Indian body; Shirley Samuels notes, "The dead body of the deer ... serves as a gift to feed those left behind, even as it implies the parallel substitution of his [Hobomok's] own conveniently dead body"—a substitution that also negates the "reality" of the couple's marriage (*Reading* 61).

Further undermining the legality of the union is the reason cited for the dissolution of the marriage: so that "Mary may be happie." "Happiness" was certainly a non-standard reason to end a marriage in seventeenth-century Anglo-American society, and the fact that it is Mary's happiness being considered would be almost unfathomable. Although Child is clearly imbuing Mary with agency in allowing her to procure her own happiness and then endowing the achievement of that happiness with value, these moves are only possible through the endorsement of an Indian, which, in colonial America, had no value. Mary technically has done no wrong by entering into marriage with an Indian; however, at the same time, Child takes pains to demonstrate that Mary's marriage is authentic. She gives Mary and Hobomok a child together. Children that resulted from the unions of white women and a racially "other" man were especially challenging to the established social order because, "[n]either white nor Indian, [they] made a mockery of racial categories, revealing their instability and impermanence" (Jacobs 34).

Because so much of Child's critique involves the subversion of binaries that undergird the white, patriarchal structures of American identity—man/woman, Christian/heathen, culture/nature, colonizer/colonized—she needs those binaries to be firmly in place and universally understood—not thrown into disarray by a character—if she is to successfully unravel them. The existence of a complex and figure like Charles Hobomok Conant, who does the work of destabilizing these very binary structures—in essence negating their existence—potentially undoes Child's interrogation of the racist and gendered paradigms in the text. How can she critique structures that one of her own characters disavows as existing? Consequently, she must ultimately downplay his presence and remove his "mixed-blood" identity from her critique.

Simultaneously, however, Child needs the figure of Charles Hobomok Conant in her narrative in order not only to validate the authenticity of her text, but also to embody her alternative solutions to the dichotomies governing Anglo-American society. By bringing in a biracial, Thomas Rolfe-like figure, a male heir who can transmit his heritage patrilineally, Child is signifying ancestral claims to the American land and unique Indian cultural identity through literal blood ties, as well as positing a way to disrupt the tyranny of Anglo-American patriarchy, through a conventionally feminine means: marriage, children, and a traditionally domestic existence. Little Hobomok is Child's link to Indian "authenticity" that validates her narrative possibilities for a differently raced and gendered American nation as well as Mary's acts of agency; however, the uncontainable nature of his biracial identity and his problematic ties to patriarchy as a man demand his withdrawal from the text.

When Hobomok does not return home after his encounter with Charles Brown, Mary is devastated, lamenting, "perhaps, like everything else that I ever loved, he is snatched away from me" (Child 147). She clearly has grown to rely on and even love Hobomok, a point that is underscored by the existence of little Hobomok, Mary's child with the Indian.[27] This child confirms, even without patriarchal or legal sanctification, the realness of Mary's marriage and the potential of such interracial unions to bring Indianness and Englishness together in a fruitful way. Further, without little Hobomok, Child's dismantling of white patriarchy would falter. He is the "proof" that Child needs to underpin her critique of colonial hegemony; he demonstrates that Indianness can in some way be incorporated into the American identity without being eradicated. However, little Hobomok simultaneously destabilizes this critique and consequently, must be contained within the text.

Once Charles Brown returns to Mary and declares his intentions to marry her and raise "the brave boy" as his own son, little Hobomok's presence becomes problematic (Child 148). The once adored and petted child of Mary, for whom she felt "more love ... than she thought she should ever again experience" when she was a member of Indian society, becomes a permanent mark of shame and guilt that Mary must carry back with her into colonial civilization (Child 136). For example, when Brown proposes that Mary be his wife "either here or in England," Mary refuses on account of little Hobomok. "I cannot go to England," she tells Brown, "My boy would disgrace me and I will never leave him" (Child 148). At the wedding, the young child's "restless motions" at the service must be restrained by his mother, with "her hand resting on the sleek head of the swarthy boy" (Child 149). Little Hobomok, who through his "mixed blood" already ties Mary to Indianness permanently—she "will never leave him"—is now a literal physical bodily extension of Mary at the public marriage ceremony through the placement of her hand on his head. He is a visible marker to all in attendance of her entanglement with Indianness that simply by virtue of his existence can never be denied or forgotten. Even Mary's stodgy, unsupportive father warms to the dark little boy, making him a "peculiar favorite" (Child 150), but only, Child is careful to explain, because of a "consciousness of blame, and ... a mixed feeling of compassion and affection" (Child 149). Little Hobomok has become a guilty problem for the family and a hurdle in the process of Mary's redemption into Anglo-American society. On one hand, he is Mary's son, a descendant of one of the hardy, founding families of the colony with prominent English ties. He is

---

[27] See Harry Brown and Carolyn Karcher for alternative critical views of Mary's marriage.

also nominally marked as Mary's descendant; as Mary explains to Charles, Little Hobomok "[a]ccording to the Indian custom, took the name of his mother ... Charles Hobomok Conant" (Child 149).

On the other hand, little Hobomok is also unquestionably Mary's *Indian* son, a direct descendant of both "savage" and elite Puritan blood who would, potentially, as a grown man reared in white society, usurp patriarchal power reserved solely for white men. He would become, for all intents and purposes, one of them. If that did occur, Child would have unwittingly reproduced in her own text the same hegemony she is writing against. Little Hobomok, if allowed to progress into active, participatory adulthood within the colony, would prove incredibly destabilizing for colonial hegemony and counterproductive to Child's own critique of patriarchy. Charles Hobomok Conant would be a living testament to the impermanence and mutability of the "stable" identity of the colonists, and in Child's own time, citizens of the early republic; he would be an Indian man who had literally become Anglo-American through blood, not just acculturation or habit. He would underscore the permeability of the membrane that separated the races in the minds of the colonizers and budding Americans and, perhaps more significantly for Child, would reify masculine authority. So Child must defuse the threat of little Hobomok by mitigating his effects upon American identity.

She does so by completely assimilating the boy into Anglo-European culture and sending him away to England, where he presumably passes as English and never returns to America. It is this removal from America and American soil that effectively diffuses the potentially crippling effects of Charles Hobomok Conant's "mixed-blooded" masculinity. By becoming a successful "Englishman" the "mixed-blooded" male child has been contained and minimized as a threat to American identity. Child writes that after the boy was left a sizable inheritance to be "appropriated to his education," he became "a distinguished graduate at Cambridge ... [then] left that infant university ... to finish his studies in England" (150). Little Hobomok's father "was seldom spoken of; and by degrees his Indian appellation was silently omitted" from his name (Child 150). Little Hobomok has been literally "removed" from Child's text. Sent away to England and separated from both his Indian heritage and his native (and Native) land, Little Hobomok, now undoubtedly "Charles," becomes a non-issue for Mary, her family, the white patriarchy of the settlement, and the reader. Any power the boy may have held in the text due to his foundational lineage, both Indian and Anglo-American, and his indigenous connection to the American landscape, both Indian and Anglo-American, is contained and neutralized by his Anglicized and distant existence in England.

However, when read in another way, Child's removal of Little Hobomok is actually her preservation of him. Unlike Thomas Rolfe who is erased in order to be forgotten and denied, Child has written Little Hobomok into a fully realized and fully accepted English existence. He is educated, financially provided for with a trust fund, and has become a noteworthy university student—all as a biracial character within the realm of "white" society. He is, as the last line of Child's narrative nostalgically notes, "the tender slip which [Hobomok] protected, [and] has since become a mighty tree" (Child 150).[28] Although seemingly shuffled aside by the author and the characters within her text, Child has allowed Little Hobomok to "succeed" in the only terms acceptable to her audience: he has become unquestionably English and excelled at it. It would have been unimaginable for Little Hobomok to assume a lifestyle that involved the incorporation of his Indian identity on any level or allowed him to remain in America. Such plot developments would have undoubtedly been viewed by Child's readers, and quite possibly Child herself, as disturbing failures, as instances of Indianness triumphing over the "superior" blood and culture of Anglo-Americanness and ultimately proving the devastation of miscegenation to American identity. Consequently, Child has to Anglicize Little Hobomok and bring him successfully into white society as a contributing citizen, but as one who exists safely beyond the confines of her textual, colonial American world. In doing so, Child has also brought her critique of Anglo-American patriarchy full circle by proving the validity of it through a favorable conclusion in which there is a space for all (white) citizens—especially women—within colonial discourses of nationalism. However, Indianness, particularly "mixed-blooded" Indianness, while serving as a point from which Child can launch her disruption of hegemony, is too disruptive of those American discourses and is removed to another nation to assume another national identity. Child is "othering" Indians and mixed-bloods in order to "un-other" white women; she is providing Anglo womanhood agency and voice through the appropriation of and silencing of Indianness.

In both the historic existence of Thomas Rolfe and the textual existence of Charles Hobomok Conant, maleness when combined with Indianness is clearly a potentially dangerous mixture for American identity. Whether it is descendants of Pocahontas eliding the "savage" biracial ancestry of their forefather or a woman writer dealing with the dual concerns of race and patriarchy embedded in one of her characters, Anglo-American consciousness struggles to contain "mixed-blooded" male identities. Such identities hover beyond the grasp of the secure binaries that defined the Anglo-American nation and self: "civilized"/"savage," self/other, English/Indian, man/beast. They complicated the systems by which they could be marked and understood by Anglo-Americans, and in doing so complicated and destabilized the same systems by which Anglo-Americans could identify or understand themselves. "Mixed-blooded" masculinity existing within Anglo-American society was a combination that necessarily relegated itself to obscurity, and removal, or, in the case of Thomas Rolfe, flat-out erasure. It was simply too transgressive, too threatening to remain an unchecked addition to American identity, so, quite simply, it was removed from historic record and consciousness.

---

[28]   This final, ambiguous passage of *Hobomok* has also been interpreted by many scholars as referencing the Puritan colony as the "tender slip" protected by Hobomok. However, Harry Brown, like myself, notes the possibility that Hobomok's son could also be the tender slip, but diverges from my own opinion by noting that such a suggestion would "publicly imagine the unimaginable possibility that we are all half-breeds" (61). I see Child's ending as affirmative rather than ominous.

Just as actual, historic Indians of various tribes were removed from their ancestral lands in the American South and east in the early nineteenth century when Child was writing in order to "make room" for white settlers, white civilization, and "progress," so, too, are these biracial males removed from the discourses concerning American identity. Figures like Thomas Rolfe and characters like Charles Hobomok Conant posed too many questions and emphasized too many of the cracks in the raced and gendered paradigms that structured Anglo-American identity to remain in plain view unmediated. Their nineteenth-century counterparts, the Cherokees, Chickasaws, Creeks, Choctaws, and Seminoles, were simply too "present," taking up too much valuable land, for the physical manifestation of that Anglo-American identity to be realized. All, however, were removed from historical record, from authorial/reader consciousness, and from literal, physical occupation of the land in order to accommodate the budding, yet fragile and ambivalent, development of the American self. Although in several of her post-*Hobomok* works, Child returns to "the theme of interracial marriage that she had instinctively recognized as both the crux of America's racial and sexual contradictions" and even actively campaigns against Indian dispossession, she quite easily dispossesses the "mixed-blooded" Charles Hobomok Conant (Karcher xxxiii). By transforming him into a successful Englishman living on English soil, Child has summarily undone her authorial "problem" of biracial masculinity and its effects on feminine agency and American identity. She has simply removed it to the domain of another nation, replacing it with the voice and agency of Anglo womanhood.

Conclusion
Curtains, Earrings, and Indians:
Texts of Today

Many summers ago, when this study was still a work in progress, I was leafing through a JC Penney sale catalogue. When I got to page 71 of the catalogue, my attention was riveted. There, beneath the headline "White Sale! It's our lowest price ever!" was the Indian of the Massachusetts Bay Colony seal (Arlington). I truly couldn't believe my eyes, but, indeed, there he was with his bow and arrow, and his banner-like plea for help staring back at me from, of all places, curtain panels. Reading the description a bit more closely, I learned that the Indian on the seal was a part of a fabric series manufactured by Penney's dubbed "Arlington," which, according to the catalogue, was a pattern that had the "[t]raditional look of toile with [a] patriotic American theme" (Arlington). Patriotic. Really?

Scattered across a white background of the fabric were images of the Liberty Bell, Mount Vernon, Federal Hall, Independence Hall, and the Bay Colony seal, all arranged in an artistic toile pattern with filler images of leafy trees and tri-corne topped men in horse-drawn buggies. You could choose full-length pole-top draperies, tailored or ascot valances, or even balloon curtains in the "Arlington" pattern and, even better, you could buy coordinating pieces in a check print to complete the ensemble. There were three color choices for the toile and check prints as well: black, navy, or spicy red(!), all on the same white background. The entire line was marked down to 25–40 percent off; something the JC Penney catalogue writer wittily noted was "an historically low price!" (Arlington).

I didn't know what to make of this. I tore page 71 from the catalogue and carried it around with me for quite a few days trying to figure out how this fraught symbol of imperialism, colonialism, and even racism made its way onto fabric that was then randomly made into curtains. Why not a bedspread or placemats? Why not a dress or tote bag? And why would this particular symbol be chosen as one representative of American patriotism? Were we really still using Indianness (and coordinating fabrics) to decorate our homes and define ourselves as Americans in the twenty-first century? The implications of these curtains were dizzying and fascinating to me.

I had a similar experience when I went to Jamestown for the first time in the summer of 2007. I was attending the biennial conference of the Society of Early Americanists and the Omohundro Institute of Early American History and Culture. The conference was held in Williamsburg, Virginia, on the campus of the College of William and Mary and included activities at Historic Jamestowne to commemorate the 400th anniversary of its settlement as the first permanent English colony in the New World. I had never been to either Williamsburg or Jamestown at that time, and was excited to see both. However, I was really looking forward to seeing the fabled earrings of Pocahontas, the focus of Chapter 4, which, at that time, I was in the process of researching and writing.

The earrings were on display in a museum gallery and they were breathtaking. I had previously only seen grainy internet images of the earrings that were made from some obscure, early twentieth-century newspaper photograph. I couldn't make out much about them from those images. In person, though, they were delicate and finely detailed with opalescent white shells and beautiful, ornate silver work. They were gorgeous examples of supposedly seventeenth-century jewelry that may—or may not—have had direct ties to Pocahontas herself. Despite the fact that I knew all about the disputed background of the earrings, it was still amazing and exciting to see them personally. I knew immediately that one of my next stops would have to be the gift shop so I could see—and let's be honest, *buy*—the replicas of these royal earrings. For a mere 40 dollars (now 50), I was able to purchase a bit of history, a bit of Indianness, a bit of royalty, and wear it in my ears. Not unlike the Arlington curtain panels from JC Penney's—which I must confess I also bought; how could I not?—these earrings seemed to promise me, an Anglo woman in the twenty-first century, an intimate, physical connection to Indianness, a connection that would somehow make me more patriotic, more historically grounded, and more American.

As I pondered these purchases, I realized that Indianness, whether stamped onto fabric or molded into earrings, is still the same commodity as it was 400 years ago; it is still appropriated, adopted, adapted, and utilized in complex ways to make white (or at least non-Native) Americans feel more American. Indianness is enmeshed with Americanness in ways that education, scholarship, tolerance, and even 400 plus years of "corrective learning" can't untangle. No matter how progressive America thinks it has become in terms of accepting and valuing "otherness," remnants of our past appropriations of Indianness still remain; in fact, they flourish. Beyond my earrings and curtains, there are clothing retailers who still regularly introduce their "Navajo" (or "Aztec" or "Tribal") clothing lines every few seasons featuring geometric patterns, faux leather, and southwestern colors. Lingerie designers still march scantily clad models down the catwalk in feathered headdresses, fringed panties, and turquoise jewelry. Sports teams still doggedly cling to racist and outdated team names and mascots, claiming their monikers show "honor" and "pride."[1] Just as the Indian on the Massachusetts Bay Colony seal found his way back into twenty-first-century consciousness by the way

---

[1]   The retail chain Urban Outfitters introduced a "Navajo" clothing line in 2011 that received much backlash, especially from the Navajo nation. In 2012 at their annual fashion show, Victoria's Secret sent model Karlie Kloss down the runway in a Plains Indian style headdress and a fringed bra and panty set, while wearing a lot of turquoise jewelry. The Washington Redskins, one of many, many national and local-level sports teams with racist names, was at press time still fighting the overwhelming public pressure to abandon their racist name and symbol. Obviously, there are many, many other examples of this sort of appropriation of Native American identity in American and world culture today; these few cited here work to underscore my specific point.

of "patriotic" home décor, and Pocahontas reemerged in our imaginations through fashionable (and "affordably" priced) earrings, so, too, does Indianness—or rather the Anglo-imagined version of Indianness—still inform much of American identity. And, ironically enough, it still very often informs a specifically *female* American identity as testified to by the stereotypically feminine commercial objects I stumbled across: curtains and earrings, the stuff of domesticity and femininity.

Clearly then, the early American images and constructions of Indianness (as well as the female writers who engaged them) that I have worked to unpack and untangle in this project are not relics of history. I am not engaging in some arcane study of America's distant past, but instead, working with concepts that America is obviously not done with yet. Americans are still not sure who exactly they are and how Indianness fits into their "American" identity, yet they do seem to universally know that Indianness belongs to them. It's theirs for the taking. But it's not just any version of Indianness that gets claimed. Americans desire the romanticized Indian of long ago, the lovingly remembered "Noble Savage" of the past who still lives on in literature, images, movies, and even commercial products. They want the Edenic Indian of Massachusetts Bay who pleads for and receives salvation from the charitable colonists. They want the glamorous earrings that were once the property of the Indian princess Pocahontas who so loved the colonists she gave up everything to become one of them. In short, Americans want the Anglo-constructed fantasy of "good" Indianness. The Indianness of present reality, which often struggles with the very real issues of poverty, alcohol and drug abuse, and higher rates of school dropouts and suicide—the ugly legacies of conquest—isn't the vision of utterly romantic indigenity the average American craves. That present reality is just too hard for Americans to acknowledge or even conceive of, because with acknowledgment comes culpability and with culpability comes change. Modern Americans would have to fully recognize and take responsibility for the fallout from centuries of colonization, occupation, and removal and then do something to make it "right." The implications of such a moment are almost unimaginable for American identity and consequently, simply unthinkable. So, instead, it is the Indianness of the past, the idealized vision of Native nobility from America's glorified and distant history before the aftermath of colonization was fully revealed, that dominates American imagination rather than the historic Native American individuals like James Printer and Thomas Rolfe who resisted Anglo hegemony or created hybrid, binary-challenging identities. Americans still want to lay claim to Indianness and the perceived "authentic" narrative of indigenity it imparts, whether they do so through consuming products, claiming a glorified Native ancestry, or, by doing as the authors and artists of this study did—writing about and visualizing Indianness in fantastical, often racist, and two-dimensional ways.[2]

---

[2]   Indianness is still very much an appropriated topic in American narrative-based pop culture, appearing everywhere from the Indian werewolves (based on the Quileute tribe of the Pacific Northwest) in the *Twilight* series of books by Stephenie Meyer (published 2005–2008), to the mixed-blooded character of Connor in the 2012 video game *Assassin's Creed III: Revelations*, to the feathered and war-painted "Reavers" in the 2002 Joss Whedon

Native American scholars and theorists have been struggling to get out from under the weight of these romanticized constructions of Indianness and to redefine Indian identity in productive and realistic ways. Scholars such as Gerald Vizenor (Anishinaabe), Robert Allen Warrior (Osage), Thomas King (Cherokee), Jennifer Nez Denetdale (Diné), Jace Weaver, and Andrea Smith work to deconstruct the "imagined" versions of Indianness established by colonial and, in the cases of Smith and Denetdale, patriarchal hegemonies that still influence American imagination today.[3] These "postindian warriors of survivance," to use Vizenor's phrase, have continued the work begun hundreds of years ago by people like James Printer and Pocahontas—real, historical personages who were skillfully able to assert their own subject identities through the innate cracks existent in the imperial machinery. The field of Native Studies also seeks to alleviate the pressure of Anglo-created constructions of Indianness by attempting to define not only the field itself, but also by contextualizing the concept of the "Indian," and moving him/her out of the distant past and beyond the steam-rolled images and caricatures.

Without a doubt, many of these enduring and racist constructions of "Indians on paper" stemmed from the artistic and narrative renditions of Indianness that flooded early America. The colonial seals, the engravings, the portraits, and the narratives of/about Indians all shaped Anglo-American perceptions of Americanness and Indianness, so much so that many Anglo women writers took up these themes and used the disruptive and ambiguous position of Indians in the Anglo-American mind to assert their own authorial identities. These women writers deployed the figure of the iconographic, "imagined" Indian as leverage, as the ground from which they could launch not only themselves, but also their critiques of the hegemonic structures that regulated early American society. Women writers such as Mary Rowlandson, Ann Eliza Bleecker, the pseudonymous Unca Eliza Winkfield, and Lydia Maria Child certainly exploited and appropriated Indianness, manipulating it and the colonial-imagined specter of it in order to highlight the fractures in colonial certainty and to write themselves into existence. However, in engendering their own unique existences, these women very intentionally foreclosed on the possibility of an Indian one. They wrote the realities of Native identity *out of* existence in order to write their own identities as Anglo women authors *into* existence.

---

television series *Firefly*, and even to the arguably "Indian" aliens in James Cameron's Academy Award winning movie *Avatar* (2009). While these few examples are beyond the scope of this particular study, they do reflect a very similar pattern of narrative appropriation and ideological silencing of Native reality that the texts examined here demonstrate.

[3]   Although there has been some debate surrounding both Jace Weaver's and Andrea Smith's claims to Cherokee identity—and Weaver has stopped listing this tribal affiliation on his official documents—both do significant work on Native identity and colonialism. Smith's body of work in particular steadfastly seeks to dismantle colonialist constructions, and her personal "authenticity" as a Native woman is an interesting conversation in and of itself that highlights many of the claims about female authorial voice and authority that I examine here.

However, despite their appropriations and racisms, these women writers also wrote about Indianness in ways that opened it up. They expressed their own connections to and relationships with Indianness in these texts. The authorial moves made by these women authors transcend acts of pure appropriation to complicate and intensify Anglo-American relationships with Indianness. These texts introduced Indian characters that, while often based on crude, racist stereotypes, were also complex refutations of those same stereotypes. In the writings of these women authors, the possibility truly exists (at least narratively) that Indians can be "savages" *and* protectors of white womanhood, enemies *and* lovers, captors *and* friends, Indian *and* white. The intriguing and complex assertions of Native, Anglo-American, and feminine identity in these texts bring Indianness and Americanness closer together and make explicit the *a priori* connections between them, connections that had been in existence from the earliest visual and written depictions of the New World. These women authors were hammering out the identities not only of themselves, but also of the nation—and conspicuously including Native Americans in that negotiation. So while trafficking in more of the same colonialist fantasies about Indianness as the dominant culture, these women were also inscribing new possibilities for Indianness and women, possibilities that expose the linkages between them and then work to open that association rather than contract it. The writings of these women—Rowlandson, Bleecker, "Unca Eliza Winkfield," and Child—serve to generate new subjectivities and social identities—such as the Anglo woman author, the Writerly or Christian Indian, the female historian, and the mixed-blooded American—within the colonial/ early republican iconographic and narrative framework. The scripted nature of the colonial project and its aftermath becomes exposed when these women "write back" to empire, creating texts that utilize, explore, and definitely critique the interconnectedness of Indianness and Anglo-Americanness in the formation of American identity in early America.

Works Cited

Abrams, Ann Uhry. *The Pilgrims and Pocahontas: Rival Myths of American Origin*. Boulder, CO: Westview Press, 1999. Print.

Abzug, Robert H. *Cosmos Crumbling: American Reform and the Religious Imagination*. Oxford: Oxford University Press, 1994. Print.

Allen, Paula Gunn. *Pocahontas: Medicine Woman, Spy, Entrepreneur, Diplomat*. San Francisco: Harper San Francisco, 2003. Print.

Amory, Hugh. *First Impressions: Printing in Cambridge, 1639–1989*. Cambridge, MA: Harvard University Press, 1989. Print.

———. "Printing and Bookselling in New England, 1638–1713." *The History of the Book in America, Volume One*. Ed. Hugh Amory and David D. Hall. Cambridge: Cambridge University Press, 2000. 83–116. Print.

Anderson, Karen. *Chain Her By One Foot: The Subjugation of Native Women in Seventeenth-Century New France*. New York: Taylor and Francis, 1994. Print.

Anonymous. *The Female American; or, The Adventures of Unca Eliza Winkfield*. 1767. Ed. Michelle Burnham and James Freitas. Second edition. Toronto: Broadview Press, 2014. Print.

Anonymous. *A True Account of the Most Considerable Occurrences …*. London, 1676. Print.

Arlington Curtains. Advertisement. *JC Penney Catalogue*. Fall 2004. Print.

Armstrong, Catherine. *Writing North America in the Seventeenth Century: English Representations in Print and Manuscript*. London: Ashgate Publishing, 2007. Print.

Ashcroft, Bill, Gareth Griffiths, and Helen Tiffin. *The Empire Writes Back: Theory and Practice in Post-Colonial Literatures*. London: Routledge, 1989. Print.

Assassin's Creed III: Revelations. Ubisoft. 2012. Video Game.

Association for the Preservation of Virginia Antiquities. "Results of Impurity Analysis of Antique Silver." Conducted by the Assay Office: London, England. 2006. Print.

The Authorized King James Bible. C.I. Scofield, D.D., Gen. Ed. New York: Oxford University Press, 1967. Print.

Avatar. Dir. James Cameron. Perf. Sam Worthington, Zoe Saldana. Twentieth Century Fox, 2009. DVD.

Axtell, James. *The Invasion Within: The Contest of Cultures in Colonial North America*. New York: Oxford University Press, 1985. Print.

Barbour, Philip. *Pocahontas and Her World*. Boston: Houghton Mifflin, 1970. Print.

Basch, Norma. *In the Eyese of the Law: Women, Marriage, and Property in Nineteenth-Century New York*. Ithaca, NY: Cornell University Press, 1982. Print.

Baym, Nina. *American Women Writers and the Work of History, 1790–1860*. New Brunswick, NJ: Rutgers University Press, 1995. Print.

Bellin, Joshua David. *The Demon of the Continent: Indians and the Shaping of American Literature*. Philadelphia: The University of Pennsylvania Press, 2001. Print.

Benzoni, Girolamo. *La Historia del Mondo Nuovo. Discovering the New World: Based on the Works of Theodore De Bry*. Ed. Michael Alexander. New York: Harper and Row, 1976. Print.

Bergland, Renee. *The National Uncanny: Indian Ghosts and American Subjects*. Hanover, NH: University Press of New England, 2000. Print.

Berkhofer, Robert. *The White Man's Indian: Images of the American Indian From Columbus to the Present*. New York: Knopf, 1978. Print.

Beverly, Robert. *The History and Present State of Virginia*. 1705. Ed. Louis B. Wright. Chapel Hill: University of North Carolina Press, 1947. Print.

Bhabha, Homi. "Of Mimicry and Man: The Ambivalence of Colonial Discourse." *The Location of Culture*. London: Routledge, 1994. 121–31. Print.

———. "The Other Question: Stereotype, Discrimination, and the Discourse of Colonialism." *The Location of Culture*. London: Routledge, 1994. 94–120. Print.

———. "Signs Taken for Wonders: Questions of ambivalence and authority under a tree outside Delhi, May 1817." *The Location of Culture*. London: Routledge, 1994. 145–74. Print.

Bleecker, Ann Eliza. *The History of Maria Kittle. Women's Early American Historical Narratives*. Ed. Sharon M. Harris. New York: Penguin Books, 2003. 1–35. Print.

Boehmer, Elleke. "Stories of Women and Mothers: Gender and Nationalism in the Early Fiction of Flora Nwapa." *Motherlands: Black Women's Writing from Africa, the Caribbean and South Asia*. Ed. Susheila Nasta. London: Women's Press, 1991. 3–23. Print.

Bohaker, Heidi. "Nindoodemag: The Significance of Algonquian Kinship Networks in the Eastern Great Lakes Region, 1600–1701." *William and Mary Quarterly* 63:1 (2006): 23–52. Print.

Boone, Elizabeth and Walter Mignolo, eds. *Writing Without Words: Alternative Literacies in Mesoamerica and the Andes*. Durham, NC: Duke University Press, 1994. Print.

Bowen, Scarlet. "*Via Media*: Transatlantic Anglicanism in *The Female American*." *The Eighteenth Century* 53.2 (2012): 189–207. Print.

Bragdon, Kathleen. "Gender as a Social Category in Native Southern New England." *Ethnohistory* 43.4 (1996): 573–92. Print.

Breitwieser, Mitchell. *American Puritanism and the Defense of Mourning: Religion, Grief and Ethnology in Mary White Rowlandson's Captivity Narrative*. Madison: University of Wisconsin Press, 1990. Print.

Brooks, Lisa. *The Common Pot: The Recovery of Native Space in the Northeast*. Minneapolis: University of Minnesota Press, 2008. Print.

Bross, Kristina. "'Come Over and Help Us': Reading Mission Literature." *Early American Literature* 38.3 (2003): 395–400. Print.

———. *Dry Bones and Indian Sermons: Praying Indians in Colonial America.* Ithaca, NY: Cornell University Press, 2004. Print.

Brown, Harry J. *Injun Joe's Ghost: The Indian Mixed-Blood in American Writing.* Columbus: University of Missouri Press, 2004. Print.

Brown, Kathleen M. *Good Wives, Nasty Wenches and Anxious Patriarchs: Gender, Race and Power in Colonial Virginia.* Chapel Hill: University of North Carolina Press, 1996. Print.

Buell, Lawrence. "American Literary Emergence as a Post-Colonial Phenomenon." *American Literature, American Culture.* Ed. Gordon Hutner. New York: Oxford University Press, 1999. 592–612. Print.

Bulbeck, Chilla. *Re-Orienting Western Feminisms: Women's Diversity in a Postcolonial World.* Cambridge: Cambridge University Press, 1997. Print.

Burnham, Michelle. *Captivity and Sentiment: Cultural Exchange in American Literature, 1682–1861.* Hanover, NH: University Press of New England, 1997. Print.

———. Introduction. *The Female American; or, The Adventures of Unca Eliza Winkfield.* By Anonymous. 1767. Ed. Michelle Burnham and James Freitas. Second edition. Toronto: Broadview Press, 2014. Print.

———. "The Journey Between: Liminality and Dialogism in Mary White Rowlandson's Captivity Narrative." *Early American Literature* 28.1 (1993): 60–75. Print.

Calhoon, Robert McCluer. *The Loyalists in Revolutionary America: 1760–1781.* New York: Harcourt Brace Jovanovich, Inc., 1965. Print.

Carruth, Mary C. "Between Abjection and Redemption: Mary Rowlandson's Subversive Corporeality." *Feminist Interventions in Early American Studies.* Ed. Mary C. Carruth. Tuscaloosa: University of Alabama Press, 2006. 60–79. Print.

Castiglia, Christopher. *Bound and Determined: Captivity, Culture-Crossing, and White Womanhood from Mary Rowlandson to Patty Hearst.* Chicago: University of Chicago Press, 1996. Print.

Castillo, Susan and Ivy Schweitzer, eds. *The Literatures of Colonial America: An Anthology.* Malden, MA: Blackwell Publishers, 2001. Print.

Cesarini, Patrick J. "'What has become of your praying to God?': Daniel Gookin's Troubled History of King Philip's War." *Early American Literature* 44.3 (2009): 489–516. Print.

Chamberlain, John. *The Chamberlain Letters.* Ed. Elizabeth Thomson. London: John Murray, 1966. Print.

Child, Lydia Maria. *Hobomok and Other Writings on Indians.* Ed. Carolyn Karcher. New Brunswick, NJ: Rutgers University Press, 2001. Print.

Chow, Rey. "Sacrifice, Mimesis, and the Theorizing of Victimhood." *Entanglements, or Transmedial Thinking about Capture.* Durham, NC: Duke University Press, 2012. 81–105. Print.

Cogley, Richard. *John Eliot's Mission to the Indians Before King Philip's War.* Cambridge, MA: Harvard University Press, 1999. Print.

Cohen, Matt. *The Networked Wilderness: Communicating in Early New England.* Minneapolis: University of Minnesota Press, 2010. Print.

Conboy, Katie, Nadia Medina, and Sarah Stanbury, eds. *Writing on the Body: Female Embodiment and Feminist Theory.* New York: Columbia University Press, 1997. Print.

Cronon, William. *Changes in the Land: Indians, Colonists and the Ecology of New England.* New York: Hill and Wang, 1983. Print.

Cummings, Prentiss. "Concerning the Great Seal of the Commonwealth." 29 Apr. 1885. *House of Representatives of the Commonwealth of Massachusetts.* Print.

Davenport, Millia. *The Book of Costume.* Vol. 2. New York: Crown Publishers, 1948. Print.

Davidson, Cathy N. *Revolution and the Word: The Rise of the Novel in America.* New York: Oxford University Press, 1986. Print.

Day, Sara. "'With Peace and Freedom Blest!' Woman as Symbol in America, 1590–1800." *American Women: The Library of Congress.* 2001. Web. 17 Mar. 2008.

De Bry, Theodor. *Grandes Voyages.* Vol. 4, *America.* Frankfurt, 1634. Library of Congress. Web.

Dean, Catherine E. *Jamestown.* Postcard History Series. Charleston, SC: Arcadia Publishing, 2012. Print.

Deane, Charles, ed. *A Discourse of Virginia.* By Edward Maria Wingfield. Worcester, MA: American Antiquarian Society, 1860. Google Books. Web.

Deloria, Philip J. *Playing Indian.* New Haven, CT: Yale University Press, 1998. Print.

Deloria, Vine, Jr. *Custer Died for Your Sins.* New York: Avon, 1969. Print.

Derounian-Stodola, Kathryn Zabelle, and James Arthur Levernier. *The Indian Captivity Narrative, 1550–1900.* Twayne's United States Authors Ser. 605. New York: Twayne Publishers, 1993. Print.

Díaz, Mónica. *Indigenous Writings from the Convent: Negotiating Ethnic Autonomy in Colonial Mexico.* Tuscon: University of Arizona Press, 2013. Print.

Dillon, Elizabeth Maddock. *The Gender of Freedom: Fictions of Liberalism and the Literary Public Sphere.* Stanford, CA: Stanford University Press, 2004. Print.

Donaldson, Laura E. *Decolonizing Feminisms: Race, Gender and Empire Building.* New York: Routledge, 1993. Print.

Doolen, Andy. *Fugitive Empire: Locating Early American Imperialism.* Minneapolis: University of Minnesota Press, 2005. Print.

Drake, James D. *King Philip's War: Civil War in New England, 1675–1676.* Amherst: University of Massachusetts Press, 2000. Print.

Egerton, Mary Margaret Stanley, the Countess of Wilton. *The Book of Costume: or Annals of Fashion (1846) by A Lady of Rank.* 1846. Trans. and ed. Pieter Bach. Lopez Island, WA: R.L. Shep, 1986. Print.

Ellison, Julie. *Cato's Tears and the Making of Anglo-American Emotion*. Chicago: The University of Chicago Press, 1999. Print.

———. "Race and Sensibility in the Early Republic: Ann Eliza Bleecker and Sarah Wentworth Morton." *Early American Literature* 65 (1993): 445–74. Print.

Faery, Rebecca Blevins. *Cartographies of Desire: Captivity, Race and Sex in the Shaping of an American Nation*. Norman: University of Oklahoma Press, 1999. Print.

Faugeres, Margaretta V. *The Posthumous Works of Ann Eliza Bleecker in Prose and Verse. To Which is Added, A Collection of Essays, Prose and Poetical, by Margaretta V. Faugeres*. New York: T. and J. Swords, 1793. i–xviii. Print.

Finch, Martha L. "'Civilized' Bodies and the 'Savage' Environment of Early New Plymouth." *A Centre of Wonders: The Body in Early America*. Ed. Janet Moore Lindman and Michele Lise Tarter. Ithaca, NY: Cornell University Press, 2001. Print.

Firefly. Creator/Executive Producer Joss Whedon. Twentieth Century Fox, 2002. DVD.

Fischer, David Hackett. *Albion's Seed: Four British Folkways in America*. New York: Oxford University Press, 1989. Print.

Fleming, E. McClung. "From Indian Princess to Greek Goddess: The American Image, 1783–1815." *Winterthur Portfolio* 3.1 (1967): 37–66. Print.

Fuller, Mark. "KLTH 45 Pocahontas—Town Hall Collections." Message to author. 20 Nov. 2014. Email.

Galvin, William Francis, Secretary of the Commonwealth of Massachusetts. "The History of the Arms and Great Seal of the Commonwealth of Massachusetts." Boston: Massachusetts Public Records Division, 1999. Web.

Gardner, Philip. *Master Plots: Race and the Founding of American Literature, 1787–1845*. Baltimore, MD: Johns Hopkins University Press, 1998. Print.

The Geneva Bible. Genevabible.org, November 2002. Web. 2 Mar. 2011.

Giffen, Allison. "'Till Grief Melodious Grow': The Poems and Letters of Ann Eliza Bleecker." *Early American Literature* 28 (1993): 222–39. Print.

Goldie, Terry. *Fear and Temptation: The Image of the Indigene in Canadian, Australian, and New Zealand Literatures*. London: McGill-Queen's University Press, 1989. Print.

Gookin, Daniel. "An Historical Account of the Doings and Sufferings of the Christian Indians in New England." 1677. Reprinted in *Archaeologia Americana: Transactions and Collections of the American Antiquarian Society 2* (1836): 423–534. Print.

Gray, Kathryn N. *John Eliot and the Praying Indians of Massachusetts Bay: Communities and Connections in Puritan New England*. Lewisburg, PA: Bucknell University Press, 2013. Print.

Greenough, Chester Noyes. *Algernon Sidney and the Motto of the Commonwealth of Massachusetts*. Boston: Massachusetts Historical Society, 1918. Print.

Hamlin, William M. "Imagined Apotheoses: Drake, Harriot, and Raleigh in the Americas." *Journal of the History of Ideas* 57.3 (1996): 405–28. Print.

Hamor, Ralph. *A True Discourse of the Present Estate of Virginia*. London, 1615. Richmond: Virginia State Library, 1957. Print.

Harriot, Thomas. *A Briefe and True Report of the New Found Land of Virginia: The Complete Theodor De Bry Edition*. 1590. Intro. Paul Hulton. New York: Dover Publications, 1972. Print.

Harris, Sharon M. *Executing Race: Early American Women's Narratives of Race, Society, and the Law*. Columbus: The Ohio State University, 2005. Print.

———. Introduction. *Women's Early American Historical Narratives*. New York: Penguin Books, 2003. Print.

Higham, John. "Indian Princess and Roman Goddess: The First Female Symbols of America." *Proceedings of the American Antiquarian Society* 100.1 (1990): 45–80. Print.

Historic Jamestowne. "White Mussel Shell Earrings." Historic Jamestowne, Williamsburg, Virginia: Visitor Center Museum, n.d. Exhibit information card.

Honor, Hugh. *The New Golden Land: Images of America from the Discoveries to the Present Time*. New York: Pantheon Books, 1975. Print.

Hopkins, Alfred. "Some American Military Swords." *The Regional Review* 4.1 (1940): 1–6. *National Park Service*. Web. 16 Nov. 2007.

Howe, Mary Ellen. Telephone interview. 5 Apr. 2008.

Hubbard, William. *A Narrative of the Troubles with the Indians in New-England, from the First Planting Thereof in the Year 1607, to his Present Year 1677, but Chiefly of the Late Troubles in the Two Last Years, 1675 and 1676: To which is Added a Discourse about the Warre with the Pequods in the Year 1637*. Boston: John Foster, 1677. Print.

Hulme, Peter. "Including America." *Ariel: A Review of International English Literatures* 26.1 (1995). 117–23. Print.

Hulton, Paul. "Introduction to the Dover Edition." *A Briefe and True Report of the New Found Land of Virginia: The Complete 1590 Theodor De Bry Edition*. By Thomas Harriot. New York: Dover Publications, Inc., 1972. vi–xv. Print.

Ingram, Penelope. "Can the Settler Speak? Appropriating Subaltern Silence in Janet Frame's *The Carpathians*." *Cultural Critique* 41 (1999): 79–107. Print.

———. "Racializing Babylon: Settler Whiteness and the 'New Racism.'" *New Literary History* 32.1 (2001): 157–76. Print.

Jacobs, Margaret D. "The Eastmans and the Luhans: Interracial Marriage between White Women and Native American Men, 1875–1935." *Frontiers* 23.3 (2002): 29–54. Print.

Jameson, J. Franklin. *The American Revolution Considered as a Social Movement*. Princeton, NJ: Princeton University Press, 1926. Print.

Jennings, Francis. *The Invasion of America: Indians, Colonialism, and the Cant of Conquest*. New York: W.W. Norton and Company, 1975. Print.

Jethro, Peter. "Letter to John Leverett." *The Sovereignty and Goodness of God*. By Mary Rowlandson. Ed. Neal Salisbury. Boston: Bedford Books, 1997. 133–4. Print.

Jones, Matt B. "The Early Massachusetts-Bay Colony Seals: With Bibliographical Notes Based Upon Their Use in Printing." *Proceedings of the American Antiquarian Society* 44 (1934): 13–44. Print.

Joseph, Betty. "Re-playing Crusoe/Pocahontas: Circum-Atlantic Stagings in *The Female American*." *Criticism* 42.3 (2000): 317–36. Print.

Kaplan, Amy. "'Left Alone with America': The Absence of Empire in the Study of American Culture." *Cultures of United States Imperialism*. Ed. Amy Kaplan and Donald Pease. Durham, NC: Duke University Press, 1993. 3–21. Print.

Karcher, Carolyn L. *The First Woman in the Republic: A Cultural Biography of Lydia Maria Child*. Durham, NC: Duke University Press, 1994. Print.

———. Introduction. *Hobomok and Other Writings on Indians*. By Lydia Maria Child. Ed. Carolyn Karcher. New Brunswick, NJ: Rutgers University Press, 2001. Print.

Katzew, Ilona. *Casta Painting: Images of Race in Eighteenth-Century Mexico*. New Haven, CT: Yale University Press, 2004. Print.

Kerber, Linda. "Separate Spheres, Female World, Women's Place: The Rhetoric of Women's History." *Journal of American History* 75 (1989): 9–39. Print.

King, Thomas. *The Truth About Stories: A Native Narrative*. Minneapolis: University of Minnesota Press, 2005. Print.

Kolodny, Annette. *The Lay of the Land: Metaphor as Experience and History in American Life and Letters*. Chapel Hill: University of North Carolina Press, 1975. Print.

Kot, Paula. "Engendering Identity: Doubts and Doubles in Lydia Maria Child's *Hobomok*." *Women's Studies* 28.1 (1998): 79–105. Web. Humanities International Complete. 3 June 2014. Print.

Kutchen, Larry. "The 'Vulgar Thread of the Canvas': Revolution and the Picturesque in Ann Eliza Bleecker, Crevecoeur, and Charles Brockden Brown." *Early American Literature* 36 (2001): 395–425. Print.

Landsman, Ned C. *Crossroads of Empire: The Middle Colonies in British North America*. Baltimore, MD: Johns Hopkins University Press, 2010. Print.

Le Corbeiller, Clare. "Miss America and Her Sisters: Personifications of the Four Parts of the World." *Metropolitan Museum of Art Bulletin* 19.8 (April 1961): 209–23. Print.

Lee, Maurice, Jr. Introduction. *Dudley Carleton to John Chamberlain: 1603–1624. Jacobean Letters, by Dudley Carleton*. New Brunswick, NJ: Rutgers University Press, 1972. Print.

Lemay, J.A. Leo. *Did Pocahontas Save Captain John Smith?* Athens: University of Georgia Press, 1992. Print.

Lepore, Jill. *The Name of War: King Philip's War and the Origins of American Identity*. New York: Vintage Books, 1998. Print.

Levine, Philippa, ed. *Gender and Empire*. Oxford: Oxford University Press, 2004. Print.

Littlefield, George Emery. *The Early Massachusetts Press 1638–1711*. Vols. 1 and 2. New York: Burt Franklin, 1907. Print.

Long, Oscar F., Captain. *Changes in the Uniform of the Army: 1774–1895.* US Army Quartermaster's Department, 1895. Web. 11 Nov. 2007.

Loring, John. *Tiffany Pearls.* New York: Abrams, 2006. Print.

Lougheed, Pamela. "'Then he began to rant and threaten': Indian Malice and Individual Liberty in Mary Rowlandson's Captivity Narrative." *American Literature* 74.2 (2002): 287–313. Print.

Maas, David Edward. *The Return of the Massachusetts Loyalists.* New York: Garland Publishing, Inc., 1989. Print.

Maddox, Lucy. *Removals: Nineteenth-Century American Literature and the Politics of Indian Affairs.* Oxford: Oxford University Press, 1991. Print.

Mandell, Daniel R. *King Philip's War: Colonial Expansion, Native Resistance, and the End of Indian Sovereignty.* Baltimore, MD: The Johns Hopkins University Press, 2010. Print.

Massachusetts Bay Colony Seal. 1629. SC1/series 138X. Massachusetts Archives, Boston. Digital image.

Massachusetts Bay Colony Seal. 1676. Broadside printed by Samuel Green. Detail from *At a Council, held at Charlestown, June the 20th, 1676.* Massachusetts Historical Society, Boston. Digital image.

Massachusetts Bay Colony Seal. 1678. Broadside printed by John Foster. Detail from *At the second sessions of the General Court held at Boston in New-England.* Massachusetts Historical Society, Boston. Digital image.

Massachusetts Bay Colony Seal. ca. 1678. Photograph of impression on paper. From the Stewart Mitchell Papers Box 2, folder 28. Massachusetts Historical Society, Boston. Photograph.

Massachusetts Bay Colony Seal. N.d. Photograph of wax impression. From the Stewart Mitchell Papers Box 2, folder 28. Massachusetts Historical Society, Boston. Photograph.

Massachusetts Seal, Pre-1898. SC1/series 138X. Massachusetts Archives, Boston. Digital image.

Mather, Increase. *A Brief History of the War with the Indians ....* 1676; Albany, 1862. Print.

Matter-Seibel, Sabina. "Native Americans, Women, and the Culture of Nationalism in Lydia Maria Child and Catharine Maria Sedgwick." *Early America Re-Explored: New Readings in Colonial, Early National, and Antebellum Culture.* Ed. Klaus H. Schmidt and Fritz Fleischmann. New York: Peter Lang Publishing, 2000. 411–40. Print.

McClintock, Anne. "The Angel of Progress: The Pitfalls of the Term 'Post-Colonial.'" *Social Text* 31/32 (1992): 84–98. Print.

———. *Imperial Leather: Race, Gender, and Sexuality in the Colonial Conquest.* New York: Routledge, 1995. Print.

———. "'No Longer in a Future Heaven': Gender, Race and Nationalism." *Dangerous Liaisons: Gender, Nation and Postcolonial Perspectives.* Ed. Anne McClintock, Aamir Mufti, and Ella Shohat. Minneapolis: University of Minnesota Press, 1997. 89–112. Print.

McMurran, Mary Helen. "Realism and the Unreal in *The Female American*." *Eighteenth Century: Theory and Interpretation* 52.3–4 (2011): 323–42. Print.

Meserve, Walter T. "English Works of Seventeenth-century Indians." *American Quarterly* 8.3 (1965): 264–76. Print.

Meyer, Stephenie. *Twilight, New Moon, Eclipse,* and *Breaking Dawn*. New York: Little, Brown and Company, 2005–2008. Print.

Middlebrook, Louis F. *The Seals of Maritime New England*. Salem, MA: Essex Institute, 1926. Print.

Mielke, Laura L. *Moving Encounters: Sympathy and the Indian Question in Antebellum Literature*. Amherst: University of Massachusetts Press, 2008. Print.

Mills, Bruce. *Cultural Reformations: Lydia Maria Child and the Literature of Reform*. Athens: University of Georgia Press, 1994. Print.

Minh-ha, Trinh T. *Woman, Native, Other: Writing Postcoloniality and Feminism*. Bloomington: Indiana University Press, 2009. Print.

Mohanty, Chandra Talpade. "Under Western Eyes: Feminist Scholarship and Colonialist Discourses." *Boundary 2* 12:3–13:1 (1984): 333–58. Print.

Mollo, John. *Military Fashion: A Comparative History of the Uniforms of the Great Armies from the 17th Century to the First World War*. New York: G.P. Putnam's Sons, 1972. Print.

Montrose, Louis. "The Work of Gender in the Discourse of Discovery." *Representations* 33 (Winter 1991): 1–41. Print.

Moore, Warren. *Weapons of the American Revolution ... and Accoutrements*. New York: Promontory Press, 1967. Print.

Morgensen, Scott Lauria. *Spaces Between Us: Queer Settler Colonialism and Indigenous Decolonization*. Minneapolis: University of Minnesota Press, 2011. Print.

Mossiker, Frances. *Pocahontas*. New York: Knopf, 1976. Print.

Murray, David. "Crossblood Strategies in the Writings of Gerald Vizenor." *Loosening the Seams: Interpretations of Gerald Vizenor*. Ed. A. Robert Lee. Bowling Green, KY: Bowling Green State University Popular Press, 2000. 20–37. Print.

Namias, June. *White Captives: Gender and Ethnicity on the American Frontier*. Chapel Hill: University of North Carolina Press, 1993. Print.

Nelson, Dana D. *The Word in Black and White: Reading "Race" in American Literature, 1638–1867*. New York: Oxford University Press, 1992. Print.

Neumann, George C. *The History of Weapons of the American Revolution*. New York: Bonanza Books, 1867. Print.

The New World. Dir. Terrence Malick. Perf. Colin Farrell, Q'orianka Kilcher. New Line Cinema, 2005. DVD.

Newman, Andrew. "Captive on the Literacy Frontier: Mary Rowlandson, James Smith and Charles Johnston." *Early American Literature* 38.1 (2003): 31–65. Print.

————. *On Records: Delaware Indians, Colonists, and the Media of History and Memory*. Lincoln: University of Nebraska Press, 2012. Print.

Newman, Eric P. *The Early Paper Money of America: Colonial Currency 1696–1810*. Iola, WI: KP Books, 2007. Print.

Niles, Grace Greylock. *The Hoosac Valley: Its Legends and Its History*. New York: B.P. Putnam's Sons, 1912. Print.

Norton, Anne. *Alternative Americas: A Reading of Antebellum Political Culture*. Chicago: University of Chicago Press, 1986. Print.

Oliver, Andrew, Ann Millspaugh Huff, and Edward W. Hanson. *Portraits in the Massachusetts Historical Society: An Illustrated Catalog with Descriptive Matter*. Boston: Massachusetts Historical Society, 1988. Print.

Orleck, Annelise. Introduction. *The Politics of Motherhood: Activist Voices from Left to Right*. Ed. Alexis Jetter, Annelise Orleck, and Diana Taylor. Hanover, NH: University Press of New England, 1997. 3–20. Print.

Palfrey, John Gorham. *History of New England*. Boston: Little, Brown, 1899.

Palmer, Vera. "Pocahontas's Earrings." *Richmond-Times Dispatch*. 17 Mar. 1935. Web. 11 May 2007.

Pearce, Roy Harvey. "The Significances of the Captivity Narrative." *American Literature* 19 (1947): 1–20. Print.

Perdue, Theda. *"Mixed Blood" Indians: Racial Construction in the Early South*. Athens: University of Georgia Press, 2003. Print.

Perdue, Theda and Michael D. Green, eds. *The Cherokee Removal: A Brief History with Documents*. Boston: Bedford St. Martin's, 1995. Print.

Person, Leland, Jr. "The American Eve: Miscegenation and a Feminist Frontier Fiction." *American Quarterly* 37.5 (1985): 668–85. Print.

Peterson, Harold L. *Arms and Armor in Colonial America, 1526–1783*. New York: Bramhall House, 1956. Print.

Pocahontas. Dir. Mike Gabriel and Eric Goldberg. Perf. Irene Beddard and Mel Gibson. Disney, 1985. DVD.

"Pocahontas Jewelry Returns to London." *Museum of London Group*. 10 June 2005. Web. 11 May 2007.

"Pocahontas Revealed: Images of a Legend." *Nova*. PBS. April 2007. Web. 23 Jan. 2008.

"Pocahontas's Earrings." *APVA Museum Store*. N.d. Web. 12 May 2007.

Price, David A. *Love and Hate in Jamestown: John Smith, Pocahontas, and the Heart of a New Nation*. New York: Alfred A. Knopf, 2003. Print.

Prudames, David. "Pocahontas's Earrings Go on Show at Museum in Docklands." *Twenty-Four Hour Museum*. 10 June 2005. Web. 12 May 2007.

Pulsipher, Jenny Hale. *Subjects unto the Same King: Indians, English, and the Contest for Authority in Colonial New England*. Philadelphia: University of Pennsylvania Press, 2005. Print.

Purchas, Samuel. *Purchas, His Pilgrimes*. 4 vols. London: William Stansbury for Henry Fetherstone, 1625. Print.

Quarles, Marguerite Stuart. *Pocahontas: Bright Stream Between Two Hills.* Richmond, VA, 1939. Print.

Rasmussen, William M.S. and Robert S. Tilton. *Pocahontas: Her Life and Legend.* Richmond: Virginia Historical Society, 1994. Print.

Records of the Virginia Company of London. Ed. Susan Myra Kingsbury. Washington, DC: US Government Printing Office, 1933. Print.

Reese, William. "First One Hundred Years of Printing in America." *Proceedings of the American Antiquarian Society* (1990): 1–20. Print.

Reilly, Matthew. "'No Eye has Seen, or Ear Heard': Arabic Sources for Quaker Subjectivity in Unca Eliza Winkfield's *The Female American.*" *Eighteenth-Century Studies* 44.2 (2011): 261–83. Print.

Revere, Paul. *1775 Revere Seal.* SC1/series 138X. Massachusetts Archives, Boston.

Ribeiro, Aileen and Valerie Cumming. *The Visual History of Costume.* London: B.T. Batsford, Ltd., 1989. Print.

Richter, Daniel. *Facing East from Indian Country: A Native History of Early America.* Cambridge, MA: Harvard University Press, 2001. Print.

Rifkin, Mark. *Manifesting America: The Imperial Construction of U.S. National Space.* New York: Oxford University Press, 2012. Print.

Robertson, Karen. "Pocahontas at the Masque." *Signs* 21.3 (1996): 551–83. Print.

Rountree, Helen. *Pocahontas, Powhatan, Opechancanough: Three Indian Lives Changed by Jamestown.* Charlottesville: University of Virginia Press, 2005. Print.

———. *Pocahontas's People.* Norman: University of Oklahoma Press, 1990. Print.

———. *The Powhatan Indians of Virginia: Their Traditional Culture.* Norman: University of Oklahoma Press, 1989. Print.

Rowlandson, Mary. *The Sovereignty and Goodness of God.* Ed. Neal Salisbury. Boston: Bedford Books, 1997. Print.

Said, Edward. *Orientalism.* New York: Vintage Books, 1978. Print.

Salisbury, Neal. "Embracing Ambiguity: Native Peoples and Christianity in Seventeenth-Century North America." *Ethnohistory* 50.2 (2003): 247–59. Print.

———. Introduction and Appended Materials. *The Sovereignty and Goodness of God.* By Mary Rowlandson. Boston: Bedford Books, 1997. Print.

———. "Red Puritans: The 'Praying Indians' of Massachusetts Bay and John Eliot." *The William and Mary Quarterly* 31.1 (1974): 27–54. Print.

Samuels, Shirley. *Reading the American Novel, 1780–1865.* Hoboken, NJ: John Riley and Sons, 2013. Ebook.

———. *Romances of the Republic: Women, the Family, and Violence in the Literature of the Early American Nation.* New York: Oxford University Press, 1996. Print.

Sanchez-Eppler, Karen. *Touching Liberty: Abolition, Feminism, and the Politics of the Body.* Berkeley: University of California Press, 1993. Print.

Sayre, Gordon M. Introduction. *American Captivity Narratives.* Ed. Gordon M. Sayre. Boston: Houghton Mifflin Company, 2000. 1–17. Print.

Scheckel, Susan. *The Insistence of the Indian: Race and Nationalism in Nineteenth-Century American Culture.* Princeton, NJ: Princeton University Press, 1998. Print.

Schloesser, Pauline E. *The Fair Sex: White Women and Racial Patriarchy in the Early American Republic.* New York: New York University Press, 2001. Print.

Schueller, Malini Johar, ed. *U.S. Orientalisms: Race, Nation, and Gender in Literature, 1790–1890.* Ann Arbor: University of Michigan Press, 1998. Print.

Schueller, Malini Johar and Edward Watts, eds. *Messy Beginnings: Postcoloniality and Early American Studies.* New Brunswick, NJ: Rutgers University Press, 2003. Print.

Schultz, Eric B. and Michael J. Tougias. *King Philip's War: The History and Legacy of America's Forgotten Conflict.* Woodstock, VT: The Countryman Press, 1999. Print.

Sederholm, Carl H. "Dividing Religion from Theology in Lydia Maria Child's *Hobomok.*" *American Transcendental Quarterly* 20.3 (2006): 553–64. Print.

Sieminski, Greg, Captain. "The Puritan Captivity Narrative and the Politics of the American Revolution." *American Quarterly* 42.1 (1990): 37–9. Print.

Slotkin, Richard and James K. Folsom. *So Dreadfull a Judgment: Puritan Responses to King Philip's War, 1676–1677.* Middletown, CT: Wesleyan University Press, 1978. Print.

Smith, Bruce R. "Mouthpieces: Native American Voices in Thomas Harriot's *True and Brief Report of ... Virginia,* Gaspar Perez de Villagra's *Historia de la Nuevo Mexico,* and John Smith's *General History of Virginia.*" *New Literary History* 32:3 (2001): 501–17. Print.

Smith, John. *The Generall Historie of Virginia, New England, and the Summer Isles. The Complete Works of Captain John Smith (1580–1631).* Ed. Philip Barbour. Vol. 2. Chapel Hill: University of North Carolina Press, 1986. 33–475. Print.

———. "A Map of Virginia. With a Description of the Countrey, the Commodities, People, and Government and Religion." *The Complete Works of Captain John Smith (1580–1631).* Ed. Philip Barbour. Vol. 1. Chapel Hill: University of North Carolina Press, 1986. 121–90. Print.

———. "The Proceedings of the English Colonie in Virginia." *The Complete Works of Captain John Smith (1580–1631).* Ed. Philip Barbour. Vol. 1. Chapel Hill: University of North Carolina Press, 1986. 191–283. Print.

Smith, Sidonie. *Subjectivity, Identity, and the Body: Women's Autobiographical Practices in the Twentieth Century.* Bloomington: Indiana University Press, 1993. Print.

Smith-Rosenberg, Carroll. *Disorderly Conduct: Visions of Gender in Victorian America.* New York: Oxford University Press, 1985. Print.

Spivak, Gayatri. "Can the Subaltern Speak?" *Marxism and the Interpretation of Culture.* Ed. Cary Nelson and Lawrence Grossberg. Urbana: University of Illinois Press, 1988. 271–313.

St. George, Robert Blair, ed. *Possible Pasts: Becoming Colonial in Early America.* Ithaca, NY: Cornell University Press, 2000. Print.

Staden, Hans. Hans Staden's *Veritable History and Description of a Country Belonging to the Wild, Naked and terrible People, Eaters of Men's Flesh, Situated in the New World, America. Discovering the New World: Based on the Works of Theodore De Bry*. Ed. Michael Alexander. New York: Harper and Row: 1976. 90–121. Print.

Stein, Jordan Alexander. "Mary Rowlandson's Hunger and the Historiography of Sexuality." *American Literature* 81.3 (2009): 469–95. Print.

Stern, Julia. *The Plight of Feeling: Sympathy and Dissent in the Early American Novel*. Chicago: University of Chicago Press, 1997. Print.

Stevens, Laura. *The Poor Indians: British Missionaries, Native Americans, and Colonial Sensibility*. Philadelphia: University of Pennsylvania Press, 2004. Print.

———. "Reading The Hermit's Manuscript: *The Female American* and Female Robinsonades." *Approaches to Teaching Defoe's Robinson Crusoe*. Ed. Maximillian E. Novak and Carl Fisher. New York: Modern Language Association of America, 2005. 140–51. Print.

Sweet, Nancy F. "Dissent and the Daughter in *A New England Tale* and *Hobomok*." *Legacy* 22.2 (2005): 107–25. Web. *Project Muse*. 3 June 2014.

Szasz, Margaret. *Indian Education in the American Colonies, 1607–1783*. Albuquerque: University of New Mexico Press, 1988. Print.

Thomas, Isaiah. *The History of Printing in America: With a Biography of Printers and an Account of Newspapers*. 1874. Barre, MA: Weathervane Books, 1970. Print.

Thornton, Tamara. *Handwriting in America: A Cultural History*. New Haven, CT: Yale University Press, 1996. Print.

Tilton, Robert. *Pocahontas: The Evolution of an American Narrative*. Cambridge: Cambridge University Press, 1994. Print.

Toulouse, Teresa. *The Captive's Position: Female Narrative, Male Identity, and Royal Authority in Colonial New England*. Philadelphia: University of Pennsylvania Press, 2007. Print.

Townsend, Camilla. *Pocahontas and the Powhatan Dilemma*. New York: Hill and Wang, 2004. Print.

Ulrich, Laurel Thatcher. *Good Wives: Image and Reality in the Lives of Women in Northern New England, 1650–1750*. New York: Vintage Books, 1980. Print.

US National Archives and Records Administration. *Magna Carta and Its American Legacy*. US Archives and Records Administration. N.d. Web. 19 Dec. 2007.

Vaccaro, Kristianne Kalata. "'Recollection … Sets My Busy Imagination to Work': Transatlantic Self-Narration, Performance, and Reception in *The Female American*." *Eighteenth-Century Fiction* 20.2 (2007): 127–50. Print.

VanDerBeets, Richard. *The Indian Captivity Narrative: An American Genre*. Lanham, MD: University Press of America, 1984. Print.

Vasquez, Mark G. "'Your Sister Cannot Speak to You and Understand You As I Do': Native American Culture and Female Subjectivity in Lydia Maria Child and Catharine Maria Sedgwick." *American Transcendental Quarterly* 15.3 (2001): 173–9. Print.

Vaughan, Alden T. *Narratives of North American Indian Captivity: A Selected Bibliography*. New York: Garland, 1983. Print.

Vaux, Molly. "'But Maria, did you really write this?': Preface as Cover Story in Lydia Maria Child's *Hobomok*." *Legacy* 17.2 (2000). Web. *Project Muse*. 3 June 2014.

Vizenor, Gerald. *Manifest Manners: Postindian Warriors of Survivance*. Middletown, CT: Wesleyan University Press, 1994. Print.

Waldstreicher, David. *In the Midst of Perpetual Fetes: The Making of American Nationalism, 1776–1820*. Chapel Hill: University of North Carolina Press, 1997. Print.

Warkentin, Germaine. "In Search of 'The Word of the Other': Aboriginal Sign Systems and the History of the Book in Canada." *Book History* 2 (1999): 1–27. Print.

Warrior, Robert Allen. *Tribal Secrets: Recovering American Indian Intellectual Traditions*. Minneapolis: University of Minnesota Press, 1994. Print.

Watts, Edward, ed. *Writing and Postcolonialism in the Early Republic*. Charlottesville: University Press of Virginia, 1998. Print.

Weaver, Jace. *That the People Might Live: Native American Literatures and Native American Community*. New York: Oxford University Press, 1997. Print.

Weierman, Karen Woods. *One Nation, One Blood: Interracial Marriage in American Fiction, Scandal, and Law, 1820–1870*. Amherst: University of Massachusetts Press, 2005. Print.

Wheeler, Roxann. "The Complexion of Desire: Racial Ideology and Mid-Eighteenth-Century British Novels." *Eighteenth-Century Studies* 32.3 (1999): 309–32. Print.

———. *The Complexion of Race: Categories of Difference in Eighteenth-Century British Culture*. Philadelphia: University of Pennsylvania Press, 2000. Print.

Wilcox, R. Turner. *The Mode in Hats and Headdress*. New York: Charles Scribner's Sons, 1945. Print.

Windrow, Martin and Gerry Embleton. *Military Dress of North America: 1665–1970*. New York: Charles Scribner's Sons, 1973. Print.

Winship, George Parker. *The Cambridge Press 1638–1692*. Philadelphia: University of Pennsylvania Press, 1945. Print.

Wood, Gordon S. "Framing the Republic, 1760–1820." *The Great Republic: A History of the American People*. By Bernard Bailyn, Gordon S. Wood, David Brion Davis, and David Herbert Donald. Lexington, MA: D.C. Heath and Company, 1992. 209–371. Print.

Woodbury, Mary. *Pocahontas*. ca. 1730. Oil on paper. Massachusetts Historical Society, Boston. Digital image.

Woodward, Grace Steele. *Pocahontas*. Norman: University of Oklahoma Press, 1969. Print.

Wyss, Hilary. *English Letters and Indian Literacies: Reading, Writing, and New England Missionary Schools, 1750–1830*. Philadelphia: University of Pennsylvania Press, 2012. Print.

———. *Writing Indians: Literacy, Christianity, and Native Community in Early America*. Amherst: University of Massachusetts Press, 2000. Print.

Wyss, Hilary and Kristina Bross. *Early Native Literacies in New England: A Documentary and Critical Anthology*. Amherst: University of Massachusetts Press, 2008. Print.

Young, Alfred F. *Liberty Tree: Ordinary People and the American Revolution*. New York: New York University Press, 2006. Print.

Yural-Davis, Nira and Floya Anthias. Introduction. *Woman-Nation-State*. Ed. Nira Yural-Davis and Floya Anthias. London: Macmillan, 1989. 1–15. Print.

Index